From Satchmo to Miles

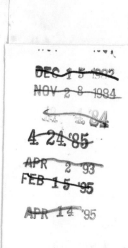

LEONARD G. FEATHER

STEIN AND DAY/*Publishers*/New York

From

Satchmo

to

Miles

ACKNOWLEDGMENTS

Portions of the Louis Armstrong and Norman Granz chapters originally appeared in *Esquire* and are reproduced by permission.

The Duke Ellington chapter and most of the Ella Fitzgerald chapter originally appeared in *Playboy* magazine; © 1957 by *Playboy*.

Portions of the Lester Young chapter originally appeared in *Playboy* magazine; © 1959 by *Playboy*.

Most of the Count Basie chapter appeared in a booklet included in the album *The Count Basie Story* and is reproduced through the courtesy of Roulette Records, Inc.

Portions of the Billie Holiday chapter appeared in a booklet included in the album *Billie Holiday: The Golden Years, Volume II*; reproduced through the courtesy of Columbia Records.

Portions of the Dizzy Gillespie and Charlie Parker chapters appeared in the book *Inside Bebop* (later known as *Inside Jazz*); reproduced by permission of Consolidated Music Publishers, Inc.

Portions of the Louis Armstrong, Billie Holiday, and Charlie Parker chapters first appeared in *Down Beat* and are reproduced by permission of Maher Publications.

Portions of the Louis Armstrong and Billie Holiday chapters appeared in the *Melody Maker*, a member of the IPC Business Press Ltd., and are reproduced by permission.

The Oscar Peterson chapter is reproduced by permission of *Nugget* Magazine.

The Don Ellis chapter and portions of the Ray Charles chapter are reproduced through the courtesy of *Cavalier* magazine.

The postscript to the Norman Granz chapter appeared in somewhat different form in the *Los Angeles Times*; © 1971 *Los Angeles Times*, reprinted by permission.

The Miles Davis chapter appears through the courtesy of *Penthouse* magazine.

First STEIN AND DAY PAPERBACK edition 1974

First published in 1972

Copyright © 1972 by Leonard Feather

Library of Congress Catalog Card No. 70-187311

All rights reserved

Published simultaneously in Canada by McGraw-Hill Ryerson Limited

Designed by David Miller

Printed in the United States of America

Stein and Day/*Publishers*/Scarborough House, Briarcliff Manor, New York 10510

ISBN 0-8128-1703-6

Author's Foreword

SOMEONE POINTED out to me not long ago that to the best of his knowledge I have been writing about jazz uninterruptedly, either in England or the United States, longer than anyone else around. Seniority tends to creep up on one very gradually, and this reminder of the passage of time came as something of a shock. It was nonetheless true, so far as I know, and it has a direct bearing upon the nature and composition of this book.

Inside Bebop, published in 1949, and a subsequent volume, *The Book of Jazz from Then Till Now,* dealt primarily with the history of jazz, together with examinations of the art by means of musical illustrations. My other books (the *Encyclopedia of Jazz* series) were reference works, and as such were concerned with facts; historiography, technicalities, and personalities were secondary.

From Satchmo to Miles, however, incorporates firsthand observations of a dozen figures, all of whom, I feel, have been vital to the development and advancement of jazz. I knew them first as disembodied sounds on a record, second as unfamiliar figures in a club or on a concert stage, and finally as personal friends. In several instances—particularly with Armstrong, Ellington, Billie Holiday, Parker, and Gillespie—there was also a working relationship through concerts, recordings, and other ventures with which we were jointly concerned.

These experiences helped provide a clearer, closer view than would otherwise have been possible.

Except for some of the material in the Parker-Gillespie section (for which I was fortunate in obtaining permission to use certain passages from the long-unavailable *Inside Bebop*), these are portraits of human beings first, analyses of musicians or musical history only peripherally if at all. The chapters are arranged chronologically, which in this instance is a synonym for logically. To some extent they focus on most of the important developments in jazz through the decades.

I admit to having chosen these personalities very selectively. If you look for Benny Goodman and Stan Kenton, whose importance I would not wish in any way to belittle, either explicitly or implicitly, perhaps it should be pointed out that their exclusion does not mean that an essential aspect of jazz in the past forty years has been neglected. Count Basie is at least as valid a representative of the swing era as Goodman; Don Ellis in many ways offers a present-day parallel to Kenton.

In acknowledging the help of those who paved the way to making this book possible, I must first thank John Hammond. Had it not been for his friendship through most of my adult life, and the knowledge I gained from him in the early years, I might never have been in this country, let alone in print on the bookshelves.

Thanks are also due to the various editors and others wno first printed some of this material: Doug Allen of *Cavalier* and *Nugget;* Charles Burr of Columbia Records; Ray Coleman of the *Melody Maker;* Arnold Gingrich of *Esquire;* Jack Kessie of *Playboy;* Morris Levy of Roulette Records; Charles Suber of Maher Publications (*Down Beat*); Eric Protter of *Penthouse,* and Gordon E. Williams of Consolidated Music Publishers, Inc.

Special thanks are also due to Frankie Nemko and Sylvia O'Gilvie for their typing and proofreading assistance, and to Jane Feather for her complete freedom from matrimonial prejudice in offering editorial opinions and suggestions.

Most of all I am grateful for the inspiration and friendship of the artists themselves. The first two were directly responsible for drawing me to jazz. After the magic of Armstrong and Ellington had worked on me, the others, one by one, sustained and refreshed and reinvigorated my interest in, and involvement with, this liveliest of the twentieth-century arts.

—North Hollywood, California, 1972

Louis Armstrong with Hoagy Carmichael

Ed Lawless

With Louis:
FROM LONDON TO LOS ANGELES

1929

IN THE early years Louis Armstrong's most dedicated admirers
—to whom his work was not entertainment alone, but part
of a vital and fast-growing art form—were the people all
over the world to whom jazz was inaccessible except through
the secondhand experience of a few three-minute photograph
records.

The Louis Armstrong story began for me in 1929 at a
record shop in Kensington, London, where a school friend
introduced me to Louis' "West End Blues." I thought this
miniature masterpiece unique in its warmth and beauty, unlike any of the conventional dance music of my London childhood. From the long, perfectly formed opening cadenza
through Louis' gentle wordless vocal and Earl Hines's driving
piano solo, down to that gloriously conceived and perfectly
executed outchorus with Louis' high C held miraculously for
four bars—all the way to Zutty Singleton's click-off coda,
"West End Blues" was incomparably moving.

It is almost impossible for an American jazz fan today to
react to Armstrong's music as I did then. If a young man
steeped in modern literature from James Joyce to James Jones
is suddenly exposed to Thoreau or Dickens, his pleasure may
be limited. Similarly, a jazz fan initiated by Miles Davis and

Ornette Coleman may not be able to understand Louis in the proper context.

There may well be no absolute values in art, and few unqualified masterpieces; yet even today Armstrong's youthful contributions approach perfection closer than those of any other improvising pioneer. Or so it seems to me still. From the moment I heard "West End Blues," I was committed to jazz, and lived for the next record release or trans-Atlantic news item.

Although Joe Glaser, boss of the Sunset Cafe in Chicago, billed him in 1926 as "The World's Greatest Trumpet Player," Louis' American public in the late 1920s was concentrated almost entirely in the urban ghettos, where his records and broadcasts were popular. But all over Europe jazz fans were rebelling against the lack of attention paid to their music. Aside from the *Melody Maker* and a French magazine called *Jazz Tango Dancing*, there was no place to read about jazz, no *Down Beat,* no U.S. publication that took jazz seriously (the black American press, as I was to find out later, was no exception).

Had it not been for the pressure exerted by a few men like Edgar Jackson (the original *Melody Maker* editor), Hugues Panassié, and Charles Delaunay, there might have been no jazz records released in Europe during those seminal years. In particular, the efforts of these men created an international interest in the Armstrongs and Ellingtons, whose artistic importance was downgraded at home.

Although by 1929 he was technically a star, Louis had little security. He and the other members of the Carroll Dickerson orchestra, which he had been fronting, left Chicago to try their luck in New York, where they scuffled and eventually disbanded. Around this time, Louis had a genuine hit with "Ain't Misbehavin'," which he sang in the *Hot Chocolates* revue staged by Connie Immerman at Connie's Inn.

During the next two years, jazz recordings of popular songs predominated over instrumental blues, and the range and vitality of Armstrong's horn, together with the warm intimacy of his voice, brought him to new musical peaks. His audience grew to include more whites, and he enjoyed a successful first visit to the West Coast. His band, on the air nightly from Sebastian's Cotton Club, attracted the patronage of white stars. This idyll ended abruptly when he and a white drummer friend, Vic Berton, were caught smoking what were then known as reefers. After ten days in jail Louis was dismissed with a suspended sentence. Later that year he was arrested again and held briefly along with several sidemen—this time for no better reason than that a white woman, his manager's wife, was traveling in the band bus—a situation abhorrent to the police chief of Memphis, Tennessee.

By now young trumpeters all over the world were copying Armstrong choruses note for note. Demand for him was particularly strong in New York and Chicago, yet during much of 1930 and all of 1931 Louis stayed mysteriously away from both cities. Certainly there was trouble in Chicago with his second wife, Lil Hardin (he and Alpha Smith were together for seven years before he divorced Lil and married Alpha in 1938); apparently, too, he was caught in the factional rivalry of the underworld. "I ain't going to New York," he is supposed to have said during this period, "but I ain't staying in Chicago neither." Years later he elaborated: "In Chicago . . . every time you looked around it seemed there was a gun in your side." On top of this, Louis was involved in a lawsuit against Tommy Rockwell, the booking agent, and Connie Immerman. The details are vague, but after a brief visit to New York he took the train west again, played a few dates in California and did not return east until the summer of 1932, when he had a contract to play in England.

Louis Armstrong's situation was common to black artists during the Prohibition years. He was being manipulated by the rival gangs that controlled many of the speakeasies where musicians worked. Although his records would become classics, his musical genius was, at the time, secondary to his role as a pawn in a sinister game he scarcely understood. In retrospect it would appear that his trans-Atlantic trip on the S.S. *Majestic* was figuratively as well as literally a breath of fresh air.

1932

Nobody in London knew what kind of band Louis would bring with him, nor what to expect on that warm Monday evening in July of 1932. We only knew that this almost mythical American figure whose horn and voice had fascinated us on an occasional 78 was, miraculously, coming to life. The Palladium's curtains parted and Louis, fronting a makeshift band composed mostly of black musicians recruited on the continent, launched into "Sleepy Time Down South." The memory of this would last a lifetime: a legend become flesh and blood.

Louis and his girl, Alpha, were lionized wherever they went. The band drew big crowds at music halls all over the country. They encountered very little racial discrimination; very few Negroes were to be found in England at that time. Louis and Alpha had a small flat in Holborn which I would often visit to play records and devour whatever news and gossip Louis could give me about the music world across the Atlantic. I remember asking about some of the records Satch had made with the Les Hite band. "Their drummer is a wonderful kid," he said. "Only nineteen, going to be a great musician—watch out for him! His name's Lionel Hampton." I never heard the name again until 1935, when, like many other Armstrong predictions, this one came true.

Although his pickup band did not do him justice (it was soon replaced by an all-white group of British musicians), Satchmo's first British tour was a personal triumph. His bookings were extended so far that he did not return home until November, at which time the American press did not see fit

to carry a single word about his foreign conquests. Not surprisingly, by the following summer he was off for Europe
again, where he remained through 1934.

During his Continental country-hopping he was plagued
by a series of managerial troubles. An innocent when it came
to business matters, he found himself torn between contracts.
At one point he had an American manager with a chronic
drinking problem; late in 1934 a Frenchman claimed to be his
representative, while an English agent also had a supposedly
exclusive contract with him. Satch became a storm center;
suddenly, in January of 1935, *Melody Maker* announced that
he had evaded all these complications by sailing for home.
He had had his taste of deification, of escape from sleazy
dance halls to the concert stage, of being received with pomp
and circumstance by dignitaries. That was the last Europe was
to see of him for more than thirteen years.

1936

I was reunited with Louis backstage at the Oriental
Theatre in Chicago, in the summer of 1936. "We're going on
a tour of one-nighters," he said. "Why don't you ride along
in the bus with the fellers in the band so you can see what's
going on? We'll be playing St. Louis for one night, then
Kansas City. After that I'll be heading for Hollywood to make
a movie."

Having seen nothing of the United States except Manhattan and Chicago's Loop, I gladly accepted and prepared to
leave town with Luis Russell's orchestra, the band Armstrong
was fronting. It was an exhausting trip for the musicians,
seated bolt upright in the humid heat of the night (there were
no air-conditioned buses in those days). Louis and Alpha arrived by train an hour ahead of us. All of black St. Louis
seemed to be aware of Satch's advent: cars streamed by with

large placards announcing his dance date, and there was scarcely a storefront that did not proclaim the trumpet king's first visit in several years to the Mound City.

Over dinner in a small ghetto restaurant I showed Louis a clipping announcing nightly trips on the "Colossal Excursion Queen," the *Saint Paul*, steaming down the Mississippi to the tune of Creath and Marable and Their Famous Big Band. I wondered whether this was the same Fate Marable whose name I had heard in connection with Louis' childhood.

"Sure, that's my boy Fate!" said Louis. "Charlie Creath's his partner. I used to work them boats with Fate in . . . must have been 1919. We were the first colored band that ever played the boats. Old Pop Foster was swinging along with us, too, and Baby Dodds on drums. Baby's running two or three taxis now—he's doin' all right. Would you like me to take you along there? I'll introduce you to Fate, and you can go on the trip and come back to the dance afterward." After dinner we took a cab down to the wharf, where hundreds of cars were lined up, their roofs glittering in the sunset alongside the pier where the *Saint Paul* lay anchored.

Aboard the boat the prodigal son's triumphant return was celebrated. Marable, a very light-skinned man in his midforties, his lips pursed in a smile of satisfaction, could hardly wait to leave the piano and reminisce with Louis. The blackskinned, handsome young Creath led the band as it plowed through a series of uninspired pop songs. As the boat was about to leave, Louis returned to the Coliseum, where Creath, Marable, and I joined him after the ride.

We were just in time. After a set by Russell's band, Louis himself strode onstage, greeting the multitudes like a heavyweight about to retain the world's championship. It looked as though the city's entire black population had turned out to honor him. I was crushed by a solid barrage of fans who stormed the stage, beseeching Louis for autographs and shrieking requests—mostly for hit songs of the day like

"Shoe Shine Boy." Louis gave them the kind of show they expected, including a horrendous ballad version of "Old Man River" by a singer named Sonny Woods. There were many moments of pure inspiration, too, which were no less appreciated.

By three o'clock the huge hall was dark. Surrounded by a clutch of old and newfound friends, Louis made his way to a local tavern where, seated beside a mysterious automatic music machine (I later found it was called a "jukebox"), we alternately talked and listened. At one point, Marable asked: "Louis, why don't you come back and play on the boats someday, for old times' sake? Why don't you play *with* a band, not just in front of one?" Under the influence of a few drinks, Louis allowed honesty to overcome discretion. "Man," he said, "you know I'd love it. I'm just doing what Mr. Glaser thinks is best for me. It's all strictly for the glory of the cash."

This was the first time I had heard Louis indicate that he would rather go back to his roots than remain a strictly show-business entertainer. And it was then that I first recognized three different personalities, each of which was the "real" Louis Armstrong, according to the given situation, and each of which I would recognize many times over the next thirty-five years. Now I was seeing Louis I, the back-o'-town New Orleans Negro among his old cronies. Louis II, Commodore Hornblower, the discographers' idol, the jazzman's jazzman, was a much more public figure. A few months later Louis III, the beloved and inimitable show-biz personality, the comic genius the world took to its heart, would emerge in Hollywood's *Pennies from Heaven.*

1939—42

In the late 1930s, although Louis was blowing his way into the top reaches of show business via Hollywood, there were no concert dates, and his recordings too often limited him to novelty songs or collaborations with such artists as the Polynesians (a steel-guitar group) and the Mills Brothers. Yet he earned as much as $10,000 a week in theaters, and followed *Pennies from Heaven* with a few more movies and a stage show. The latter was a jazz version of *A Midsummer Night's Dream*, in which he was cast as Bottom. Maxine Sullivan played Titania; Eddie Condon and Benny Goodman led combos at either side of the stage.

I caught *Swingin' the Dream* at the Center Theatre in Rockefeller Center. Although sometimes corny, it was a happy innovation, and Louis enjoyed himself thoroughly. ("Man," he said to me during intermission, "if Old Shakespeare could see me now!") His happiness was short-lived; the show, panned by critics, closed after eleven nights.

So it was back to the vaudeville theaters and the one-night stands. It's no wonder that during the next couple of years Satch, as just another bandleader in a succession of swing-era figures, spent much of his time between one-nighters in dressing rooms and small-town hotels writing long letters to friends —letters offering insights into his character, spelling, punctuation, and free-flowing style that were as personal as his horn and voice.

One letter I received in 1941 ran to fourteen single-spaced pages and 8,000 words, rambling through such topics as the konking of his sidemen's hair; a dance date and a fight that erupted around the bandstand; a long, lame joke about a Negro who wanted to join the RAF; an account of a visit to an alligator farm in Florida; three full pages on the weight problems of his musicians; a report on a visit with Bunk Johnson in New Iberia, Louisiana, and half a page about the correct pronunciation of pecan.

Satch had little to say about music itself, but upon being asked to name his favorite trumpeters he produced an answer of lasting value:

> Huntington, W. Va.,
> August, 5th, 1941

Planes fly
the birds flew
Dig this jive
I'm writing you

Dear Brother Feather:

Now this question about my opion about the Trumpet Players that I admire—that is actually asking an awful lot of me . . . Because theres, so many Trumpet Players that I admire until there would not be room enough'to mention them on this paper . . .

But—as you wished—my friend I'll do my damdest . . . First I'l' name my boy Bunny Berrigan . . Now there's a boy whom I've always admired for his Tone-Soul-Technique-his sense of "Phrasing:etc. . . . to me-Bunny can't do no wrong in music . . .

Harry James is another youngster whom won Ol Satch right along side of a million other fans . . . His "Concertos, etc, makes, him in my estimation a grand Trumpet Man . . . And He can Swing Too . . .

Roy Eldridge is another youngster after my own heart . . . He has' power—and pair of chops that's out of this man's world . . .

Now for a number one' 'First Chair Man—I am sure that I have him right here in my Orchestra . . . And that man is non other than-"Shelton"Scad" Hemphill . . . Because anytime any 'Phrasing-Attacking-giving each note it's full value—Scad's Got It . . .

Erskine Hawkins is another youngster whom has power on his Trumpet and should stay on the mound a long long time.

Well, Leonard, now I'll just be like the little boy whom sat on a'block of Ice-MY TALE IS TOLD. . . . Goodnight and Godbless you . . .

Am Redbeans and Ricely Yours,
Louis Armstrong

A year or so later Louis, eager to keep in touch with his friends in England, sent a batch of news to me in New York with a request that I transmit it to the *Melody Maker:*

I have gotten married since the last time I was in England . . . I married a girl whom was over there with the Blackbirds show at the time I was touring England with my band . . . Her name is Lucille Wilson . . . She was one of the Lew Leslie's Chorus girls at that time . . . Swell gal I must say . . . Lucille and I gotten married in St. Louis Missouri October 12th, 1942 . . . USA. We were married at the home of my vocalist Velma Middleton . . . We bought our home out in Corona Long Island . . . So peaceful and quiet. . . . After Balling all night having fun in New York's Manhattan I go home in Long Island—get my good rest . . .

I have a new manager since I was in England . . . His name—Mr. Joe Glaser . . . I worked for Mr. Glaser way back in the good old days in Chicago as far back as 1926—when I was just a member of the Carroll Dickerson's Orchestra. . . . He'll just about be the last manager that I'll have . . . We'll be together just that long. . . . . .

Nightie night and heres wishing that I'll see youall real soon and God Bless everyone of you . . .

Am Brussell Sproutsly Yours,
Louis Armstrong

Louis, always proud of his musicians, resented the least aspersion cast on them. From 1943 to 1947 I was involved with most of the rare times he worked in a smaller and more informal setting, and it was sometimes frustrating to find his loyalty to the band outweighing (in my view) considerations of musical compatibility.

The first such occasion was the inauguration of the *Esquire* jazz concerts and polls. No matter how low he sank in the popularity polls (in 1943 *Metronome* gave him only 86 votes and he finished a poor fourth), the critics who formed *Esquire's* panel never considered him passé, and he won the first place Gold Award both as trumpeter and singer the first year the poll was held. A small group of the winners was to be presented at the Metropolitan Opera House. Louis soon warmed to the invigorating company of Roy Eldridge, Jack Teagarden, Barney Bigard, Coleman Hawkins, Art Tatum, Al Casey, Sid Catlett, and Oscar Pettiford, but it was not until the second year's concert, when he took part in a unique three-city jam session with Benny Goodman and Duke Ellington (via coast-to-coast live radio), that he showed signs of regaining the pristine form of his Hot Five days.

From time to time I hinted to Louis and Joe Glaser about the orchestra's expendability: the foremost virtuoso of jazz, I felt, should leave the commercial forum of big-band swing and return to his natural habitat—small combo music. It was late in 1946 before this was accomplished, and then only temporarily. Charles Delaunay, working through RCA to produce some material for the Swing label in France, deputized me to cut an Armstrong date for him in Los Angeles.

I found Louis at the Dunbar Hotel on Central Avenue, about to start shooting on a movie, *New Orleans.* The next day, at the Hal Roach Studios in Culver City, he rehearsed with a small group that was to play and act in the earlier sequences of the story. The men were trombonist Kid Ory, clarinetist Barney Bigard, pianist Charlie Beal, banjoist Bud Scott, bassist Red Callender, and drummer Zutty Singleton.

The tunes were simple and familiar, and the men were under orders to work until 6 P.M., so most of the time was spent jamming and gabbing. When Beal wasn't around, I sat in. Zutty sent my ego sky-high by insisting that I play the record date, and when Louis agreed, I happily acceded. Vic Dickenson replaced Ory; the rhythm section was strengthened by the addition of a guitarist, Allan Reuss. Beal played on "Sugar" and "I Want a Little Girl," and I took his place on

"Blues for Yesterday" and "Blues in the South." Louis was in his element, using no arrangements, his tone purer than ever, his phrasing a remarkable blend of staccato and legato.

Nevertheless the big-band business continued to rear its brassy head. A couple of months later I approached Glaser with the suggestion that it was about time for Armstrong to play at Carnegie Hall. Incredibly enough, this had never been suggested, although a decade earlier Louis had been accepted in several European concert halls. Satch wanted to present his whole touring orchestra, including singers Velma Middleton and Leslie Scott. I preferred a small jazz group. Finally Louis wrote to me, agreeing to a compromise:

Dear Leonard:

'Man—I've been trying so hard to write you a letter—but owing to the fact that they have been bouncing us around so fast one would swear that we were a bunch of adagio dancers, etc. . . Ha ha . .

Concerning the concert you and the Boss Mr. Glaser are planning for me and my gang . . . Well I'll tell ya planning concert,s alright—but if any an every old Tom Dick & Harry will be interfering I'd just sooner forget about the concert . . . They have all been awfully messy anyway-from what I can gather . . . So if you boys intend on doing the thing-for 'God's sake-don't have a lot guys whom think they know whats going down- . . . -the'yr no where. . . . . It really wouldn't be a bad idea to have the seven piece band (the one I used in the picture)in that concert . . . There was Kid Ory Trombone. . . . Barney Bigard Clarinet . . . Bud Scott Guitar . . . Zutty Singleton Drums—Myself trumpet-Those are the New Orleans boys-the ones I've just mentioned . . . Red Calender Bass Charlie Beal Piano. . . . . We really did romp. . . .

Nightie night my man and God Bless Ya . . .

Red beans and ricely,
Louis Armstrong

Since it was financially impractical to bring in musicians from the West Coast, we agreed that the first half of the concert would feature Louis in a small setting provided by the band from Cafe Society Uptown, where clarinetist Edmond Hall and his sextet were appearing. The date for Carnegie Hall was set for Saturday, February 8, 1947.

With coproducers Bob Snyder and Greer Johnson we devised a pattern that split the show into four segments intended to reflect Louis' career in four locations: New Orleans, Chicago, New York, and Hollywood. The Hollywood segment was a means to justify the big band and its vocalists; Leslie Scott could sing and Miss Middleton could clown with Pops. By way of compensation, however, this section included a surprise appearance by Billie Holiday in a duet with Louis, and a guest shot by drummer Sid Catlett.

By the end of the program it was obvious to the most myopic observer which of these settings belonged naturally to Louis. A few months after the concert the large orchestra was disbanded and the first great Louis Armstrong All Stars combo was born. (Years later Louis told me: "I had eighteen men and they were a nice bunch of cats. I didn't want to see them all out of work. Well, we fought it for a long time, but it had to be done, because the trend was changing.")

Once the die was cast, Louis took naturally to his new group. And although he said little about it, the combo, unlike the big band, was interracial. The revised formula was to serve Louis well for the rest of his professional life.

1949

In the London days Louis had spoken to me of his ambition to be "King of the Zulus" (at the segregated Negro parade) during the Mardi Gras celebrations in his home town. I told him that I hoped some day to visit New Orleans at Mardi Gras time while Louis was there. The following letter was in response to my request for some reminiscenses on the subject:

Lake Manitau.
Rochester, Indiana

Mary had a little bear
The, bear was mighty fine
Everywhere-Mary went
You'd see her, bear behind.

Dear Leonard, 'Man-I guess, you've been wondering what on earth has happened to Ol,Satchmo, he,s taking so long to answer my letter . . . You asked me, what was the Mardigras, And what was it like,in the old days . . . Well, I can,t very well tell you about, all of the olden days . . But I can sum up a pretty good memory of what I saw in the days when 'I was a little boy . . . And, etc. . . And, 'Brother, thats taking you way back *as-is*

I can remember the mardigras as far back as five years old . . . I remember the first time I saw my mother and father, mask . . . You talking about a sharp masqurader, or masqu-radress; I'll never forget how sharp my mother was . . . In those days the women would go the limit to look good on mardigras day . . . They would buy the very best in silk - satins and laces . . . The best silk stockings that were made in those days. . . . They wore masks the image of a face . . . And they would carry a - small switch-in their hands . . Thats what they use to let you know that they know you, then they,ll give you a little peep from under their masks, and, from then on, or, maybe not, they,ll take you into a saloon and buy you a drink, well, - some drinks. . . . .

I,ll never forget the first time I saw Mayann-Maryann,s my mother . . . They call her mayann for short . . . Not that she,s that short'. . . . Anyway-----I sure was proud of my mother, in her short, silk mardigras outfit . . With her lil,ol,-big leg self her silk stockings running all up to her------you,d be surprised-how beautiful those women used 'to look . . . And still do . . . The Zulus Club was the first colored carnival club to get together in New Orleans . . . The Club has been-for generations consist of the fellows in my neighborhood . . . The members were - coal cart drivers, bar tenders—waiters, Hustlers, etc, people of all walks of life . . . Nobody had very much . . . But they loved each other . . . And put their best foot forward as to making a real fine thing of the Zulus Aid and Social Club . . . Its, been

my life long ambition to become King of the Zulus, some
day . . .

The day the King ride in the parade, his float would pass the
City Hall . . . Thats where they - usually build a reviewers
stand . . . The Mayor would invite his choice guests to sit
there with him and 'dig the King on his float . . . And, listen
to those jazz brass bands swinging away like mad . . . Those
base drum beating four beats to the bar . . . The music is so
good, until, while standing there watching the parade pass
by, you,ll find your feet moving in rhythm with each band
that passes . . .

On Mardigras day, everybody do a little masking of some what
. . . Even when I was a kid, I'd black my face, pick up some old
raggidy clothes, and burlesque'somebody . . .

My father was a guy who masked evry year . . . He used to
mask in a big white monkey suit . . . The trouble with a guy
who'll pass you in a monkey suit, he,s liable to hit you in the
'chops with their tales . . . Because their tales have marbles in
them . . . A lick in the 'chops with those' tails would make them
swell up, just like, 'two beef hearts . . .

Well Leonard old, boy, I could go on and on talking about
the good old days of the New Orleans Mardigras . . . Something
that everybody in the world have to see if they can . . . Give
my regards to your family . . .

Here,s 'Satchin Atcha' . . .
Louis Armstrong

In March of 1949, Louis' lifelong ambition was realized.
The Zulu Club named him King of the Parade.

My three days in New Orleans were a wide-awake dream
spent in a carnival-crazed city, a visit packed with excitement
and strange racial paradoxes. When I arrived the Zulus were
preparing to present Louis that night in a concert at Booker
T. Washington Auditorium. At the concert I saw black spectators seated in the left and center aisles while the whites were
over in the right aisle; but on the stage I saw Louis and Jack

Teagarden with their arms around each other, radiating interracial brotherhood as they sang a duet. I saw white officials
shaking hands with Louis onstage, congratulating him and paying tribute to his talent; I saw Satch bursting with pride at
being given an honorary citizenship and the keys to New
Orleans by the mayor. I knew there were hundreds of places
to which those keys would not admit him.

("The day before mardigras day, I payed the Mayor a visit,
and had quite a few pictures made with him in his office. I
met him through a friend of mine . . . Negro by the name of
'Bo Zo . . . He,s always on the ball with everybody, even the
Mayor . . . After the Mayor and I had a long chat before the
microphone—before an office full of people, the Mayor asked
me . . . he said—Satchmo—I read in the *Time* Magazine
where you said—all you wanted to do was to be the king of the
Zulus, and you were ready to die—is that true? . . . I said—
'yes Mr. Mayor,—but there ain't no use of the Lord taking me
Literally' . . . . WOW . . . .")

Throughout my visit I saw Louis looking at me from the
cover of *Time* on every white newsstand in town. I saw front-
page stories in every local white newspaper about Louis, the
Zulus, and the parade; but I also saw black citizens wearing
the "Zulu King" lapel button on which was caricatured a
Negro face so grotesque that there would have been an up-
roar if whites had distributed it. I was refused a ride late at
night by a frightened Negro cab driver who said "he couldn't
drive white folk"; yet in broad daylight I followed the Zulus'
parade with Lucille Armstrong and a mixed group of friends
in an open car, and nobody said a word.

On the night before Mardi Gras Louis and the band traveled by bus to New Iberia, Louisiana, 147 miles away, for a
one-night stand. When they got back to New Orleans at 6
A.M. on Tuesday, it was time for Louis to start putting on his
makeup for the parade, which was to begin at 9. After the
parade he had a dance date in town for the evening, and the

next morning the band would leave for Jackson, Mississippi. It meant almost three days with little sleep for Satch, but he bore up magnificently.

Louis' makeup for the parade masked him in blackest black-face, with huge white patches around his eyes and mouth, a long black wig, a crown, a red velvet gown trimmed with gold frills, and no personal identity left beyond the unmistakable Armstrong smile, which he flashed at the crowds along the parade route. They were packed so tightly that it was almost impossible to raise an arm to salute the King.

As Louis joined in a champagne toast with Bernice Oxley, a buxom local girl who had been named Queen of the Zulus, a frail little old woman edged her way through the crowd. She was Mrs. Josephine Armstrong, a bemused but proud and happy lady who, at the age of ninety-one, could witness the tribute paid her grandson. The mood of that day was best described in a letter from Louis written some time later:

("I had six Zulu,s on my float helping me-throw coconuts to the crowd. . . . Big Sid Catlett was in my band at the time . . . He and Velma Middleton (my vocalist) were in the car in back of my float . . . They were riding with the big executives of the club . . . But things were a little too dull for them . . . So, Velma Middleton got out of the car an started giving out hand bills for the dance we played that nite. Big Sid, also followed the parade on foot . . .

The brass band was right in front of my float . . . The brass band was Paul Barbarin,s band . . . Paul played the bass drum . . . And, My My, Whatta drumer. Ever now and then, Paul(while walking) would turn around(while still beating (the drum) and - back up while he,d be swinging. It sounded so good until I wanted to get down off of that float and beat out a couple of good ol, good ones with them . . .")

The Zulu parade was harshly criticized, particularly in the black press, as an exercise in Uncle Tomfoolery and a capitulation to the white concept of a simplistic black life style. A good case could be made for this view; yet it cannot be argued that the occasion was a source of genuine happiness for Louis.

Relatives, friends, and fans had come from all over the United States to pay homage to him (even Hugues Panassié had flown in); in a sense, it was one of those rare events for which blacks and a few integrationist whites found it worthwhile to submit temporarily to the humiliations of a Jim Crow city.

Louis was often attacked by shrill and unthinking critics for some of his social actions and inactions. In the final analysis it was a monstrous injustice to dismiss him out of hand as a Tom rather than to understand him in terms of his background. Certainly Louis III, as seen on TV, might be called a Tom. Yet Louis I the black American—and Louis II the jazzman—would have nothing to do with discrimination, as his integrated bands made clear. Discreet and noncommittal he may have been most of the time, yet there was a latent anger that bubbled to the surface when provoked strongly enough. Watching TV one day in 1957, Louis saw whites jeering and spitting in the face of a young black child who was attempting to enter a white school; he issued an impassioned denunciation of President Eisenhower, Governor Faubus, and racism in general, which concluded: "Because of the way they are treating my people in the South, the Government can go to hell." And during the years after his Zulu appearance, when New Orleans reimposed strict segregation laws, he refused to go home until he could present his full sextet, black and white together.

1954

After dropping the big band and subsequently establishing himself domestically as a respected jazz artist (albeit one who worked ceaselessly at entertaining his audiences), Louis was seldom able to spend time at his home in Corona, Long Island. One particular visit to his modest, comfortable house stands out in my mind. After we had listened to records for a while, Louis said: "Let me show you my tape library. Man,

I got thousands of 'em!" And indeed he had—airchecks, old jazz records dubbed on tape, miscellaneous conversations, all carefully filed and cross-indexed. He had spent endless hours working on the tape transfers with the help of a friend, Charlie Graham, who had set up the elaborate hi-fi rig.

Louis' sister Beatrice ("Mama Lucy"), who happened to be in town from New Orleans, prepared a fine Creole gumbo dinner. After dinner Louis and I sat in the backyard on a long bench, chatting amiably in the pleasant summer evening. At one point Louis pulled out a gold cigarette case and flipped it open: "Help yourself, man." The case was filled with (to revive a term long since obsolete) sticks of tea. Though I had always stayed away from pot because the legal risk seemed disproportionate to the pleasure, I reflected that turning on with Louis would make a nice memory years later. Oddly enough, it was the only time Louis ever asked me to do so, and not until after Joe Glaser's death was he willing to talk freely to newspapermen about his own lifelong use of pot.

Later in the evening I interviewed him for a *Down Beat* "Blindfold Test" while he was preparing to leave for a job. I followed him around with the record player and tape recorder as he talked. "Now that's what's causing music to go bad today," he said after listening to a performance of West Coast jazz by Shorty Rogers. "Didn't any of those guys end up their solos on the nose. They tried to be out of this world. They're playing for musicians." It occurred to me that, more than anything else, playing for musicians was what had helped to elevate Louis' stature throughout the world. His comments sounded like Louis III, the show-biz Louis, not the jazz Louis II.

I had caught my best glimpse of Louis I, the black hometown boy, during the 1949 Zulu parade. During much of the evening at home with him in Corona, I felt at ease with Louis II. But Louis III returned the next day when he went to work at Basin Street, a nightclub off Broadway. On opening night Louis sat sprawled on a hard wooden chair in his dressing room. He had a patch of cotton over his mouth, another over one eye, and an eyecup over the other eye. His head was inclined far back as he bathed the eye while "Doc" Pugh, his gloomy-faced Negro valet, prepared his clothes.

"I'm tired today," said Louis. "Been down to Columbia Records. They had some nice open spots on the tapes, where I could fill in behind my vocals—dubbed in some horn accompaniment." He hummed a few bars and chuckled. "Man, a cat came in from Columbia and said we gotta make some more of these. It was an album of W. C. Handy's blues. Mr. Handy came in too, and listened to all the records.

"They're perfect! They're my tops, I think. I wouldn't call them Dixieland—to me that's only just a little better than bop. *Jazz* music—that's the way we express ourselves." He picked up his horn and blew a long, lingering legato phrase. "You know what this is?" he said. "It's 'Duna'—'Little Stars of Duna Call Me Home.' I remember playing that with Erskine Tate back at the Vendome Theatre in Chicago. I like to warm up my chops with things like that—brings back memories of those pit-band days. One day," he said as Pugh helped him to struggle into his jacket, "they offered me an extra $25 to do that number on stage, and I was too scared to do it."

It was almost time for Louis' first show, and by now the dressing room was crowded with uninvited strangers: an Argentine newspaperman, a photographer from a Negro magazine, and a drunken woman who had been standing in a corner listening.

"Go on talking, don't stop," said the woman. "I just love to hear you talk. Isn't he just superb?" she said to nobody in particular.

"Come on, let's get the pictures," Louis said a little impatiently to the photographer.

It was clear that Louis II's time was running out and that Louis III had to do a show. He conferred hastily with Pierre "Frenchy" Tallerie, a corpulent, dour white man who for many years was the band's road manager. Then, pulling himself up determinedly from the uncomfortable chair, Pops strode out of the dressing room and walked onstage as the crowded club applauded him.

Red Buttons, the comedian, was on hand; so were such in-people of the day as Betsy von Furstenberg, John Hodiak, and Don Budge, along with a clutch of executives from Decca and Columbia. Aly Khan was there with Joan Fontaine. They had all come to see Louis III, and that was just what he gave them. He played his theme, "When It's Sleepy Time Down South," then told the audience, "We're gonna lay some of them good ol' good ones on ya." Soon he had clarinetist Barney Bigard taking a vocal. He introduced Billy Kyle, his pianist, as "Liberace in Technicolor," and the audience loved it. He grinned, mugged, and joked with members of the audience.

This was the Louis III who wrote in his book, "I have always loved my white folks," and proved it by giving them just what they expected; the Louis of whom Murray Kempton once said, "He endures to mix in his own person all men, the pure and the cheap, clown and creator, god and buffoon." It was the Louis who, guest-starring on the Dorsey Brothers' television show, had said over a network microphone, "Don't play it too fast, and not too slow—just half-fast." It was the Louis III who, during a joint concert tour with Benny Goodman, insisted that Velma Middleton do the splits and followed it up with an unprintable joke. This was Louis the Inimitable Personality—"Louis, like the River Mississippi," as Kempton said, "pure like its source, flecked and choked with jetsam like its middle, broad and triumphant like its end."

1961

Louis rounded out his sixth decade by conquering new worlds. A joyful return to Britain in 1956, after an absence of twenty-two years, was followed by an African tour, preserved on film by Edward R. Murrow in his remarkable documentary

Satchmo the Great. The All Stars visited South America as well as appearing in films made in Hollywood, Newport, Denmark, and Germany. By now Louis was recording every type of popular music and jazz, with groups ranging from the Oscar Peterson Trio to the Dukes of Dixieland.

In the winter of 1960–61 he returned to Africa for a big tour, followed by a trip to Mexico. I visited Louis and Lucille in Palm Springs, California, where he was working at the Chi Chi Club, and learned a little about his latest successes.

"What was so nice about Africa," said Lucille, "was that Louis didn't just entertain. He was entertained, too, by the native music and dances of each country. The artists would meet us with their band at the airport, or put on a special show for us wherever we were staying."

"Don't forget about Mexico City," added Louis. "They had a band at the airport there too—native cats with guitars. The people were beautiful to us. Of course it was rush, rush, rush, but I kept my chops in shape and the people loved us."

"Louis," I said, "you've enjoyed just about every possible honor and you've visited almost every country. Don't you ever feel like cooling it a little?"

"Well, when I take time off," said Satch, "I want to make it a whole year. I'd like to just sit home and edit some more of my tapes. And I'd like to go around and catch all the bands and singers. Let me be a civilian for a change! Might even settle down in Las Vegas someday—so many places there to dig some real great entertainment.

"Even if I take that year off, I'll want to keep my chops up so I can always come back and blow some more. People are always asking me when am I gonna quit. I tell them, musicians don't quit; they just stop when there ain't no more gigs!"

Louis did not live to take his year's sabbatical. Except for brief bouts of illness he was active until the summer of 1968; by then his gradual but eventually very noticeable weight loss had begun to worry his old friends and fans. In September he was admitted to Beth Israel Hospital for a thorough examination.

1969

Louis' final years were characterized by attacks of serious illness alternating with incredible recoveries. Released from the hospital in January of 1969, he was back within a month. "Mr. Louis Armstrong decided he wanted to stay up all night as if he were a 21-year-old kid," Joe Glaser said. "And Mr. Armstrong is now back in the hospital." Then, as if aware that his words seemed harsh and unfeeling, he added: "Don't worry, Leonard, Louis'll be out soon. He's taking care of himself this time."

Ironically, Glaser himself was admitted to the same hospital in April after suffering a stroke. It was a heavy blow to Louis' morale. "I went to see him, but he didn't *know* me," Louis said later. Louis was released in June, but Glaser died after lingering for two months without regaining consciousness.

Soon afterward, I received a handwritten letter:

June 28, 1969

Dear Leonard:

I am writing my letters on the back of my Diet Charts (if you'll notice) because I have so many of them, and with so many Charts and my own personal writing paper, man that will really Clutter up the Joint . . .

We are just about cooling down over the passing of our dear Pal Mr. Glaser. Lucille and Myself went to the church Service where he was laid out. A real nice funeral. Everybody was there. The family, the Members from the Office and the head men from all over the Country, and all of his Admirers and Acts were there. Dr. Alexander Schiff managed all of the funeral arrangements. He was with Mr. Glaser at the hospital the whole time . . . The Family came from Chicago and when the service was over they flew the body to Chicago for burial.

There were so many people there I could only wave at them . . .

I am just waiting - resting - blowing just enough to Eula-gize the Chops, in other words, to keep my embrasure up "ya dig" thats a beeg word that I very seldom use. Anyway it all sums up that I'm about to feel like my Old Self Again. I Never Sqawk About Anything. I feel like this—As long as a person is Still Breathing, he's got a Chance, Right? Lucille's fine, sends a big hello to you and your wife. Thanks again. Here's swinging Atcha,

Louis Armstrong "Satch"

Late in 1969, Louis worked his first gig in more than a year: he taped a theme for the film *Her Majesty's Secret Service*. But he was under strict orders from his physician, Dr. Schiff, not to blow his horn. His occasional appearances were limited to singing.

1970

Although tributes and celebrations had long since become his way of life, few if any were more important to Satch than the seventieth birthday celebration arranged by his old friend Floyd Levin, head of the Southern California Hot Jazz Society. Louis arrived at Los Angeles airport on the evening of June 30 and found, to his surprise, something he normally expected only at foreign airports: a big brass band, and hundreds of fans jamming the arrival area. Lucille did her best to whisk him away from the surging crowd and the Armstrongs left for their hotel after a brief press conference.

The concert was held at the Shrine Auditorium on the night of July 3, after a year of planning by a coalition of California Dixieland clubs. Almost 50 traditionalist jazzmen had been rounded up to represent various phases of the Satchmo story. I opened the proceedings by introducing the master of ceremonies, Hoagy Carmichael, who brought the guest of honor to the stage. At the sight of Louis, the crowd of 6,000 rose to its feet; the applause was as heartfelt and as long-lasting as one of Pops' high-C finales.

Seated in a rocking chair in front of a New Orleans French Quarter backdrop, Louis and Hoagy sang an unaccompanied duet—"Rockin' Chair," which they had recorded together in 1929. They then commented on a series of slides, which showed the wooden backyard building where Louis was born; thirteen-year-old Louis playing in the Waifs' Home band; the 1918 riverboat ensemble, and King Oliver's Creole band in 1923, with Louis on second cornet. As these reminders flashed on the screen, Louis reminisced freely while a succession of combos filed onstage to amplify his stories with music. (The riverboat band included, fittingly, many men who had been playing for years in a boat on a simulated Mississippi at Disneyland.)

Later, in a recreation of the Oliver band, Louis heard an old buddy, Andy Blakeney, who had replaced him with Oliver in 1924. The Armstrong Hot Five was represented by Teddy Buckner's group. Another combo, announced as the "Ambassador Satch Band," had four Armstrong alumni: Barney Bigard, Tyree Glenn, Joe Bushkin, and Red Callender.

As the midnight deadline approached, Louis reappeared to croak "Sleepy Time Down South," followed by "Blueberry Hill"; then he hypnotized the happy crowd into a sing-along, clap-along "Hello Dolly!" with Tyree Glenn up front playing the obbligato.

The evening was climaxed when an 800-pound cake, 11 feet high, was wheeled onstage. Satchmo had to climb up seven steps to take a slice off the top. In all it was a night filled with joy and love, in which the only missing element was the sound of Satchmo's horn. The question nagged at all of us: would he ever play again? "I still practice an hour a day, every evening before dinner," he told me. "Dr. Schiff says maybe I'll be ready in a couple of months."

Ready or not, his mere presence meant instant nostalgia to his fans. Everyone at the Shrine had his own private memory of Louis; perhaps a long-forgotten dance in a Depression-era ballroom; perhaps a forty-year-old Hot Five record that had triggered a career in music; perhaps the recollection of departed giants who had become part of the Armstrong legend —Joe Oliver, Jack Teagarden, Edmond Hall, Billy Kyle.

The next afternoon, on his actual birthday, Louis relaxed quietly with Tyree Glenn, Barney and Dorothe Bigard, Floyd Levin, and a few other friends in the sunlit penthouse apartment of Bobby Phillips of Associated Booking Corporation, the organization Joe Glaser had headed until his death.

Perhaps because Dr. Schiff was present, or perhaps because Louis wanted us all to know how seriously he took his doctor's injunction, he even refused to toot a note on a small toy trumpet that was handed him as a gag during the birthday party.

Looking back at the nostalgic joys of the previous evening, Louis turned to Levin and said: "Man, I've had a lot of wonderful honors in my life, but last night was the biggest thrill of all." So it had been for many of us whose pleasure was dimmed only by the belief that Louis had long since blown his final chorus.

As it turned out, the impossible took a little while. Two months later the International Hotel in Las Vegas announced: "The Pearl Bailey Show, with Louie Bellson and His Orchestra. Special Guest Attraction—Louis Armstrong." Pearl Bailey had the unprecedented pleasure of sharing her customary standing ovations with a legend brought back from limbo, and the overtones of this evening made it unforgettable.

It was not just Louis himself we applauded as he ambled onstage to the opening stanza of "Sleepy Time Down South"; it was the fact that he was once again able to play his horn, for the first time after two years of illness.

Satchmo and his combo (most of his 1968 men were back with him) cruised through their traditional show, with the usual "Indiana" for openers, followed by "Someday," "Tiger

Rag," and "The Saints," among others. His horn had lost none
of its incandescence. His sound might have been stronger, but
we told ourselves that time would take care of that. Each note
was perfectly on target and Armstrong-pure.

The teaming of Pearl and Louis was a delight as they
traded choruses, from "Bill Bailey" to "Blueberry Hill." "Didn't
We?" with occasional vocal murmurs from Satch, was Miss
Bailey's most affecting ballad. For a finale the two of them
went through a mutually stimulating series of choruses on
"Exactly Like You." "There was an awful lot of love in the
house tonight," Miss Bailey said later.

More than thirty-eight years had gone by since my first
personal exposure to the Armstrong horn. It was just as well
that nothing alerted me, during this evening of celebration, to
the fact that this was, for me, the last time.

1971

(From an obituary in the Los Angeles *Times,* July 1971)
Many will characterize Louis Armstrong's passing as the
death of an era; yet the end of the Satchmo saga is in fact
much more than that.

It reminds us jarringly that no matter how far jazz improvisation may have come in the past half-century, it might
well have reached a dead end, or at best would have taken a
far less adventurous course, had it not been for the inspiration of Louis' lustrous, straight-talking trumpet and uniquely
hobbled vocal cords.

How much progress, in fact, had the art of the jazz solo
made before the first contributions recorded by Louis as a
sideman with King Oliver in 1923? You could answer by pos-
ing an analogous question: How far had transportation developed before the invention of the wheel?

Until Louis arrived, most jazzmen lumbered along, armed
with a fairly limited technique, an awareness of the harmony

of a given tune, and a vague intuitive ability to ad-lib in and around the chords. They were, for the most part, happy primitives.

Louis was different in every respect. He developed, in the earliest years, a command of the horn and a pure, legitimate trumpet sound that nobody before him had achieved. His idols were not only fellow jazzmen, but concert-trumpet virtuosi such as B. A. Rolfe.

He conceived each solo not as a series of trial runs through the chords but as a cohesive entity, as much a melody in its own right as the original tune on which the improvisation was based.

Stylistically he was the first link in a chain. Most experts feel that Armstrong led directly to Roy Eldridge, who in due course was the motivating power behind Dizzy Gillespie, who in turn inspired Miles Davis.

Placed in the context of a present-day abstraction by Davis, Satchmo's solos on such classics as "Knockin' a Jug," "Mahogany Hall Stomp," "Rockin' Chair," and "Confessin'" may seem primordial in their simplicity; yet of the thousands of jazz records made during the 1920s and early 1930s, his works, in their declarative beauty, have withstood almost alone the shattering test of time.

Trumpeters, then and now, have revered him for his unequaled sublimation of the blues idiom ("West End Blues," "Muggles," and others among his early masterpieces were based on this traditional jazz form); for his expansion of the range of the horn (musicians in the early days would sit unbelieving in the audience, counting off the high C's at the end of "Tiger Rag"), and later for his unprecedented role in transforming popular songs of the day into valid jazz media, a facet of his talent that was established worldwide with his 1929 record of "I Can't Give You Anything but Love."

Dizzy Gillespie had called him "The cause of the trumpet in jazz." Clark Terry once said: "Without him we wouldn't have had anything to follow." Roy Eldridge said: "Anything I achieved was due to the time I spent listening to Pops."

His influence was by no means limited to trumpeters. Earl Hines, his principal aide in most of the classic Armstrong Hot Five records of the late 1920s, gained a reputation as "the trumpet-style pianist" as elements of Louis were incorporated into his solos. As saxophonist Benny Carter commented, "No matter what instrument we play, there's a lot of Louis in all of us."

For those who knew only the Louis who grinned and clowned his way through movies and TV shows, it is hard to form a true perspective of his contribution. Phrases casually tossed off in an early version of "You Rascal You" or "Dipper Mouth Blues" may have endured as clichés employed by composers and arrangers in studio orchestras who do not know, or have forgotten, the source of their unconscious borrowing.

Singers acknowledge a similar debt. The line from Louis to Billie Holiday, Ella Fitzgerald, even Frank Sinatra, can be traced just by studying their phrasing and by comparing them with other singers who emerged around the time Louis scatted his way through "Heebie Jeebies."

Armstrong was the first to justify what has become the hoariest platitude applied to every singer who has since attempted to emulate his initiative: he really used his voice as if it were an instrument.

Louis was a pervasive influence from the crucial Chicago period (1923–29) through the early years in New York. Admittedly, by the late 1930s, when he was touring with a cumbersome and generally uninspired big band, he had fallen in line with the requirements of the swing era and of the show-business world into which he had been orbited; yet, if beyond this point he may be said to have adjusted to a new image as a giant of popular music, his jazz creativity was never far below the surface.

To most musicians his last great works were two albums

recorded in the mid-1950s with the small group he had led since breaking up the big band in 1947: *Satch Plays Fats,* an anthology of Fats Waller songs, and *Louis Armstrong Plays W. C. Handy.* On these occasions there seemed to be a fire under Louis that had burned only fitfully when he sang "Blueberry Hill" or jived with Bing Crosby.

Now that Louis is gone, the artist who will remain with us, hopefully in the form of carefully assembled reissues, will not be the goodwill ambassador who hobnobbed with royalty; rather he will be the prevaudeville Louis, the dedicated, seminal artist who earned the awed admiration of fellow jazzmen and who, more than any other performer before or since his original impact, affected the entire course of an indigenous American music.

Leonard Feather

The Duke

DUKE ELLINGTON is to composed and orchestrated jazz what Louis Armstrong is to jazz improvisation. Ellington was the first to show signs of bringing the music out of its primarily intuitive early stages into a new phase marked by orthodox musicianship and, in the best sense of the word, sophistication.

My relationship with Ellington has brought me from time to time so close to the music, the man, and the mystique enveloping him that my attitude, given an almost lifelong admiration for him and his orchestra, has most often been subjective. At other points I have remained far enough removed to evaluate the Duke more objectively.

In the early 1940s I worked for him, handling publicity, writing press releases, working on special events (principally his initial Carnegie Hall concert), and in the process finding myself drawn into the orbit of the Ellington "family." This meant not only his blood relatives but all those who, fired by their love for his music, became a sort of self-appointed palace guard for the man. The family included everyone from his doctor to his booking agent to a cadre of fans, all of whom attached themselves to him in friendships of varying intensity and predictably wound up as defenders of the Ellington faith, following every move made by Duke and all his sidemen and showing up with loyal regularity at any event, important or trivial, in which he was involved.

A master of the art of playing associates off against one another, Ellington enjoys the game thoroughly, safe in the knowledge that in the final analysis, to use his own perennial cliché, we will all still love him madly.

It is a reflection of the fidelity of the Ellington adherents that there has been since 1958 a very active Duke Ellington Society, a sort of high-level fan club that holds monthly meetings in New York, inviting as honored guest speakers just about anyone who has ever been a part of the orchestra from his music copyist to the third trombonist. The Ellington Society members are by and large mature men and women who have followed Duke and bought his records for periods ranging up to forty-five years. The object of their affection, although obviously flattered by the existence of this organization, has remained generally aloof from active participation and has rarely appeared at meetings. (Curiously, the only other significant fan organization now devoted to a bandleader is that of the late Glenn Miller.)

Ellington the man is an enigmatic figure with a steel-trap mind that few, if any, of those closest to him have ever succeeded in prying open. It is significant that in Stanley Dance's book *The World of Duke Ellington* (1970), only four brief opening chapters comprise quotes from the maestro; the rest of the book is a series of interviews profiling dozens of sidemen, accounts of trips made by the band, lists of records, and similar secondhand items. In a nine-line introduction Ellington wrote: "Stanley . . . has been a part of our scene for a long time, maybe longer than he cares to remember. However I am sure he has not revealed more than he ought"—a remark that may be interpreted as kidding on the square. Ellington gave even shorter shrift to a book by Barry Ulanov published a quarter of a century earlier and written without his cooperation or consent.

Like other distinguished men Ellington finds himself surrounded by people who need him, who have something to gain from his patronage. They form a protective shield that has long enabled him to keep, at least outwardly, his imperturbable cool.

Logically the man who may be closest to him and who certainly has spent more time with him socially than any other individual, aside from his immediate family, over the past decade or two, is someone who has nothing to gain from his closeness except the pleasure of the friendship. He is Harold "Bob" Udkoff, a wealthy swimming-pool manufacturer whose home in Encino, California, has been the setting for many parties at which Ellington was the de facto guest of honor. Udkoff, who became an Ellington fan as a teen-ager, has been a part of Duke's entourage on most of the orchestra's overseas jaunts in recent years, including the trip to the U.S.S.R. in late 1971.

Although he would not dream of capitalizing on his friendship by doing so, Udkoff as much as anyone could write the definitive book: one that could give us a Duke's-eye view of the world and an honest, intimate, inside picture of Ellington the total, admirable, fallible, scrutable human being who bleeds when pricked and cries inwardly when hurt, who knows how to employ the invective of impatience as well as the magniloquence of diplomacy.

My own observations clarify the extent and nature of Ellington's accomplishments and attempt to shed some light on the man behind them.

Edward Kennedy Ellington knows he is a great man. If and when he denies his greatness, he does so in the knowledge that a great man must include modesty among his most conspicuous characteristics.

What Duke Ellington knows, and has gladly accepted since around 1925, is that his peer has yet to be found among jazz composers, arrangers, and conductors. Cushioned by this knowledge, lulled by it into a permanent state of emotional ease, Ellington drifts through his daily life as though in a dream —in a world where such unpleasant realities as boxoffice failures, moochers, swindlers, racism, junkies, and the need to meet deadlines simply do not exist. When one of these problems touches him he shrugs it off, looks the other way, or finds some stratagem through which to convince himself that the incident or unpleasantness never took place, or happened to somebody else.

Barry Ulanov, in *Duke Ellington* (published in 1946 and long out of print), made it clear that the Duke's self-confidence is not of recent origin:

When he was late in getting up for school, his mother or his Aunt Florence would shake him and push him and rush him out of bed into his clothes. Once dressed, Duke would change his tempo. He would come downstairs slowly, elegantly. At the foot of the stairs he would stop and call to his mother and his aunt.

"Stand over there," he would direct, pointing to the wall. "Now," he would say, "listen. This," he would say slowly, with very careful articulation, "is the great, the grand, the magnificent Duke Ellington." Then he would bow. Looking up at his smiling mother and aunt, he would add, "Now applaud, applaud." And then he would run off to school.

The great, the grand, the magnificent Duke Ellington has been on display before a worldwide audience for some four and a half decades. Most experts place the starting point of fame at December 4, 1927, the night the ten-man Ellington orchestra opened at the Cotton Club, which was to Negro show business what the Palace was to vaudeville. (The Palace itself was to open its stage to the band less than two years later.) Ellington was then, and is now, an imposing figure. An inch over six feet tall, sturdily built, he had an innate grandeur that would have enabled him to step with unquenched dignity out of a mud puddle. His phrasing of an announcement, the elegance of his diction, the supreme courtesy of his bow, whether to a duchess in London or a theater audience in Des Moines, has lent stature not only to his own career but to the whole of jazz. Since the music he represented was stifled for many years by several kinds of segregation—social, esthetic, and racial—this element certainly played a vital part in bringing to jazz its full recognition, just as his music itself brought the art he epitomized to a new peak of maturity.

Although he and his band have slipped from first place in some of the popularity polls, musicians and critics remain almost unanimous in their respect for Ellington and in their conviction that nothing and nobody—no matter how loud the fanfare, how fickle the votes—can replace or surpass his position as the greatest figure in the sixty-year dynasty of jazz. None but Ellington can claim the reverent respect of an eclectic unofficial fan club composed of Woody Herman, Milton Berle, Arthur Fiedler, Peggy Lee, Percy Faith, Deems Taylor, Pee Wee Russell, Lena Horne, Lennie Tristano, Benny Goodman, Guy Lombardo, Dave Garroway, Cole Porter, Morton Gould, Lawrence Welk, Andre Kostelanetz, and Gordon Jenkins, all of whom not only tossed verbal bouquets at Ellington on the occasion of the silver anniversary of his Cotton Club debut but also listed five of their favorite Ellington records. No other bandleader alive could persuade such a galaxy even to *name* five of his records, far less select the five best.

The Ellington orchestra, aside from a few leaves of absence (including a Hollywood jaunt for its movie debut in a mediocre Amos and Andy feature, *Check and Double Check*), spent all of 1928, 1929, and 1930 at the Cotton Club. In later years it was to subside into a pattern more familiar to dance orchestras, that of the floating band with occasional home bases. Ever since then, Ellington and his sidemen have been accustomed to the necessity of interminable one-night stands, with only an occasional one- or two-week stint at a major city and, very rarely, a few days of comparative leisure in New York to complete a recording date. Duke has been constantly under pressure from well-meaning friends and relatives who point out that his income might actually be boosted if he were to keep the band on salary, and on tour, for three or four months out of each year and spend the rest of his time at ease in New York, stretching his legs and mental muscles, writing music for shows, and possibly acquiring the permanent television program that has long been one of his dreams. But Ellington without his musicians would be lost. "I want to have them around me to play my music," he has often said; "I'm not worried about creating music for posterity, I just want it to sound good right now!"

Ellington's background upsets most of the convenient legends that envelop jazz giants. Born not in New Orleans but in Washington, D.C., he was raised not in poverty but in relative security, the son of a butler who worked at the White House and at many great parties held in the capital's embassies. Despite the rigid Jim Crow system that held fast in Washington, Ellington grew up a well-adjusted child.

Duke's nickname was awarded him in obvious deference to his polished style and manner by a young neighbor, Ralph (Zeb) Green. Zeb and Duke's mother both liked to play piano, but apart from a few piano lessons when he was seven, Ellington had little interest in music until his middle teens. Before then, studying at Armstrong High in Washington, he became absorbed in art, revealed a nimble talent for sketching, and won a poster contest sponsored by the NAACP. The kicks he got out of making posters and working with colors paled as he developed a more intense concern for tone colors; by the time the Pratt Institute of Applied Arts in Brooklyn had offered him a scholarship, his interests had switched to music and he turned the offer down.

During this period the ragtime surrounding Ellington provided ample evidence that jazz had long been flourishing far from New Orleans, often wrongly credited as its sole birthplace. Talking of the "two-fisted piano players" of that era, he recalls "men like Sticky Mack and Doc Perry and James P. Johnson and Willie 'The Lion' Smith . . . With their left hand they'd play big chords for the bass note, and just as big ones for the offbeat . . . they did things technically you wouldn't believe." He had little time for the garrulous Jelly Roll Morton, whose reputation was built on Jelly's own ego rather than on musical values: "Jelly Roll played piano like one of those high school teachers in Washington; as a matter of fact, high school teachers played better jazz."

Ellington's informal music education, acquired from pianists he heard around Washington and later in New York, combined with his meager formal training, enabled him to make a substantial living out of music almost from the outset. Engaged in sign-painting by day and combo gigs by night, he was well enough fixed financially to get married in June 1918 to Edna Thompson, whom he had known since their grade-school days. The following year Mercer Ellington was born. In 1919, by supplying bands for parties and dances, Duke was making upward of $150 a week. He attributes much of this early success to his decision to buy the largest advertisement in the orchestra section of Washington's classified telephone directory.

Ellington's first sojourn in New York in 1922—with Sonny Greer, Toby Hardwicke, Elmer Snowden, and Arthur Whetsel —was the only period in his life marked by real poverty. Jobs were so scarce, Duke remembers, that at one point they were forced to split a hot dog five ways. With the help of Ada Smith, who was later to achieve fame in Europe under the cognomen "Bricktop," the band opened at Barron's in Harlem under Snowden's nominal leadership. When they moved into a cellar club called the Hollywood at Forty-ninth and Broadway, Duke became the leader and Freddy Guy took over Snowden's banjo chair. This was their first downtown job, and it was during their incumbency at the Hollywood, later known as the Kentucky Club, that they made their first records.

The Kentucky Club era, which lasted four and a half years, provided a storehouse of warm memories for the band: wild breakfast parties after the job; the patronage of Paul Whiteman and his musicians, working a block down Broadway at the Palais Royale; $50 and $100 tips; Duke's first attempt to write the score for a show (*The Chocolate Kiddies* in 1924, which never made Broadway but ran for two years in Berlin); and the uninhibited bathtub gin celebrations by Duke, Bubber Miley, and Toby Hardwicke in the face of Prohibition.

It was the late Ted Husing, a prominent radio announcer of the day and one of the band's early and regular ringsiders, who helped to secure its first broadcasts at the Kentucky Club. "East St. Louis Toddle-O," a minor-to-major lament with an acute accent on plunger-muted brass, became the band's radio theme.

"I'll never forget the first time I heard Edward's music," says Duke's sister, Ruth. "Of course, we'd heard him at home, playing ragtime, but here he was playing his own music with his own band on the radio from New York, coming out of this old-fashioned horn-speaker. I think radio had just about been invented . . . or at least just launched commercially.

"It was quite a shock. Here we were, my mother and I, sitting in this very respectable Victorian living room in Washington, my mother so puritanical she didn't even wear lipstick, and the announcer from New York tells us we are listening to 'Duke Ellington and his Jungle Music!' It sounded very strange and dissonant to us."

"Black and Tan Fantasy," on which Miley growled the famous interpolation from Chopin's "Funeral March," may have horrified the Ellington family, but it succeeded in catching the attention of a man named Irving Mills. A successful song publisher who was beginning to extend his practice by dabbling in the management of artists, Mills soon formed a corporation in which he and Duke each owned 45 percent and a lawyer the other 10 percent. It was the start of a partnership that lasted through the thirties, through the first great years of the Ellington story. Confident that his counsel and guidance were tantamount to full collaboration, Mills published the Ellington songs and also appeared on record labels and sheet music as co-composer of most of the famous Ellington hits of the thirties, among them "Mood Indigo," "Sophisticated Lady,"

"Solitude," and "I Let a Song Go Out of My Heart." Years later Mills wrote that he "withdrew" from his relationship with Duke because he sensed that Ellington had "fallen into a different attitude toward his music, and was taking off into what I thought was a wrong direction." This claim was never disputed, nor was Ellington's side of the story ever quoted. His characteristic avoidance of subjects that could not be discussed without personal recriminations precluded any public comment.

Matters about which Ellington feels more able to comment include a rundown of several high spots and traumatic moments in his career, such as the band's first gig at the Palace Theatre, when they opened the show with "Dear Old Southland." "The men hadn't memorized their parts," recalls Duke, "and the show opened on a darkened stage. When I gave the downbeat, nothing happened—the men couldn't see a note."

A somewhat later highlight, one that flickered out prematurely, was *Jump for Joy,* a 1941 musical show in which the whole band took part. "A number of critics felt this was the hippest Negro musical ever," says Duke, but the show ran only three months in Los Angeles and never reached New York.

The evening of Saturday, January 23, 1943, was auspicious not only for Ellington but for jazz itself. This was the first Ellington concert at Carnegie Hall, and it was given under conditions that could not be reproduced today. A concert by a jazz orchestra was a rare novelty then (the last comparable event had been Benny Goodman's concert five years earlier), and the orchestra played a new work, *Black, Brown and Beige,* described by the Duke as a "tone parallel to the history of the American Negro." In its original form it ran for a full fifty minutes and was easily the most ambitious, spectacular, and successful extension of Ellingtonia to longer musical forms.

The concert, a black-tie affair, was a benefit for Russian War Relief. As Ellington has pointed out, the quality of the appreciation, the attentiveness of the 3,000 who listened that night, was a "model of audience reaction that has proved hard to duplicate." Ironically, when an Ellington jubilee concert was set for November 1952, the presentation of a self-sufficient orchestra introducing original works was no longer considered desirable; it was announced that the show would also include Billie Holiday, Charlie Parker, Stan Getz, and others. The concept of a jazz concert as Ellington had visualized it was dead, although in due course Duke would bring it back, stronger and more fully accepted than ever.

Another unforgettable occasion was the chaotic scene at Newport, Rhode Island, during the three-day jazz festival in July 1956. Performing an extended and revitalized version of a fast blues entitled "Diminuendo and Crescendo in Blue," first recorded in 1938 and lengthened on this occasion to fourteen minutes and fifty-nine choruses, Ellington and his band (with particular help from the frenetic tenor sax of Paul Gonsalves) whipped the audience into such a furor that elder jazz statesmen could recall no comparable scene since the riots in the aisles of New York's Paramount Theatre two decades earlier, during Benny Goodman's first wave of glory.

For all its value to Ellington in terms of the publicity it earned him, the almost accidental Newport triumph was to mean far less to him as a milestone than an auspicious and carefully planned event nine years later. In September of 1965, at Grace Cathedral in San Francisco, an astonishing precedent was set in the conjunction of jazz and the church when Duke offered the world premiere of his first sacred concert.

Despite its obvious relationship to the music heard in black churches, Afro-Americans as well as whites had looked on jazz at best with condescension and at worst had reviled it as "the devil's music." When Ellington was granted permission to play in a cathedral, American music took a momentous step forward.

Initiated by Dean Julian Bartlett ("I've been an Ellington fan for about 100 years"), the event had the blessing of a man who had become Duke's close friend, the late Bishop James A. Pike.

An overflow crowd hesitantly applauded Ellington's first entrance as if uncertain whether reverence was compatible with hero-worship. The program included excerpts from such earlier works as *Black, Brown and Beige* and his 1963 musical show *My People* (written for and introduced at the Century of Negro Progress Exhibition in Chicago), as well as some new pieces and a selection of spirituals.

Despite acoustical problems (those of us who attended the premiere had to wait for the LP version to gain a full perspective) there were many moments of sublime beauty. The evening reached a spectacular climax in a performance of "Come Sunday," one of Ellington's most beguiling and flexible melodies, with the whole band playing, Herman McCoy's seventeen-voice choir singing, the veteran vaudevillian Bunny Briggs tap-dancing, and Jon Hendricks singing a bop vocal. Only Ellington could have conceived such a disparate set of elements and brought them into rhythmic and harmonic cohesiveness. The breakthrough was internationally acknowledged as an historic step forward in the acceptance of jazz. During the years that followed, Ellington performed this and a second sacred concert program at churches, synagogues, and concert halls in many countries.

If the events chronicled above were in one manner or another professional steps forward for Ellington, the manner in which he celebrated his seventieth birthday was perhaps the most symbolic of the changes Duke has effected in the image as well as the quality of jazz. On April 29, 1969, in the State Dining Room of the White House, the President of the United States said: "I've lifted my glass here to emperors, kings, and prime ministers, but never before has a Duke been toasted. I ask you all to join me in raising our glasses to the greatest Duke of them all."

This was one of many emotional moments during an extraordinary evening. The dinner, the first of three segments that made up the event, was followed by a concert of Ellington's music, played by a specially assembled ten-piece band, with Duke and the Nixons as front-row spectators.

Just before the concert began, Nixon presented Ellington with the Presidential Medal of Freedom, the highest civilian award. It was the first such medal to be presented during this Administration. Ellington responded with a brief and characteristically dignified speech; then, in accordance with his time-honored custom, kissed the President four times on both cheeks.

The first performer in the East Room was Nixon himself. "I haven't played piano since I've been living here; however, I'll try if you'll join me—but, please, in the key of G." And in that key, we all sang as the President played "Happy Birthday."

The band comprised Clark Terry and Bill Berry, both Ellington alumni, on trumpets; J. J. Johnson and Urbie Green, trombones; Paul Desmond and Gerry Mulligan on saxophones; Hank Jones, piano; Jim Hall, guitar; Milt Hinton, bass, and Louie Bellson, another ex-Ellingtonian, at the drums. Tom Whaley, six years Duke's senior and for many years the band's music copyist, served as conductor.

There were a few guest soloists, notably Earl "Fatha" Hines, whose version of "Perdido" almost stole the show, and Joe Williams, whose deeply moving "Come Sunday" and highly charged "Jump for Joy" took the vocal honors.

As the program ended, Nixon rose to say: "I think we ought to hear from the Duke, too." Ellington, as much a life-long diplomat as he is an apolitical individual, replied: "Let me see . . . I'll just take a name, see what it suggests, and improvise on it—say, for instance, Pat."

A brief, pensive, extemporized solo, and the concert was over, but as Nixon said, "The evening is still young; there will be refreshments, a jam session, and dancing for all who wish."

What followed was unlike anything ever before heard in the White House. Lou Rawls, Joe Williams, and Billy Eckstine

traded verses on the blues, with Dizzy Gillespie blowing ob-
bligatos. Dr. Harold Taylor, President Emeritus of Sarah Lawrence College, and long an Ellington camp follower, played
some fine, funky clarinet; so did Leonard Garment, a one-time
saxophonist in Woody Herman's band. Garment had become
Nixon's law partner and by now was a Presidential adviser
who, along with a former Nixon campaign aide named Charles
McWhorter and Willis Conover of the Voice of America, had
conceived this birthday tribute.

Marine Band members sat in with amateur and professional jazzmen as the jamming and dancing continued until
2:15 A.M. Possession of the great piano with the golden eagle
legs switched hands many times: from Ellington to his old
friend Willie "The Lion" Smith to Marian McPartland to
George Wein to Billy Taylor and even to me.

The repercussions of this occasion have been felt in many
ways. The evening may have had an indirect bearing on the
sponsorship by the U.S. State Department, better belated than
never, of Duke's first Russian tour, which took place in 1971.

It would have been easy to write off the whole affair cyni-
cally as a political ploy. True, it redounded to the President's
benefit (during the evening one well-known musician commented: "After tonight I'd vote for him if he were running for
Grand Dragon of the Ku Klux Klan"); nevertheless, what
took place that night transcended questions of either politics
or race. White jazzmen for decades had been kept almost as
completely underground in American society as their black
colleagues. While an entire art form was stigmatized as vulgar
and trivial, Bix Beiderbecke went to his grave without newspaper obituaries, a genius too far ahead of his time.

Respectability was the name of the game, and respectability is what Ellington, more than any other man living or dead,
had brought to jazz in his music, his bearing, and his impact
on society.

During the years of his undisputed acceptance as certainly
the world's foremost jazz orchestra leader and composer, El-

lington's career moved forward in three different areas. From the economic standpoint and in terms of mass popularity, he accomplished his greatest achievements as a song writer. Some of his biggest hits were written hastily in taxis, trains, and recording studios and are simple single-note lines designed to be set to lyrics; others, whether written casually or more formally, were primarily instrumentals for the orchestra but were later furnished with words. At this level Ellington is in the field with Cole Porter, Harold Arlen, and Richard Rodgers.

From the esthetic standpoint Ellington's significance as a contributor to the culture of the twentieth century lies in his orchestrations of original music for the instrument he plays best—his own orchestra. These range from simple blues and stomps to such elaborate efforts as the "Liberian Suite," "New World a Comin'," "Blue Belles of Harlem" and "Blutopia," all of which were heard during the annual Carnegie Hall series but few of which have been preserved on records. Later suites were dedicated to the Virgin Islands, the Far East, and New Orleans. In this department Ellington's counterparts are Quincy Jones, Oliver Nelson, Gil Evans, Gerald Wilson, and Don Ellis.

And there is Ellington the dance band leader, who occasionally (but not often in the past decade) tried for a hit record and came up with something like "Twelfth Street Rag" or "Isle of Capri Mambo" to sail with a prevailing wind. He was even persuaded at one point to record an LP of songs from the Disney film *Mary Poppins*. This Ellington, conscious in recent years of the implacable exigencies of the commercial world, is apt to open a dance date or even a stage show with an arrangement of "Stompin' at the Savoy," which was neither composed nor arranged by anyone in the band and has about as much of the Ellington stamp as a Guy Lombardo arrangement of "Solitude." In this sphere Ellington's contemporaries presently include Harry James, Count Basie, and Woody Herman.

Not content to limit himself to mere composing, orchestrating, and leading a band, Ellington has set his sights on many other goals. As a composer-dramatist he was responsible in 1957 for *A Drum Is a Woman,* a sort of jazz-tinged opera-cum-ballet, shown in color on CBS-TV, in which he was the slightly specious narrator. As a lyric writer he revealed his ability to achieve a simple beauty in the pyramid-lined word construction of "The Blues," the only lyricized part of *Black, Brown and Beige,* and a sophisticated brand of hip humor in a monologue he used to recite called "Pretty and the Wolf."

Since the late 1950s the accretion of the years, which in other men might have called for a gradual slowdown of activity and a graceful move toward semiretirement, seems only to have stimulated Ellington to more and greater enterprises in an ever-broadening variety of fields. Musicians less than half his age have marveled at his ability to drive or fly hundreds of miles a day to a gig, sit up after the job talking with friends or composing, go to bed at 9 A.M., rise at 4 P.M., eat a steak breakfast and be cheerfully prepared to meet his public at 8:30 P.M., then leave at 2 A.M. for a one-night stand in another state or another country.

His limitless energy and ambition have taken him into a long-delayed stab at motion-picture writing. Hollywood never sought his services during the first thirty years of his world-wide acceptance as a major American writer. The reasons were very basic: racist attitudes (black composers were rarely used except as ghost writers for whites) and the long-standing prejudice against the use of jazz in film scores, which kept white as well as black writers from attaining their objectives.

Ellington's first score, in 1959, was *Anatomy of a Murder,* in which he was also seen in a small acting role as a pianist in a bar. There have been a few other assignments since then, including a quickly forgotten Frank Sinatra film called *Assault on a Queen.* For the most part Ellington has used key men from his own orchestra along with a phalanx of Hollywood studio musicians. The most successful of his attempts to gain a foothold in this field was the 1960–61 *Paris Blues,* recorded with an augmented band, which earned him an Academy Award nomination.

Television has seldom made suitable use of his talent for scoring. He wrote the main theme and scored the first segment of the *Asphalt Jungle* series in 1960; since then his ambitions in this field have never achieved realization.

Perhaps the most frustrating facet of his omnidirectional life has been the desire to succeed on Broadway. The abortive life of *Jump for Joy* has been noted. At intervals since then, there have been rumors that he would stage his own musical show, or a straight drama, or a comedy with music, or some other such venture. One such project, an adaptation of *The Blue Angel* retitled *Sugar City*, folded before it could even boast an out-of-town opening.

Duke fitted a score to the onstage action for *Turcaret*, a play by the seventeenth-century French playwright Alain Le Sage. He conducted the performance on its opening night at the Palais de Chaillot (this was during the period when he was busy on location scoring *Paris Blues*). Closer to home and more generally recognized was his first ballet, *The River*. Commissioned by the American Ballet Theater, it was choreographed by Alvin Ailey and has been presented in New York and Washington to enthusiastic reviews.

Another area that has expanded during the past decade has been his occasional collaboration with other orchestras: appearances or recordings with the Cincinnati Symphony (generally successful), the Boston Pops at Tanglewood (hobbled by a string section that was incapable of jazz phrasing), and Ron Collier's Canadian orchestra, with Duke as guest soloist performing the works of Canadian composers.

Asked why he has ventured so often into undertakings that have tended to disappoint him, Ellington once replied, "What the hell, you have to have some direction, you've got to go somewhere looking for new things to do." In other words, having scaled every peak available to him, he has had to look for new heights to conquer. "I'm so damned fickle," he once said.

"I never could stick with what I was doing—always wanted to try something new."

Ellington's personality is riddled with paradoxes. His deep personal attachments are few but intense. When his mother died a lingering death in 1935, he was at her bedside for the last three days, inconsolably griefstricken. Two years later his father died in a New York hospital with both his children beside him. His sister, Ruth, sixteen years his junior, became Duke's closest friend and confidante. Dr. Arthur Logan, the family physician for the past thirty years, caters to his hypochondriacal tendencies. Fundamentally strong and healthy, Ellington gave up his heavy drinking around 1940 but did not stop indulging his insatiable appetite until 1956, when he embarked on a diet and reduced his contours by some thirty-five pounds.

Ellington's vanity takes strange turns. His son, Mercer, tall and good-looking like his father, has had several chaotic careers—bandleader, trumpet player, band manager, liquor salesman, record company executive, disc jockey, and general aide-de-camp to his father—and was for many years the object of Duke's vacillations between parental pride and a desire to hide from the calendar. The two have been much closer since 1965, when Mercer joined the band as trumpeter and band manager. Level-headed and amiable, he is, according to veteran sidemen, the best manager the orchestra has ever had.

Ellington's customary demeanor, with strangers or casual friends, is one of sardonic badinage or subtle sarcasm that catches the victim unaware. "We are indeed honored by the presence of such luminous company," he will say with a low bow to a song publisher whose company he would be delighted to dispense with. His capacity for small talk is endless. Complimented by a feminine guest on a striking blue-and-gray checked jacket he wore during one engagement, he promptly responded: "Yes, I was up all afternoon sitting at the loom, weaving it to impress you." It is difficult to coax him into an intellectual discussion; his reluctance to bruise any feelings and his desire to remain noncontroversial are jointly responsible.

Ellington is an incomparably affable mixer, as befits one who, alone among jazz musicians, has enjoyed the respect of Leopold Stokowski (who came into the Cotton Club, sat discussing music with Duke, and invited him to his own concert the following evening at Carnegie Hall); President Truman ("whom I found very affable and musically informed," he remarked after a private audience at the White House); the then Prince of Wales (now the Duke of Windsor: "He sat in with us on drums in London and surprised everybody, including Sonny Greer"); George, Duke of Kent ("I fluffed off the guy who kept requesting tunes all night, then found out he was the King's son"); as well as uncounted heads of state and, particularly in recent years, religious leaders of every denomination.

Some of his fans have wondered why Ellington has tended at times to follow trends set by others, particularly in view of his record of innovations. His was the first band to use the human voice as a wordless musical instrument ("Creole Love Call" in 1927); first to devote an entire work to a single jazz soloist ("Clarinet Lament" for clarinetist Barney Bigard in 1936); first to use extended forms beyond the standard three-minute length of the 78 rpm record (the six-minute "Creole Rhapsody" and twelve-minute "Reminiscing in Tempo" in the early 1930s); first to use the bass as a melody solo instrument (Jimmy Blanton, 1939); first to make elaborate use of rubber-plunger mutes that became an indispensable part of that hard-to-define element known as the Ellington sound.

Asked why he plays songs like "Birth of the Blues," or features nondescript singers rehashing "Lover Man," which reflect little or nothing of what is commonly identified with what he represents in esthetic terms, he may remark brusquely that nobody can dictate to him what is meant by the Ellington sound and that the pieces thus criticized are warmly received by the audience.

Ellington's oldest and closest friend within the band is

Harry Carney. Born in 1910, Carney joined the band at the age of sixteen, has never left it, and is usually Duke's companion and driver between one-night stands. Musically Ellington's closest ties were with Billy Strayhorn, who composed and ar- ranged for the orchestra from 1939 until his death in 1967. Ellington had an almost telepathic understanding with "Strays," whose writing for the band so closely resembled Duke's own that veteran bandmen were often unable to discern where one left off and the other began.

Ellington's grief over the passing of Strayhorn, who died at fifty-one after a two-year battle with cancer, inspired him to one of his best-remembered literary efforts. In an essay eulogizing his friend he wrote that Strayhorn "demanded freedom of expression, and lived in what we consider the most important and moral of freedoms: freedom from hate, unconditionally; freedom from all self-pity (even throughout all the pain and bad news); freedom from fear of possibly doing something that might help another more than it might help himself; and freedom from the kind of pride that could make a man feel he was better than his brother or neighbor." This litany has since been recited by Duke on many occasions as part of the "Freedom" movement in his second sacred concert.

The Ellington employment policy has always been unique. The idea of firing anyone is so repugnant to Duke that he will tolerate unparalleled insubordination. It is no less painful to him to find a sideman quitting without due cause, which in his eyes means nothing less than complete physical disability or retirement. Men stepping out to form their own groups have hurried off the bandstand to the echo of Ellington's laconic comment, "He'll be back," and in a matter of months or years this has almost always been true. (Cootie Williams waited twenty-two years before coming back home in 1962.)

Observers of Ellington rehearsals, and even of public performances at which two or three men may amble in an hour late, find it hard to believe that the apparent lack of band morale can produce such exemplary music. They are no less bewildered by the team spirit in the brass, reed, and rhythm sections, even when certain men are not on speaking terms with Ellington or each other or both.

Duke's escapism and aloofness have had the valuable effect of keeping him clear of any musical hybridization, any involvement with other musical forms. He rarely listens to classical music, but when he does, his taste runs to such works as Ravel's *Daphnis and Chloë*, Debussy's *La Mer* and *Afternoon of a Faun*, and Delius' *In a Summer Garden*.

In addition to its complete independence from classical and modern concert music, Ellington's orchestration technique cannot be said to have founded any particular school within jazz itself. Direct imitation has often been found in the recordings of Charlie Barnet, Woody Herman, and others; the impact of Ellington on Oliver Nelson and other contemporary arrangers is unmistakable. Yet there is no true parallel between Ellington and any other jazz writer. The reason is simple: Ellington's works remain inscrutable. He has never allowed his orchestrations to be published, preferring to take the secrets of his voicings on a solo journey to posterity.

The result was best summed up by André Previn, a musician who was not yet born when the Cotton Club era began. "You know," he once said, "another bandleader can stand in front of a thousand fiddles and a thousand brass, give the downbeat, and every studio arranger can nod his head and say, 'Oh yes, that's done like this.' But Duke merely lifts his finger, three horns make a sound, and nobody knows what it is!"

Bert Block

Lady Day

In 1935, AT A studio on Long Island, Duke Ellington and his orchestra made one of their rare motion-picture appearances in an all-musical two-reeler, *Symphony in Black*. It incorporated, for a few incandescent moments, the totally unfamiliar and unidentified sight and sound of Billie Holiday. She sang just twelve bars of blues. The picture was made shortly before Billie's twentieth birthday; later that year her career was launched in earnest when the first records in which she was vocalist with Teddy Wilson's small band were released. They made a profound impact on the jazz audience.

Billie was a second-generation jazz artist; her father, Clarence Holiday, had played guitar with Fletcher Henderson and Benny Carter. She and Ella Fitzgerald became prominent at the same time. Both came from broken homes; both had suffered years of poverty and Jim Crow before achieving recognition as jazz singers; yet there the resemblance ends. Their subsequent attitudes, styles, and careers contrasted as sharply as those of Charlie Parker and Dizzy Gillespie a decade later: one an emotionally unstable, supremely innovative artist destined to die young, a victim of narcotics and of social pressures; the other a greatly gifted performer, who would ultimately be acknowledged as a major jazz influence, and live to enjoy the financial rewards and professional security that should have been achieved by both.

Although some critics believe (wrongly, in my opinion) that Ella Fitzgerald is no more than an exceptionally capable popular singer, no such assessment was ever made about Billie Holiday. Every note of every lyric she sang proved her to be the complete, untrained, unadulterated, definitive jazz singer.

To the public, of course, the front-page headline, freak-show aspect of her life was uppermost; ever since her death there has been talk of a motion picture or stage show about her. Ironically the artist most often suggested as best suited for the role of Billie Holiday used to be Dorothy Dandridge, whose own tragic life ended a few years after Billie's. After Billie's posthumous admission to the *Down Beat* Hall of Fame in 1962, I wrote: "It is easy to imagine how *The Billie Holiday Story* would shape up on Broadway or in Hollywood. Who will they get to sing the sound track? Mabel Mercer? Chris Connor? Who will score the music? Lawrence Welk?" Yet in 1971 fantasy became reality: It was announced that a multi-million-dollar motion picture was to be made in which the statuesque, jazz-rooted Billie Holiday would be portrayed by the diminutive, soul-soaked Diana Ross. As if this were not enough, Miss Ross would do her own sound track. If, God forbid, our grandchildren had to base their knowledge of musical history on the biographical distortions of the motion picture industry, they would be hard put to understand the high esteem in which we held some of our idols.

There are those who listen to Billie Holiday as they would read a Scott Fitzgerald novel. Too far separated from Billie's era to feel any direct sense of communication, they can nevertheless penetrate the veil of time drawing from her gifts-and-caviar tones some understanding of what she brought to music.

Then there are those who can hear Billie more subjectively, as part of a world they once knew, and remember a unique segment of musical history that returns fleetingly to life when they listen to her records.

I once wrote:

Billie Holiday's voice is one of the incomparable sounds that jazz has produced . . . the timbre, despite its gradual deepening through the years, has remained unique. The coarse yet warmly emotional quality of this sound, and the exquisite delicacy of her phrasing and dynamic nuances, were often given added luster by the support she gained from her long association with Lester Young and other members of the Basie band on her earlier records."

If you find no message here or in her records, perhaps the only thing you can do is take a backward journey through time and be born in the twenties, so that the arrival of Billie's glorious four years of regular sessions with the Teddy Wilson combos (Brunswick-Vocalion-Columbia) will coincide with your high school or college days. And by the time she spends a full year at the Onyx on Fifty-second Street, reducing audiences of noisy drunks to silence with her gracious, dignified, gardenia-embellished beauty as she sings her brand-new hit "Lover Man," you will be in your twenties, and part of a warm and wonderful new jazz era that is growing with Billie. By the time you are in your thirties you will have been so conditioned to a love of the Holiday sound that you will excuse the little flaws, the gradual withdrawal of assurance, the fading of the gardenia. By now you are in love with Lady Day and everything she does; each tortured lyric she sings about the men who have laid waste her life will have meaning for you whether she hits the note or misses it, holds it or lets it falter.

But chances are you weren't born in the twenties, and so you must listen to the early Holiday records as you might read *Tender Is the Night,* trying to assimilate the mood of the era. Perhaps it will bring her a little closer if you know something of the young woman who was the maker of so much that we found beautiful.

Billie died at forty-four. Like many people who lead turbulent, stimulant-governed lives, she was unpredictable, moody, impassioned, paradoxical. With the possible exception of her mother, there was not a single person among those she was fond of, or who were fond of her, with whom she was not at one time or another violently at odds. But Billie could not stay angry long with anyone, nor could any of us who loved her and quarreled with her hold onto our grievances. As her close friend Maely Dufty, wife of her biographer, once said: "Billie's not a woman—she's a habit."

It would be a gigantic oversimplification to pretend that social conditions alone shaped her life, formed her vocal style, led to her death. Ella Fitzgerald's family background was at least partly comparable to Billie's, yet Ella's career, untouched by scandal, brought her undreamed-of success. For Billie it was marijuana at fourteen, a jail term for prostitution at fifteen, and heroin addiction from her late twenties to her death.

What made the two singers' lives so different from one another? What caused the self-destructiveness in Billie that ultimately proved fatal?

For anyone who knew her, it is impossible to listen to Billie's records today and not be engulfed by a wave of nostalgia. With one of her early 78s on the turntable, I flash back to a small, dimly lit Harlem apartment in 1938, where I first interviewed Lady Day.

A door opened on the first floor up; a huge woman emerged, glancing down the stairs with mixed curiosity and suspicion. "You the feller wants to see Billie?"

There was no need to ask who was addressing me. The round face and full mouth; the whole impression of Billie multiplied by three, pound for pound, told me that this was Mrs. Holiday, the patient and aggrieved mother whose life was vainly dedicated to achieving communication with her daughter.

The little living room was in almost complete darkness. Four or five men sat intently absorbed in Lights Out, a weekly radio thriller. Closest to the radio, and wallowing in an aural orgy of murder and gunfire, was the woman who, as always, was the focal point of the room. Sleek-haired, smartly dressed, elaborately made up, Billie to me was the epitome of glamour, a young woman by whose side I was neither a visiting London journalist nor a guest but simply a naive and nervous cipher in the presence of royalty.

As *Lights Out* ended, the party came to life, and Billie brought out a big stack of records, her own, Teddy Wilson's, and dozens more. On the mantelpiece were signed photographs of Teddy, Maxine Sullivan, Pha Terrell (a popular black ballad singer with Andy Kirk's band) and one of Billie herself in an ingenious frame composed of 5,000 matchsticks—she told me proudly that it had been painstakingly assembled and sent to her from jail by an admirer who was serving a twenty-year sentence. "He sent me a song along with it that he wrote and wants me to use. Maybe I'll do it on my next session."

Nothing about Billie during that evening presaged misfortune or doom. Instead, an unselfconscious camaraderie was immediately discernible in her warm, friendly manner. I asked her to play "Billie's Blues," which had a special meaning for me: as John Hammond's guest, I had first met her during the session at which it was cut. It was doubly significant to me because I had been as much in love with the blues as with Billie. Asked where she had found the unusual lyrics, she replied: "I've been singing them same blues as long as I can remember. I made up those words myself. That's how I made my whole income as a composer. A couple of months ago I got a royalty check for the record—just eleven bucks!" But she said it without a trace of the rancor that twenty years later was to run through the pages of her *Lady Sings the Blues*.

Sadie Fagan Holiday interrupted us with the story of how her daughter used to annoy an aunt with whom she lived by singing those same blues about "my man this and my man that." Billie was a child, she was told, and had no business singing about such things. "But the first song she ever sang was 'My Mammy,' and she used to sing that to me all the time!"

During my first visit to Billie's apartment, I found her

to be poised and gracious. I knew no more about her private indulgences than Mrs. Holiday did, but had I known I'm sure I would have justified them with elaborate rationalizations. I have a theory about Billie that conflicts with the conventional explanations of her life and times. I believe that if she had been taken out of the environment that was slowly beginning to swallow her up, the end would not have come when it did and her vivid patterns of gently twisted melody might still be part of our lives. Had she accepted an offer to go to England, for example, and found there a group of admirers who could give her personal and economic security, the agony and the squalor might have been avoided.

On that first evening I had tried to convince her that she and the overseas audience were ready for one another. "Well, I had one offer last year, £50 a week," she said. (That was $250, and in those days, for Billie, it was a very substantial temptation.) "But those musicians over there they can just about read and that's all, huh? I'd have to bring my own musicians with me."

I tried to reassure her by playing a few of Benny Carter's new recordings with a British band. She hadn't suspected until that moment that British musicians had even heard of swing music. When a particular passage moved her, she would say, "Man, that sure sends me!" and rock in gentle rhythm around the room. But when a passage displeased her, she would murmur, "No, I ain't comin'!"

It did indeed seem to me, even then, that Billie preferred balling to taking care of business. But this may have been the effect rather than the cause of her misfortunes; none of us knew then the frightening story of her childhood.

Billie's career at the time of our 1938 encounter was in one of its first states of temporary collapse. She had been on the road for some months as Count Basie's band vocalist; now Basie had let her go. It seemed apparent to me and to others close to the scene that many of her white audiences did not probe far enough beneath the tonal eccentricity of her style to appreciate her fully. She had refused to change her style, ignoring those who urged her to commercialize it.

All the might-have-beens of Lady Day's life cannot alter one central fact: from 1935 (the year when her long series of collaborations with Teddy Wilson was inaugurated) until her death, Billie Holiday put on record a timbre like that of no other woman, a manner of phrasing evocative at times of Bessie Smith or Louis Armstrong, and a casual air that lent gaily rhythmic meaning to the most trivial of tunes.

Of the hundreds of records she cut between her debut with Benny Goodman in 1933 and her last, stumbling effort for MGM in 1959, less than a dozen were blues. She was always referred to in the lay press as a blues or torch singer, yet essentially she was neither. There is a tendency on the part of latecomers to the art of Holiday-analysis to draw everything in terms of gloom and doom, to equate with her private life the quality she gave to her songs. This posturing was aggravated as early as 1938, when suddenly she became an object of social significance. There is a measure of truth to John Hammond's observation that "artistically, the worst thing that ever happened to her was the overwhelming success of her singing of the Lewis Allen poem 'Strange Fruit,' which amassed a host of fans among the intelligentsia and the left." I disagree, however, with John's implication that Billie's career, as a consequence, moved steadily downhill from 1939, when she introduced that song. He and I shared enough evenings at Cafe Society in the 1940's, and I spent enough unforgettable nights on tour with her in Europe in 1954, to know that her magic never quite left her until very close to the end, when her physical equipment itself collapsed.

But there is another and highly relevant reason for refuting the theory that Billie was a messenger of misery. It is to be found in one of the most durable compilations of her records: *Billie Holiday: The Golden Years*, Vol. II (Columbia C3L 40). Checking the lyrical and melodic character of the material, the happy songs and the sad, I found, not much to my surprise, that the former outnumber the latter by about two to one. That she sang twice as many salutes to love and light as odes to missing men and gloomy Sundays will come as a surprise only to those who did not know Billie during those years.

"Yes," you may say, "but she can convert the happiest rhythm songs into blues." On the contrary, the fact is that Billie often turned a melancholy refrain into something with a light, bouncing air, as is immediately demonstrated in *I'm Painting the Town Red*. When she tells us that she is painting the town red to hide a heart that's blue, you are not, if you understand Billie, listening to those corny lyrics. You are re-acting to what she does with the melody, and this, it seems to me, was her chief purpose in many of her songs.

Billie's spectrum ranged from a light treatment of medio-cre tunes to a deep probing of first-rate lyrics, as in "Solitude" and the magnificent "My Last Affair," a too-long forgotten song by Haven Johnson. Given the kind of songs that often consti-tuted her material, one can only be thankful for her "Tain't whatcha do, it's the way thatcha do it" attitude.

It has been said often that Billie rose above her surround-ings, that in later years she was saddled with batteries of pre-tentious strings and indifferent rhythm sections. Yet one must remember that her musical accompaniment from the very start ranged from superb to fair to downright mediocre.

It is impossible to describe Billie's voice: the tart, gritty timbre, the special way of bending a note downward, the ca-pacity for reducing a melody to its bare bones or, when it seemed appropriate, for retaining all its original qualities. But it is worth noting that although her actual vocal range was limited, her emotional range was not; nevertheless during the early years her sound broadened rapidly beyond the high-pitched, teen-aged hollering of the two tunes ("Your Mother's Son-in-Law" and "Riffin' the Scotch") in which she appeared as guest vocalist with a pickup recording band led by Benny Goodman. John Hammond produced this early session, as well

as many others during her evolutionary phase. His tireless, unpaid efforts in her behalf changed the pattern of her career.
From an aimless round of obscure uptown nightclubs she was
set on a course that could lead to success, despite the restrictions of being black. But just as surely as Jim Crow, she herself
was responsible for many lost opportunities.

Little by little, Billie's relationship with Hammond deteriorated. His dedication to the lustrous warmth of her voice was
not matched by her dedication to work. Hammond, for one
thing, would not allow a recording session to be interrupted
while its star participant lounged around smoking pot in the
hall. Whatever the conditions, the recording dates from 1935 to
1942 produced a series of masterpieces; for many who knew
her then, her talents were crystallized during this seven-year
span. She wrote "God Bless the Child," with Arthur Herzog,
after a quarrel with her mother, although that kindly, unsophis-
ticated woman probably never fully grasped the sardonic im-
port of Billie's lyrics. An argument between Billie and her husband, Jimmy Monroe (he had arrived home "with lipstick on
his collar"), led to "Don't Explain," another song written with
Herzog.

During this time Billie changed physically and emotionally from a chubby, pretty girl into an exquisitely beautiful
woman, tall and slender, always impeccably gowned when she
worked. Her innate sexuality informed the slightest movement
of her body, every snap of her fingers, every twist of her lips.
But this was also the time when Billie was victimized by the
cruelest, ugliest humiliations of racial discrimination. I remember particularly traveling one day from New York to Boston
for her debut with Artie Shaw's orchestra at the Roseland
Ballroom. As the first black vocalist ever to join a white orchestra, she was more than a mere token; for Shaw himself she
was a dangerous experiment, a calculated risk.

Billie did not simply wear a mask to cover her apprehen-
sion; she sensed how self-defeating it would be to nourish any
resentment toward those who felt only empathy and affection

for her. Her grievances and animosities were selective. Her unwillingness to strike out indiscriminately at the whole white world, tempting though that may have been, is poignantly expressed in the chapter of her book dealing with the Shaw ordeal. Amplifying her statement that "most of the cats in the band were wonderful to me," she relates painful incidents in which Shaw, Tony Pastor, Georgie Auld, and others fought actively to protect her against the outright crackers, the well-meaning but ignorant whites who hurt her unwittingly, and all the other hassles that were a daily part of the obstacle course of living black.

Professionally, the years after she renounced touring as a big-band vocalist ("I swear I'll never sing with a band again," she told me after leaving Shaw) were those in which her life seemed most stable. She played better nightclubs for bigger money, and received an award each year the *Esquire* jazz poll was held (1944–47).

Yet it is important to bear in mind that in 1942 the jazz fans who voted for their favorite singers in the *Down Beat* poll elected Helen Forrest (who, ironically, had been the white "protection" second vocalist with Shaw during Billie's incumbency). In 1943 they chose Jo Stafford, and in 1944, probably Billie's peak year musically and commercially, the winner was Dinah Shore. Such were the patterns of American life, and it would be naïve to think that this did not affect Lady Day's view of the world.

After her first victory in the *Esquire* poll, Billie was invited, along with a dozen other winners, to take part in a concert I had been deputized to assemble. It was not only the first jazz concert ever held at the Metropolitan Opera House, but the first gala occasion at which Billie was treated as a major artist. The following year she made the long train haul out to California, for a celebration at the Los Angeles Philharmonic Auditorium. This time Hollywood celebrities presented the "Esky" statuettes. Billie, in superb vocal form, was genuinely moved when the award was presented to her by Jerome Kern. This sort of treatment, of course, would have been accorded her more regularly if the projected European tour had actually come about; but there was always some delay, some interruption, professional or personal.

In 1946, recognized at long last by the motion-picture industry, Billie was assigned a role in a feature film, a ridiculous pseudo-jazz history called *New Orleans*. True to the pattern of Hollywood, she played a servant. I recall her attempt to cover her frustration when she broke the news to me. "I'll be playing a maid," she said, "but she's really a cute maid."

Billie sang well in the picture and had some effective scenes with Louis Armstrong. But it was the last event of any consequence before her habit and the law finally tangled. In May 1947 she was arrested in Philadelphia for narcotics violations. The district attorney observed: "She has had following her the worst types of parasites and leeches you can think of . . . in the past three years she has earned a quarter of a million dollars; last year it was $56,000 and she doesn't have any of that money."

After kicking cold turkey, Lady spent a year and a day at the Federal rehabilitation establishment for women at Alderson, West Virginia. Soon after her release she appeared in a triumphant concert at Carnegie Hall. She looked healthy to the point of overweight but she was still beautiful.

Those who knew her only through the lurid headlines may find it hard to understand that at heart Billie might have liked to be an average, well-adjusted housewife. She was a capable cook; she liked neatness and order; she yearned for "straight" social relationships. But once she was in the grip of heroin, she saw her dream disappear. After the breakup of her marriage and several turbulent relationships with men who encouraged her dependence on drugs, she became involved with a man named John Levy; in 1949 the two of them were arrested in San Francisco. (Levy died many years ago.)

Down Beat reported Billie's situation following a masterful defense by her lawyer, Jake Ehrlich: "Broke and alone after

her manager, John Levy, left her to face trial here. . . . Billie
Holiday decided to go back to work. . . . But despite the fact
that the jury said they believed Billie had been framed by
Levy, she said, 'If he was to walk into the room this minute,
I'd melt. He's my man and I love him.' The trial appeared to
confirm that a package of opium had been planted on Billie
just before the raid. Billie came to trial with a black eye she
said Levy had given her. 'You should see my back,' she added.
'And he even took my silver blue mink—18 grand worth of
coat . . . I got nothing now, and I'm scared.' "

During the 1950s some of her fears were alleviated through
the help of Norman Granz, who signed her up for his record
company and got her concert dates. Then at last, in January of
1954, the dream we had talked about sixteen years earlier became a reality: Billie was to star in a show I had been asked
to package for Nils Hellstrom, the Swedish concert promoter.
The tour would take us all over the Continent, and Billie would
then play a couple of dates on her own in England.

The man in Billie's life now was Louis McKay, later her
widower. He accompanied her on the tour and seemed able
to keep her in good mental and physical shape. The other
musicians were her pianist, Carl Drinkard; the Buddy De
Franco quartet; the Red Norvo trio; and an all-girl instrumental trio led by Beryl Booker, a talented pianist.

By 1954 Lady Day's reputation preceded and predamned
her at every step. Although the Billie Holiday who traveled
through Scandinavia, Germany, Holland, Belgium, France,
and Switzerland was not the same woman who had put fear
into the hearts of nightclub owners and of musicians who
worked for her, nevertheless such were the misgivings about
becoming involved with her that none of the three bass players and two drummers wanted to work with Billie and Drinkard. Finally Red Mitchell and the drummer Elaine Leighton
agreed to do the job—but the agreement was arrived at too
for rehearsal.

were supposed to open in Stockholm, but the airport

there was snowed under. We were all dumped off the plane in Copenhagen to straggle in by train a few hours before the first show. The critics, knowing nothing of this, gave everyone including Billie a cold reception. Morale was not improved when it was reported next day that a hypodermic needle had been found in Billie's dressing room. Later it was learned that her visitors had included a Swedish musician who was a notorious junkie, but to this day I am uncertain whether Billie was at fault that night. During the rest of the tour (except for one night when she drank before the show instead of afterward) her behavior was impeccable, whether she was using or not.

The working conditions on a tour of this kind would tax the patience, and the voice, of any artist. Photographers were a constant problem. They jumped up on the bandstand while she was singing, and in Cologne, during her poignant ending to "I Cover the Waterfront," one leapt forward and exploded a flash gun within inches of her face. The audience reacted with a barrage of titters, whistles, and derisive applause for the intruder, yet Billie behaved as though she had noticed nothing and went on with her performance.

Often, if we went to a nightclub after the show, everyone would beg her for "just one song," and weary though she might be, Billie usually obliged. One evening, after the concert in Nuremberg, Billie and Beryl Booker were invited by some officers to a U.S. Army hotel, which for years had been frequented by Hitler and the Nazi hierarchy. In the big salon where the Führer had once roared and raved, the dry-ice tones of Billie rang smooth and clear across the room.

I was not surprised by her cooperation and comportment throughout the tour. Everything contrasted sharply with her life in America. Instead of the second-rate ghetto theaters, tacky dressing rooms, and half-empty minor-league nightclubs in Detroit and Pittsburgh that typified her directionless career, she found audiences teeming with fans who had dreamed for years of seeing her, bouquets presented to her onstage and backstage, autograph hunters, deferential treatment—and never a glimpse of racism. When treated like a lady, she acted accordingly. Her morale was never better. Only once, when a newspaperman asked about narcotics, did she bridle. "I didn't come 3,000 miles to talk about that. That's past and forgotten. I don't even want to think about it."

My most vivid memory of the tour is of her indomitable pride and firmness under pressure. One morning in Brussels we missed the musicians' bus that was to take us to Frankfurt, West Germany. With Hellstrom and McKay, we chased clear across Belgium in a taxi to the German border, then had to change there for a German cab all the way to Düsseldorf— and arrived shivering at the airport to find the last plane to Frankfurt had just left. A small plane was hastily chartered. It seated only four; since I was required to appear as the show's master of ceremonies, Louis McKay had to proceed by train. With the pilot and Hellstrom up front in the freezing cold plane, Billie and I huddled in the back seat and killed a small bottle of Steinhaegen, a remedy that did little to allay our incipient frostbite. We reached Frankfurt barely in time for the show. To Hellstrom's amazement, Billie gave two magnificent performances that night, showing not a trace of the ordeal.

This incident, however, reveals one side of the Billie Holiday paradox. Two days later, after a particularly grueling day's travel, she announced that she was calling Joe Glaser in New York to arrange for her immediate return home in mid-tour. Louis McKay assured us that she was "just talking," and he was right.

Back in the United States after that generally heartening interlude, Billie found herself surrounded once again by her usual crowd of pushers and hangers-on. Significantly the very next event reported in her biography after the European tour is her arrest in Philadelphia in 1956. It was as though nothing of consequence had happened in the interim.

Later that year Billie's self-esteem was helped by the pub- of *Lady Sings the Blues* (Doubleday). Written in collaboration with William Dufty, it is a mixture of half-truths, untruths, and events seen by Billie through a haze of wishful thinking. John Hammond, Teddy Wilson, and others close to her were quick to point out the inaccuracies, as was I; yet the overall impression of the impact of racism on the life of a gifted black American woman compensates for many of the flaws and distortions.

For anyone who knows the circumstances of Billie's death, the final chapter contains two passages that cannot be forgotten: "There isn't a soul on earth who can say that their fight with dope is over until they're dead." And the concluding paragraph: "Tired? You bet. But all that I'll soon forget with my man."

By 1958 her man was gone: Louis McKay took off for California. Her voice half-shot, the rich timbre lost except on an occasional good night when she pulled herself together, Billie continued the round of clubs and theaters, her asking price down and her morale even lower.

In September she agreed to make guest appearances at two history-of-jazz concerts I was staging. Several of her old friends took part: Mal Waldron, her pianist; Georgie Auld, a friend from the Shaw band days; and Buck Clayton, whose delicate, sensitive trumpet had been so important to Billie when she sang with Basie.

One of the shows, at a theater in Wallingford, Connecticut, was recorded. Billie sang "I Wished on the Moon," the first tune she had recorded during the first Teddy Wilson small-band session inaugurating the classic series of Wilson-Holiday collaborations; she followed it with "Lover Man." The record confirms that her voice had regained its old timbre and assurance. But backstage over a drink before the show, she told my wife: "I'm so goddamn lonely. Since Louis and I broke up I got nobody—nothing." Her misery was the inevitable result of an impossible situation: Billie's basic urge simply to love and be loved, so long frustrated, by now had become hopelessly mired in a desperation that made her impossible to live with, hard to reason with, and pathetically easy to sympathize with.

A few months later she astonished us by refusing a drink and asking instead for a cup of tea. "The doctor says I have cirrhosis of the liver and I can't drink." Needless to say, the doctor's warning was soon ignored.

In mid-March, when I called at her small, ground-floor apartment on West Eighty-seventh Street to escort her to the funeral of Lester Young, her close friend in the Basie days, I saw her slip a small bottle of gin into her purse. After the services she talked dejectedly, drawing an ominous parallel between herself and Lester. "I'll be the next one to go."

Our next meeting was a few weeks later, on her birthday. Billie had decided: "I ain't celebrated my birthday in fifteen years and this time I'm going to throw me a party." Among the well-wishers were Ed Lewis and Jo Jones of the old Basie band, Annie Ross, Elaine Lorillard, the Duftys, and Tony Scott. The party lasted all night, winding up at Birdland, and Lady never stopped toasting herself; bottles were emptied with alarming speed. Many of us wondered whether there would be any more birthdays to celebrate. She had already become skinny rather than slender. Those of us who watched her follow the Prez pattern begged her, vainly, to stop. Thinner and paler with each passing day, she continued to argue that she had cut down on her drinking and was taking care of herself.

Soon after the birthday party there was an incident typical of her stubbornness, pride, and confusion. She awoke me at 2 A.M. and in a passionately angry tone of voice insisted that I come to her apartment immediately. I rushed over and found her sitting at a table nursing a bottle. It seemed that she had been told I was spreading a rumor that she had been drunk all through her engagement the previous week in Boston. "What's all this shit going on? I don't want people putting my fucking business in the street. I made every show and you can ask anybody."

I didn't have to ask; I knew what a successful week it had

been, and that was the only story I had been spreading. Within a half hour Billie's rage had shifted to the person who had indicted me.

It was agonizing to observe how uncertain she felt that anybody really cared for her, how intensely anxious that nobody derogate her. Worse, she knew that now only disparaging talk could help her at the box office. "They're not coming to hear me," she said, "they're coming to see me fall off the damn bandstand."

Not long afterward, on May 25, Billie was to appear in a benefit concert at the Phoenix Theatre for which Steve Allen and I were the emcees. I looked into her dressing room to say hello, and saw her seated at the makeup table coughing, spittle running unchecked down her chin. Looking at her, I was on the verge of tears and she knew it.

"What's the matter, Leonard? You seen a ghost or something?"

Indeed I had; a ghost so emaciated, so weak and sick, that it was impossible for me to hide my feelings. She had lost at least twenty pounds in the few weeks since I had seen her.

Steve Allen helped Billie to her feet, walking her a short distance to a microphone, which had been deliberately placed at the near corner of the stage. She managed to get through "'Tain't Nobody's Business If I Do," the song of defiance that had become a staple of her repertoire in these fading days; she sang one other tune. It was the last time she was ever to sing.

The next morning I called Joe Glaser and Allan Morrison, then the New York editor of *Ebony*, with the suggestion that the three of us as a delegation might be able to break down her long resistance to hospitalization. As we sat in her apartment Glaser did most of the talking, guaranteeing all her hospital expenses and begging her to call off an opening scheduled for Montreal the next week. "Give me another week," she said. "The doctor said these shots he's giving me will do it." We left in a mood of frustration and despair.

Billie never got to Montreal. Five days after we saw her

she collapsed, and the inevitable hospitalization followed. Then came the obscenely gruesome headlines in the sensation-hungry press: Billie, part of a society in which addiction was still a crime rather than a sickness, was arrested on her deathbed. Police were posted outside her hospital room. She lingered, rallied long enough to give us hope, then on July 17 it was over.

To the end Billie was uncertain about who her true friends were and who was trying to make money out of her. Notwithstanding possible selfish interests, many people close to her felt sincere love, regard, and pity for her right up to the end, but Billie was unable to accept any of the love offered her during those last days.

It was probably too much to hope that she would survive any longer than she did the kind of life she had led for so many years. Whether the final abandonment of the will to live came with her estrangement from Louis McKay (who flew in from California soon after her hospitalization), or with Lester's death, or with the arrest in the hospital, nobody will ever know.

Billie Holiday's voice was the voice of living intensity, of soul in the true sense of that greatly abused word. As a human being she was sweet, sour, kind, mean, generous, profane, lovable, and impossible, and nobody who knew her expects to see anyone quite like her ever again.

Ella

ELLA FITZGERALD's story is strikingly different from Billie Holiday's, even though both were initially handicapped by being poor and black. The difference was a temperamental one: Ella would no more have become identified with "Strange Fruit" than Billie would have with "A-Tisket A-Tasket." Although Billie was deeply involved in the world of popular music, such songs were not endemic to her style and personality. Ella, on the other hand, can fashion from the most trivial material a performance that appeals to mass audiences—without losing her jazz fans. Billie sometimes accepted songs of little artistic value: Ella often embraced them.

At the beginning of 1936 it was my intense pleasure to travel uptown on any evening I pleased (and I pleased on many evenings) to hear Chick Webb's music at the Savoy Ballroom. In an article for the *Melody Maker* whose prose style can be excused only in the light of its author's age, I tried to capture the experience.

Amid that dark world of Lindy Hoppers, of laughter and light ale [the Savoy serves no hard liquor], of low lights and swing music, of fellowship and fights, the arrangements of Chick Webb and his Chicks stood out like the Aurora Borealis in a sullen sky. . . . There is here something more than the pure, unalloyed swing that has been admired in the work of the early Armstrong, in Oliver and other sepia jazz pioneers. There is the sophistication . . . the artistry and painstaking rehearsal, the brilliant orchestration combined with the loop-holes for grand improvisation, combining to make the perfect swing orchestra of 1936.

Accompanying the story was a photograph I had taken of arranger Edgar Sampson and a slim, pretty Ella Fitzgerald with comments that concluded as follows:

"Please, Mr. Webb, may I sing this number?".
The audacity of seventeen-year-old, witching-eyed Ella Fitzgerald in clambering onto the Savoy bandstand, making this request, and collaring the mike, led to her immediate leap in the Webb aggregation as featured artist on records and from the ranks of unknown amateurs to permanent membership broadcasts.

Ella is a rarity: the only vocalist whose interruptions of a Sampson arrangement can be tolerated, even welcomed with open ears.

Ella Fitzgerald's life will never be made into a movie. The worlds of alcoholism, addiction, and degradation—stepping stones to Hollywood's wide screen—are alien to her. Even the story that she was raised in an orphanage is untrue.

She was born Ella Fitzgerald in Newport News, Virginia, on April 25, 1918. She never knew her real father or her native town: her mother and stepfather moved to Yonkers when she was a child, and she spent much time shuttling back and forth between her mother and an aunt.

As a young girl Ella loved to dance and sing. During lunch hours at junior high school, she would sneak to the theater with a couple of school friends to catch Dolly Dawn with George Hall's orchestra; at night she listened to the Boswell Sisters on the radio—Connee Boswell soon became her favorite.

"Everybody in Yonkers thought I was a good dancer," Ella says. "I really wanted to be a dancer, not a singer. One day two girlfriends and I made a bet—a dare. We all wanted to get on the stage, and we drew straws to see which of us would go on the amateur hour. I drew the short straw, and that's how I got started winning all these shows."

Ella's first appearance, at Harlem's Apollo, won her a prize. "Benny Carter saw the show and told John Hammond about me; they took me up to Fletcher Henderson's house, but I guess they weren't too impressed when I sang for Fletcher, because he said, 'Don't call me, I'll call you!' "

The round of amateur hours continued, and word of her reached the CBS offices. She won an audition to appear with Arthur Tracy, the "Street Singer," and a contract was drawn up in which she was promised a "build-up like Connee Boswell." The bubble burst suddenly when Ella's mother died, leaving Ella orphaned and a minor, with nobody to accept legal responsibilities for her. Hoping to find work, she was forced to resume the weary amateur hour routine. She lost a contest for the first—and last—time when she tried to sing "Lost in a Fog" and ran off the stage to an accompaniment of boos. ("The pianist didn't know the chord changes and I mean I *really* got lost!") But her long-delayed professional debut came soon afterward—a week's work at the Harlem Opera House, for $50.

"Tiny Bradshaw's band was on that show," Ella remembers. "They put me on right at the end, when everybody had on their coats and was getting ready to leave. Tiny said, 'Ladies and gentlemen, here is the young girl that's been winning all the contests,' and they all came back and took their coats off and sat down again."

The orchestra that followed Bradshaw's was that of Chick Webb, a frail, humpbacked drummer from Baltimore who, although barely literate, had risen to form one of the greatest bands of the day. Chick resolutely refused to enlarge his vocal department, which comprised a male ballad singer and a trumpeter whose vocal style resembled Louis Armstrong's.

"He didn't want no girl singer," Ella recalls, "so they hid me in his dressing room and forced him to listen to me . . . I only knew three songs: 'Judy,' 'The Object of My Affection' and 'Believe It, Beloved.' I knew them all from Connee Boswell and I sang all three of them. Chick still wasn't convinced, but he said, 'OK, we'll take her on the one-nighter to Yale tomorrow.' Tiny Bradshaw and the chorus girls had all kicked in to buy me a gown. The kids at Yale seemed to like me, so Chick said he'd give me a week's tryout with the band at the Savoy Ballroom."

"The first time she came to my office," said Moe Gale, who was Webb's manager, "she looked incredible—her hair disheveled, her clothes just terrible. I said to Chick, 'My God, what can you do with this girl?' Chick answered, 'Mr. Gale, you'd be surprised what a beauty parlor and some makeup and nice clothes can do.'" And Edgar Sampson remembers: "We all kidded her. It would be 'Hey, Sis, where'd you get those clothes?' We all called her Sis. And 'Sis, what's with that hairdo?' But Ella always took it in good spirits."

Ella was still slim during her first months with the band, despite her fondness for Southern cooking. While the Lindy Hoppers at the Savoy grew familiar with Fitzgerald in person, her voice was slowly becoming known to radio listeners everywhere as the band broadcast late-night remotes. Eventually her fame forced Chick to include her in a record date for Decca.

"I'll never forget it," said Ella. "The record was 'Love and Kisses.' After we made it the band was in Philadelphia one night when they wouldn't let me in at some beer garden where I wanted to hear it on the piccolo [jukebox]. So I had some fellow who was over twenty-one go in and put a nickel in while I stood outside and listened to my own voice coming out.

"Things went so good that by the fall of 1936 Benny Goodman had me make some records with the band for Victor. But Chick was under contract to Decca and they made them call the records back in." (There were three tunes, all collectors' items today.)

By 1937 she had become famous enough to win her first *Down Beat* poll, which she shared with Bing Crosby. Jimmie Lunceford, whose band she revered, offered her a job at $75 a week; he later retracted the bid out of respect for Webb, but Chick raised her salary to $50 and then to $125.

The Fifty-second Street era was now in full swing. Jazz clubs were blossoming, and the phrase "swing music" was on everybody's lips. The demand was for anybody who could "swing, brother, swing." Stuff Smith tried it on the fiddle, Artie Shaw had a string section in his band for a while, and Maxine Sullivan, swinging folksongs at the Onyx Club, was the new national rage as the "Loch Lomond" Lady.

If you could swing a folksong, why not extend the concept? One day the band was at a rehearsal in Boston when Van Alexander, who was doing some of the vocal arrrangements, heard Ella fooling around with an old children's rhyme. He suggested they add some lyrics and a middle part. The result was Ella's smash hit for Decca, "A-Tisket, A-Tasket." "If they'd been giving out gold records in those days I imagine we'd have gotten one," says Ella.

The Webb band and Ella were flying high with their hit records when Chick's health began to deteriorate rapidly; he had tuberculosis of the spine and only his superhuman stamina enabled him even to sit behind his drums. After playing on a riverboat outside Washington, he was rushed to Johns Hopkins for an operation. Chick's will to live carried him through a whole week, then the pain-racked little giant looked around at his friends and relatives, asked his mother to lift him up, said, "I'm sorry—I gotta go!" and died.

At Chick's funeral Ella's voice achieved a poignant beauty it could never surpass. "There were thousands of people," said Moe Gale. "It was the biggest funeral I had ever seen—and I know there wasn't a dry eye when Ella sang."

Gale decided that the band should continue, with Chick's name but with Ella fronting and with one of the saxophonists as musical director. There were more tours and records, and Ella won her third straight *Down Beat* victory.

When the band hit Los Angeles, some of its members were invited to earn an extra $6 by playing an occasional jam session run informally at a nightclub by a tall, intense young man named Norman Granz. "Sure, he used my musicians, but he didn't want me—he just didn't dig me," says Ella. ("I never used Nat Cole either," says Granz.)

The bandleading period, although successful, was not a very happy time for Ella. She had contracted a bad marriage that was ultimately annulled. The draft had decimated the band. Her career as a bandleader was soon over. Gale teamed her with a vocal-instrumental group, the Four Keys, and they had one big hit record, "All I Need Is You," before the Keys themselves were drafted. Ella then joined forces with a series of road shows.

The bop revolution never fazed Ella; she had Dizzy Gillespie in her band for a while in 1941, and her ear grasped the harmonic intricacies of the new style well enough to enable her to incorporate it into a series of wordless performances known as scat, or bop singing. "Flyin' Home" in 1946, "Lady Be Good" in 1947, and a series of follow-ups established her reputation among the same cognoscenti who combed the record shops for the latest Diz and Bird recordings.

A young bassist from Pittsburgh, Ray Brown, was an early bop musician who, after a long apprenticeship with Gillespie, began to play dates with Norman Granz. By now Granz had moved out of nightclubs and into concert halls. Ella's interest in this new kind of music began to focus on Brown. When she visited him in 1948 at a Jazz at the Philharmonic concert, admiring fans spotted Ella in the audience and asked her to sing. Granz grudgingly consented and Ella won Granz over; he offered her an immediate contract. That same year she married Ray Brown.

As soon as she boarded the Granzwagon, Ella's prestige rose even further. She remained with Granz who, even after his move to Switzerland in 1959, continued to manage her. She made a number of albums for Granz's Verve label. He teamed her with Louis Armstrong on one album, gave her a flock of Cole Porter songs for another, followed it up with Rodgers and Hart, and kept her constantly on the best-seller charts. Ella's business alliance with Granz proved more durable than her marriage to Brown, which ended in divorce in 1952.

Ella Fitzgerald has never fully recognized the extent of her fame or talent; she is constantly amazed at her reputation. She is not publicity-conscious at all, is reluctant to give press interviews, and hates cameramen as well—especially the type whose flashbulb explodes during the more tender moments of a love song. "That's the one thing that can drive her crazy at concerts," Granz once said, "that and nervousness. I have yet to see her do a show when she wasn't nervous. We can be at an afternoon concert playing to a small house in Mannheim, Germany, in the fifth week of a tour, doing the same show she's done every day, and she'll come backstage afterward and say, 'Do you think I did all right? I was so scared out there!' "

The views of Ella's managers and fans alike concerning what songs are best for her conflicted violently for many years. A frustrated ballad singer, she once burst into tears when Chick Webb ("He didn't think I was ready to sing ballads") assigned to the band's male vocalist a tune that had been specially arranged for Ella.

"She was temperamental about what she sang," says Tim Gale, Moe's brother, whose booking agency handled Ella for many years. "However, she would sing *anything* if her advisers insisted. One of her records was a thing called 'Happiness.' She cut it under protest; I brought the dub backstage to her at the Paramount, and she said, 'It's a shame. A corny performance of a corny song.' It turned out to be one of her biggest sellers.

"She once played a club in Omaha when Frankie Laine's 'Mule Train' was a tremendous hit. One of the biggest spenders in Omaha came in constantly and demanded that she sing it. She kept ducking it until finally the club boss begged her to please the money guy. Ella said to herself, 'I'll sing it in such a way that he'll never ask for it again,' and proceeded to do a burlesque so tremendous that she kept it in the act and scored riotously with it everywhere—even at Bop City."

Granz's first move on assuming the managerial reins was to steer Ella away from the jazz rooms and into the class clubs. Skeptical at first, Ella gradually took to the new plush environments when she found that audiences at the Fairmont in San Francisco or the Copa in New York were as susceptible to "Air Mail Special" and "Tenderly" as the hip crowd at Birdland.

The quantity of Ella's performances has caused more disagreements than the quality. "I'll ask her to do two ballads in a row, to set a mood," says Granz, "but some kid in the back will yell 'How High the Moon' and off she'll go. Or I'll say I want her to do eight tunes and she'll say, 'Don't you think that's too many? Let's make it six.' And she'll go out there and do the six and then if the audience wants fifty she'll stay for forty-four more. It's part of her whole approach to life. She just loves to sing."

"Every tour I ever made with her convinced me that singing is her whole life," says guitarist Barney Kessel. "I remember once in Genoa, Italy, we sat down to eat and the restaurant was empty except for Lester Young and his wife and Ella and me. So while we waited to give our breakfast order I pulled out my guitar and she and Lester started making up fabulous things on the blues.

"Another time, when we were touring Switzerland, instead of gossiping with the rest of the troupe on the bus, she and I would get together and she'd take some tune like 'Blue Lou' and sing it every way in the world. She'd do it like Mahalia Jackson and like Sarah and finally make up new lyrics for it. She would try to exhaust every possibility, as if she were trying to develop improvisation to a new point by ad-libbing lyrically, too, the way Calypso singers do."

"Ella does that even on shows," recalls another musician who toured with her for years. "If there's a heckler she'll interpolate a swinging warning to him in the middle of a number, or the mike'll go wrong and she'll tell the engineer about it in words and music.

"But she's terribly sensitive socially. Whenever she hears a crowd mumbling she feels that they are discussing her—and always unfavorably. I think she lays so much stress on being accepted in music because this is the one area of life into which she feels she can fit successfully. Her marriages failed; she doesn't have an awful lot of the normal activities most women have, such as home life, so she wraps herself up entirely in music. She wants desperately to be accepted."

This analysis may be accurate, but Ella often gives the impression that she is a happy extrovert. One of the gang to her fellow workers, she is a whiz at tonk or blackjack when the cards are pulled out on bus trips. She also has the naïvely enthusiastic qualities of one of her own fans. ("Do you know who caught the show the other night?" she said to me one day in 1960. "Judy Holliday—and she came backstage afterward to see me! And she went on and on about how she liked me! Imagine that—Judy Holliday!") Once when a restaurant owner for whom she had just tape-recorded an interview picked up the check for her dinner, she was both astonished and grateful —as if this gesture were without precedent.

Today Ella is firmly established within the jazz world as a great artist. She has kept pace with the times by sometimes adapting current tunes to her style, although her attempts to gain a foothold in the pop record market by recording with unsympathetic rock arrangements have proved less than successful, both musically and commercially.

She continues to travel frequently. In the summer of 1971, however, one of her European tours was cut short when, shortly after she had recuperated from a cataract operation on her left eye, her right eye hemorrhaged. While she recovered at home in Beverly Hills, she studied Portuguese "so when I do those Brazilian songs I'll know what I'm singing about."

The arguments concerning her stature as a jazz singer have long since subsided. With the shrinking emphasis on categorization, the central fact has stood out in sharper perspective than ever: Ella Fitzgerald's is one of the most flexible, beautiful, and widely appreciated voices of this century.

Perhaps the best assessment of it was made by Mrs. David Frisina, wife of the Los Angeles Philharmonic concertmaster, after a historic concert at the Hollywood Bowl in 1957: "Ella Fitzgerald," she said, "could sing the Van Nuys telephone directory with a broken jaw and make it sound good. And that," she added, "is a particularly dull telephone directory."

Catherine Basie, Leonard Feather, and Count Basie

Leonard Feather

Swing and Basie

IF ELLA FITZGERALD was the prototypical swing singer, Count Basie's orchestra was the instrumental epitome of swing music. The loose, easily pulsing sound of Basie's piano, so well integrated with his impeccable rhythm section, was reflected in the band's informality as a unit, the lack of tension, the vital role played by a phenomenal assemblage of improvising soloists. The illusion of complete effortlessness was a primary facet in the magic of Basie's leadership.

That Benny Goodman was acclaimed King of Swing around the time of Basie's emergence caused many heated disputes. It may be argued that Goodman had been firmly established for a year or two before Basie left Kansas City to make his first, unsuccessful attempt to storm New York. Along with dozens of the most important jazz figures of the 1930s, Basie was immensely handicapped by the many doors closed to black musicians. But the same conditions that restricted one giant to working for a pittance in a ghetto nightclub enabled the other, with the powerful assistance of John Hammond, to assemble a well-trained group, gain access to air time, and acquire a lucrative recording contract.

The original creative source of jazz, of course, was Afro-American. Later sources were predominantly American, occasionally white, almost never stemming from any source outside the United States. I remember from my adolescence that the black musicians in London, most of them West Indians, were just as incapable as their white British brothers of feeling the beat, the swing, the rhythmic essence of jazz indigenous to the black man in America. If Count Basie had not been exposed at an early age to the ragtime around him—the stride piano of Fats Waller, and, later, the teeming jazz scene in Kansas City —he might not have evolved as he did. Similarly the young Benny Goodman's exposure to the sounds of black and white jazz pioneers in Chicago, coupled with his innate musicianship and rapidly developed technique, enabled him to become an immensely exciting and authentic jazzman.

Goodman had one of the better jazz-oriented swing bands of the mid-1930s; nobody seriously questioned that he had the best white band. He was a peerless clarinetist whose orchestra generally had three or four first-rate soloists. Basie's band, at first weaker in intonation and precision, compensated for this by its spirit, and by the quality and quantity of improvisational solo work. Yet social conditions at that time precluded white musicians from joining Basie's group. At the same time, black musicians, whose life experience was so important to the soul of jazz, could not become full-fledged members of Goodman's band.

It is entirely possible that if social conditions at the time had permitted it, both Goodman and Basie would have been well served by using racially integrated orchestras. In certain key roles that called for professional expertise, whites, who had the advantage of better musical education, might have been helpful to Basie; but just as surely, the black experience that was endemic to the solos of men such as Lester Young, Buck Clayton, and Dickie Wells could have been of inestimable value to Goodman.

Today, thirty-five years later, we see it all in perspective. The racial lines have slowly eroded: Goodman, who in 1935– 36 encountered so many problems in hiring Teddy Wilson and Lionel Hampton that he was obliged to use them as an extra attraction, an act rather than part of the orchestra, has been able to hire blacks freely for many years. Meanwhile Basie, since the late 1940s, has made use of numerous white musicians from time to time. None of this alters the fact that while Goodman was wearing a crown bestowed on him by white America, Count Basie was the genuine King of Swing.

"Count Basie isn't just a man, or even just a band," Lena Horne said one night at Birdland during the early 1960s. "He's a way of life." Her comment summed up the feelings of many toward a group that had become, for many of us, the most potent symbol of an art form frequently declared dead but unwilling to lie down: big-band jazz.

The Count Basie orchestra, founded in 1935, is one of the more durable jazz entities, but by 1950 the state of the music business forced Basie to dissolve the full orchestra and tour with a septet. He reorganized a big band in 1951 and pulled himself slowly and stubbornly back; by 1954 the jazz festival, the concert tour, and the adoption of jazz by the intellectuals, along with a fast-expanding overseas market, had helped to pull jazz out of the doldrums. A year later Joe Williams added to the band's box-office power. By 1960, the year of his silver anniversary as a bandleader, Basie's international acclaim had reached proportions that would have seemed impossible a decade earlier. He had toured Europe four times, had played a command performance for the British royal family, and had completed successful engagements at the roof ballroom of the Waldorf-Astoria in New York City, where no jazz attraction of any kind had been heard before.

Basie had indeed come a long way from Kansas City. He had actually come an even longer way from Red Bank, New Jersey, where he was born on August 21, 1904, but the crucial years of his career were spent in Kansas City, and there his band was organized. Yet he had been a professional musician for more than a decade before a series of chance incidents landed him in Kansas City at the height of the Pendergast era.

William Basie grew up an only child, a brother having died

young. Bill studied piano with his mother, but his most valuable tuition came from the early gigs he played in New York and New Jersey and from the years of scuffling as combo pianist and accompanist to singers on a variety of minor jobs.

His youthful friendship with Thomas "Fats" Waller helped to increase his mastery of the piano and the organ. Waller, exactly three months older than Basie, was playing the same kind of jobs during the 1920s, although with slightly greater financial success as well as an occasional record date. He was a performer of admirable skill and originality, and an accomplished organist. Although Basie never took formal organ lessons, what he learned from Waller enabled him many years later to double on pipe organ and occasionally on the Hammond. (His organ ability is not hampered by his exceptionally small feet—he wears a size 7½ shoe.) Once Basie substituted for Waller as accompanist for an act known as Katie Krappin and her Kids. By then James P. Johnson and Waller were the kings of "Harlem stride" piano, the Prohibition era's offshoot of ragtime.

Basie's association with hard-driving Kansas City jazz began accidentally around 1926. "I was touring the Keith circuit with a vaudeville show," he says. "One night we played a gig in Tulsa, Oklahoma, and I woke up the next morning to hear this wonderful music. At first I thought somebody in the hotel had some crazy records, but then I saw it—an advertising wagon down the street, plugging a dance. It turned out to be Walter Page and his Blue Devils. I chased after this band and got to know some of the cats; I finally wound up sitting in with them at a breakfast dance. Believe me, that was some music.

"It wasn't long after that, I guess, that the show I was working with was stranded. There we were, with no show and no loot and no job—in Kansas City. I managed to land myself a job in a silent movie theater, the Eblon. It didn't pay too well and it wasn't the kind of job I liked best, but it was a gig. Later I got in touch with Walter Page, and everything changed: Walter offered me the job playing piano with the Blue Devils."

Basie's position improved during the years with Page. There were jobs, food, and, most significantly, music of a brand unmatched outside Kansas City. Several jazzmen have testified to the scene: "Some places in Kansas City never closed," declared Jo Jones. "You could be sleeping one morning at 6 A.M., and a traveling band would come into town for a few hours, and they would wake you up to make a couple of hours' session with them until eight in the morning. You never knew what time in the morning someone would knock on the door and say they were jamming down the street."

Ben Webster, afterward famous as a tenor saxophonist, played some of the wildest barrelhouse piano in town at that time. Not long after he had begun doubling on saxophone, a memorable session occurred, involving Ben, Lester Young, Herschel Evans, Budd Johnson, and Coleman Hawkins, at which one blues alone lasted two hours.

"I remember once at the Subway Club, on Eighteenth Street," and Sammy Price, the boogie-woogie pianist, "I came by a session at about ten o'clock and then went home to clean up and change my clothes. I came back in a little after one o'clock and they were still playing the same song!"

The picture is best summed up by Raymond Horricks in his survey of the band and its background, *Count Basie and His Orchestra* (Citadel). Because so many travel routes converged in Kansas City, he pointed out,

The location was a distinct encouragement to jazz . . . the influx of trade and money increased the demand for entertainment and allowed a large local jazz scene to be maintained. Yet even more important, the many routes which passed through the city caused hosts of musicians and singers to visit the place . . . the Negro section of the city became a familiar calling place for singers and musicians passing through with the big touring bands, many of whom had only a few hours to spare . . . yet who wanted to play at a private jam session with the core of resident musicians there. Some of them liked the music they heard so much that they came back and settled, swelling a local jazz school that in size was already out of all proportion to the population of the colored quarter.

Such was the Kansas City in which Count Basie played as a sideman with the Walter Page band until its breakup in 1929. He then became a second pianist with the Bennie Moten orchestra, in which Page also played, as did some future members of Basie's own group. Among the latter were Jimmy Rushing, who had sung with the Page band; trumpeters Ed Lewis and Oran "Hot Lips" Page; trombonist Eddie Durham, and saxophonist Jack Washington.

Basie recorded a couple of sides in 1929 under Page's leadership, as well as a series of 78 rpm discs with Moten during the next three years; some of these were Basie compositions. A 1930 Moten record entitled "The Count" introduced Basie's nickname to the general public.

Basie, while working for Moten, and during the first few years with his own band, experimented with the piano more fully than he does today. He had an aggressive left-hand stride —the result of Waller's influence—and showed more technique and flash than in later years. By the 1950s his "trigger-finger," single-note line had become so commercially successful that he used it as identification. Neal Hefti even began to incorporate one typical figure into his arrangements for the band, in the formalized manner of Guy Lombardo's traditional tag.

Basie once expressed his feelings about his role as an instrumentalist in an interview with Bill Coss: "The chief thing I do is pace-setting—you know, tempos . . . and I feed the soloists. Other people use the piano for solos—guys who can really play it—but I use it as part of the rhythm section."

Upon Bennie Moten's sudden death in 1935, his brother Buster, an accordionist, became the leader. "I didn't stay with the band more than about a week after Bennie died," says

Basie. "Then I got a call from the Reno Club. They had a five-piece group there and they wanted me to bring in one of my own. I said I'd like to have nine men, so the boss told me OK. We opened with three saxes—Buster Smith and another alto player, and Slim Freeman on tenor; three trumpets—Dee Stewart, Joe Keyes, and Carl (Tatti) Smith; plus Walter Page on tuba, myself, and the drummer Willie (Mac) Washington. Then there was Lips Page, who worked in the Reno show as a single, and sometimes he'd sing or play with us and maybe sit in with the trumpet section.

"I got $21 a week and the sidemen got $18, plus whatever we could pick up from the kitty. The tips brought it up to enough to live on, just about. But I would have been happy just to be on the Kansas City scene at that time, even without my own band. Being a leader made it even more of a kick.

"Jimmy Rushing worked at the club too, and when we did a Sunday night broadcast out of there on a small local station, he went on the air with us. That was when John Hammond heard the band."

The group that Hammond heard on his automobile radio, in what may have been the most momentous chance audition in jazz history, included two invaluable new sidemen: Jo Jones on drums and Lester Young on tenor saxophone. Hammond discerned, beyond the group's instability and roughness, a freshness and dynamism that set the band apart from anything yet heard on the East Coast jazz scene. He resolved immediately to enlarge the Basie group and bring it east. Hammond began by initiating a booking at the Grand Terrace in Chicago, a Negro club that used elaborate shows. For Basie it was a first step into the big time.

In the memory of some who recall it vividly, the Grand Terrace engagement was a fiasco. "They had us playing the *Poet and Peasant* Overture as our big show number," says Basie ruefully. "The band just didn't make it, and there was nothing in the show that gave us a real chance to display ourselves properly." ("Maybe they didn't play the show so well,"

Basie's veteran road manager Henry Snorgrass commented, "but they still managed to set Chicago on fire with their own music.")

The beginning of Basie's long and influential recording career was a quintet date arranged by Hammond that took place in Chicago, October 9, 1936. Because Hammond had just revived the dormant boogie-woogie piano art form by bringing Meade "Lux" Lewis out of obscurity, Basie cut "Boogie Woogie," with a blues vocal by Rushing. Harry White's memorable song "Evenin'," the current pop hit "Shoe Shine Boy" (from the Grand Terrace show), and the Gershwin standard "Lady Be Good" completed the session. The quintet consisted of Tatti Smith, Lester Young, Basie, Jo Jones, and Walter Page; three months were to pass before the full orchestra gained access to a recording studio.

At Hammond's suggestion the band had been enlarged to include a trombone section—Dan Minor, Eddie Durham, and George Hunt—as well as a fourth saxophonist, Herschel Evans, and Jimmy Rushing as regular vocalist. The men worked hard on arrangements of pop tunes in order to broaden its appeal, and were obliged to play tangos and rhumbas for their first New York engagement, at Roseland. "Woody Herman was playing opposite us," Basie remembers. "He was breaking in his band too, but he was *in* there—he had it made. We had a rough time at Roseland, but the manager there stuck with us —he believed in what we wanted to do."

On January 22, 1937, the first session by the full band was waxed in New York City. (The word "waxed" was literally appropriate in those pretape days, when no ten-inch wax master could accommodate more than about three minutes of music, thus effectively reducing the impact of the band, which liked to stretch out on many of its exciting performances.) The dance hall job was celebrated in "Roseland Shuffle"; Buck Clayton, whose cup-muted trumpet was to become one of the band's most identifiable sounds, was heard in "Swingin' at the Daisy

Chain"; Rushing demonstrated his way with a pop song in the then-current "Pennies from Heaven"; and Basie acknowledged his debt to Fats Waller with "Honeysuckle Rose."

Basie's rehearsals in the old days were disorganized, to say the least. Arrangers would stand around in the crowded, stuffy basement of the Woodside Hotel in Harlem where the band lived, hoping that sooner or later the Count would get around to their own scores. (Buster Harding, Don Redman, Jimmy Mundy, and Andy Gibson were among the frequent visitors who contributed to the book.) In his anxiety to give every arranger a chance to be heard, Basie placed himself in danger of never truly rehearsing anything; yet somehow the band muddled through a fair quota of charts every time, and a few got played and recorded while others were returned to the writers or discreetly placed in the back of the book and forgotten. The legend that the musicians carried the music in their collective heads rather than in manuscript is true only of the very early years, when "head arrangements" predominated. By 1940, almost all the new performances were based on written arrangements.

What gave the band its unique incandescence in the 1930s, of course, was not its ability to rehearse, but its esprit de corps. "It's always been a family feeling, from the thirties right on," says guitarist Freddie Green, a Basie sideman for thirty-five years.

Jo Jones felt that much of the credit for the band's early success belonged to the late Lester Young, whose tenor sax certainly was the most influential solo voice. "It was a whole new impact on the band," said Jones, "a reflection of Prez's different background and environment compared to the way Coleman Hawkins came up. Until Prez came along, Coleman was the only tenor player everybody talked about. But Lester's sound wasn't newly developed when he joined Basie. I have a home recording of Prez made in 1930 and he was getting just the same tone quality back then."

"Prez wasn't just a tenor influence," says Joe Newman. "He was a great influence on my trumpet playing as I'm sure he was on a lot of other people who don't play tenor."

"It was such a fresh, touching sound—more flexible; you could feel it," says Freddie Green.

There was great mutual admiration rather than rivalry between Prez and his tenor teammate. "Listening to Herschel and Lester," says Jo, "was like watching a tennis match. You just dug them both—and it wasn't a question of one cutting the other. It was like what do you want for breakfast, ham and eggs or bacon and eggs?"

And Harry "Sweets" Edison said, "When I first joined the band we had maybe six arrangements in the entire book. Now since I was going to make music my career, I wanted to read music and learn more about it. But they kept playing and playing until I didn't know where I was. Finally I said, 'Hey, Basie, where's the music?' and he answered, 'What's the matter? You're *playing*, aren't you?' So I said, 'Yes, but I want to know *what* I'm playing.' And I said, 'When the band ends I don't know what note to hit.' Then Basie told me, 'If you hit a note tonight and it sounds right, just play that same note tomorrow!'"

The band's morale was high. "You get tired even talking about those old one-nighters," said Edison. "You'd get in a town and have to wake people up at 4 A.M. to get a room in a private house because there were no hotels."

"It's all true," agreed Jo, "yet even at our lowest ebb we all thought and felt as one man. I was with the band fourteen years and not one single time did I see a fight."

Both old and new band members have given the same explanation for this phenomenon. Freddie Green says: "Basie is a real leader—the ideal leader." Sweets Edison adds: "He was always so tactful that no matter what went wrong, it never got to the point where anybody in the band wouldn't feel like playing."

Musically Basie's personal tastes are catholic; he harbors

a natural inclination to look for the positive side in anything he hears. His knowledge of classical music is limited; his life-long jazz idol is Duke Ellington. (When the owner of a short-lived Broadway club put the Ellington and Basie bands in the same show for a couple of weeks in the early 1950s, Basie was modest to the point of self-effacement in assessing the situation.) The two men, in a spirit of mutual respect, have never tried to steal musicians from one another, although by chance a few men have worked for both (notably Clark Terry and Paul Gonsalves).

Although cautious about becoming personally involved, Basie has followed new jazz developments with interest through the years. He was intrigued by the bop movement of the 1940s, and during that time the foremost bop trombonist, J. J. Johnson, was a member of his brass section. But his characteristic absentmindedness has sometimes stood in the way of his music. In 1945 Sarah Vaughan, still almost unknown and eager for a job as vocalist with the band, applied for an audition while Basie was playing New York's old Roxy Theatre. Basie casually assigned her a dressing room backstage, where she played audition piano for half a dozen other singers, then just as casually dismissed her, voice unheard.

Most important to the band after Basie himself was Marshal Royal, "the Burgomeister," to whom many admirers gave credit for the polished precision and other virtues that marked the new Basie band. Royal's association with Basie, which lasted until 1970, began in a peculiar manner. When the band was playing the old Florentine Gardens (Cotton Club) in Hollywood in 1949, each man had to take a night off to conform to union rules. The nights off being staggered, Royal would sub for a different member of the reed section every evening —one night lead alto, the next night tenor, the next night baritone. Another curious substitution occurred the following year when economic conditions forced Basie to break up the big band and form a septet. While in Hollywood with the combo, he was reunited with Billie Holiday, in a two-reeler film. Basie was permitted to have his white clarinetist, Buddy De Franco, play the sound track, but was not allowed to show him on camera. Because Hollywood clung to the belief that integration on the screen would hurt bookings in the South, Royal replaced De Franco for the visual work. In February of 1951 Royal took over Buddy's chair permanently. Basie had not yet decided to reorganize the big band, but in April the plan was initiated and Royal started lining up men in New York.

"It wasn't a hard job recruiting men then," he remembers. "There were always good people available. We played some one-nighters to break in, then went into the Strand Theatre on Broadway. We cut up a lot of the old arrangements, changed some tempos, played others as is, and took arrangements from just about everybody."

This was the beginning of the new Basie band, the one that brought him even greater recognition and financial success than the original. Comparing the two bands, Royal says: "The emphasis in the old band was essentially on soloists; now it's more on ensembles, and the soloists sometimes are secondary. There was more emphasis on highness then and there's more on depth today—as a result the voicings in the arrangements are spread wider. Of course there are five saxes instead of the original four, and eight brass instead of six."

By 1954 the new Basie band had found a receptive audience for music supplied by a new generation of writers; their reputation was further enhanced by Joe Williams, who was to remain as vocalist until 1960.

For the first time since Jimmy Rushing's long tenure in the old band, Basie had a singer who was not merely a commercial asset, but a true artist whose talents blended perfectly with those of the other men. And from today's viewpoint, the evolution of this "second" Basie orchestra can be divided into three parts: pre-Joe Williams, Joe Williams, and post-Joe Williams.

When Williams left in 1960 to work as a single, attempts to replace him were not successful. Moreover the post-1960 period saw a slow and subtle shift in Basie's public. The overseas tours became annual events, while at home Las Vegas was the band's focal point—they played there two or three times a year.

Many of the people who hear Basie today have blurred recollections of the original band playing at their college proms twenty years ago; these audiences seldom are aware of such things as which sidemen come or go. By 1972 the Basie band had undergone an almost total change of personnel; when Marshal Royal left they were especially hard hit. Still, Basie's former sidemen return from time to time, most notably tenor saxophonist Edrie "Lockjaw" Davis, the official straw boss in recent years; Al Grey with his plunger trombone, and occasionally, Sweets Edison. The loss of Sonny Payne, a flashy and popular drummer, was more than compensated for by Harold Jones, a spirited yet more controlled young percussionist.

For the past decade or so the Count's music has varied greatly according to such circumstances as the availability of arrangers or the sudden need for material to fill out an album. Quincy Jones, Benny Carter, and Billy Byers wrote original instrumentals for albums; later Sammy Nestico, a swing-era trombonist, became the closest thing Basie had to a staff writer. Gradually the band worked more and more as a supporting attraction to various popular singers—some good, some mediocre. From the mid-1960s on, when a series of personal appearances and recordings with Frank Sinatra proved mutually stimulating, there were many similar engagements for which Basie was teamed with Tony Bennett, Sammy Davis, Ella Fitzgerald, and enough others to reduce the problems inherent in keeping a big jazz orchestra alive and moving fifty weeks a year.

At the same time the group has continued to record albums on a scattershot basis for any company that could come up with the prerequisite five-figure advance. Basie has recorded not only with Sinatra, Bennett, Davis, and Miss Fitzgerald, but also with pop singer Jackie Wilson (for this atrocity a rock guitarist was added—it didn't help); with Arthur Prysock, Kay Starr, the Mills Brothers, Bing Crosby, and a group called the Alan Copeland Singers.

Instrumentally there have been such popular but fast-forgotten LPs as *Hits of the 50s and 60s* and even two collections of Beatles songs. A partially successful but rare attempt at new, more demanding work was produced by Bob Thiele of Flying Dutchman Records in 1971. Arranged and conducted by Oliver Nelson, and entitled *Afrique,* the album brought the band together with such guest soloists as Hubert Laws on flute and Buddy Lucas on harmonica; Nelson himself played saxophone on some tracks. Instead of the old familiar round of blues the orchestra took on challenging compositions by Nelson, Pharoah Sanders, Albert Ayler, and Gabor Szabo.

Some critics feel that because of certain indiscriminate pop associations, and Basie's frequent work for square, elderly audiences, the band's creative days are over. John Hammond, though still friendly with the man he had discovered thirty-five years earlier, hears a distinct deterioration. The band is often associated with "establishment jazz"; Whitney Balliett has dismissed it as "civil-service swing."

On the other hand Stanley Dance, a veteran chronicler of the early jazz years, wrote four years ago:

The Basie band is an American institution, a jazz institution. Its policy has changed only superficially in more than three decades. It still stands for forthright, swinging music, and the responsibility for it belongs to the man who, in Duke Ellington's words, is "still the most imitated piano player around."

The truth probably lies somewhere in between these two views. Basie on a one-night stand may repeat the lackluster motions common to most bands forced to travel extensively. In Las Vegas he gives the customers what they want rather than making them want what he prefers to give. But during a 1972 visit to Donte's in North Hollywood, one of the hippest jazz clubs in the United States, the musicians were in perfect form: the packed house contained half a dozen Basie alumni, scores of musicians, and veteran Basie camp followers. Given these conditions, the band roared from the first bar. Before long Basie was pulling out all the stops. The white in his graying hair had spread noticeably; he walked a little slower as he left the stand after each set, yet the implacable energy of the orchestra was still there, unmistakably sparked from the keyboard by this 67-year-old survivor of the swing era battlefield.

For a few fast-vanishing hours, cramped at our tables, not six feet from the upper reaches of Basie's piano, Fifty-second Street was alive again for those of us who remembered. We were back once more at the Famous Door, listening to a group of young, energy-packed innovators who had set their own pace for big-band jazz. At such moments this incomparable ensemble offers the best evidence still at hand that the values Bill Basie and his original group of catalysts inculcated during the great days of discovery will not die so long as the singular Basie esprit de corps remains a part of our world of jazz.

Filipacchi

Prez

THOSE FANS WHO play his old records, recalling the days of his powerful musical influence, still sing a blues for Lester Young. They remember his sound emerging languidly from the Basie band—his saxophone, in wheaty-toned pleas, groping for beauty in 12- or 32-bar sighs. With inimitable delicacy he transformed the most banal tunes into dramatic, personal soliloquies, wondrous speeches emerging from a kaleidoscopic life colored by gin and bourbon and cheap wine and pot. When he stumbled, he often fell, scratching for answers, scratching for beauty.

When they toured as members of the Count Basie band, Billie Holiday loved him and gave him his name. "I always knew Lester was the greatest," she said, "so when it came to a name for him, that had to be the greatest too. In this country, kings or counts or dukes don't amount to nothing. The greatest man around then was Franklin D. Roosevelt, and he was the President. So I started calling him the President. Later it was shortened to Prez."

During the definitive stage of his career (essentially from the late 1930s to the early 1950s) many saxophonists agreed that Lester was indeed the president.

"I was about twelve or thirteen," remembers Al Cohn, one of today's most successful Prez-influenced tenor men, "and at that time clarinet was *the* instrument in jazz. I'd found nothing interesting in the saxophone. Then I began rummaging through the nine-cent bargain counters in those stores that sold used 78s, and someone told me about a band—Count Basie. Well, when I heard 'Jumpin' at the Woodside' and 'Dark Rapture' I switched overnight. Prez was the reason I became a saxophone player."

"Lester had his own sound and style, even way back around 1933 in Kansas City," said Coleman Hawkins. "The kids today are too young to have heard him when he was real great—his best days were just around the time I came from Europe in 1939, when I first heard him with Basie. And none of those imitators could ever really get anywhere."

"Prez got that soft tone, so different from Hawkins', because that's the way he wanted everything in life," says a former Prez sideman. "I got him a pair of shoes once, and one day I came in and found them in the wastebasket. Then I realized they were hard-soled shoes, and he would always wear moccasins or slippers. It had to be soft and gentle or Prez wanted no part of it."

Prez himself was soft and gentle, and infinitely lonely. Confronted with one-nighters, deadlines, booking agents, and nightclub drunks, he recoiled repeatedly into his own quietly decaying world, destroying himself more with each retreat. He shuffled toward perfection, grasped it momentarily, lost it, and resumed his ambling way.

"Lester's approach to everything he did in life was concerned with beauty," says pianist Billy Taylor. "He liked things pretty, and the word had a special meaning for him. The highest compliment he could pay anyone was, 'That was real pretty.'"

Beauty was always the goal. It existed apart from Prez's way of life, which was something else. He read comic books. He was a Giants fan. He drank gin with a sherry chaser, or Courvoisier with beer. He consumed buttermilk and Cracker Jack, or sardines and ice cream. For years he could sleep only in a room filled with light and the sound of a radio at full volume. Once, at Birdland, armed with a water pistol, he battled members of the Basie band. He spent much of his off-stand time listening to vocal recordings; Sinatra was his man.

On the stand Prez was his own man, and jazz was his language. Often obscure in his speech, he spoke lucidly and warmly through his horn, and when he did, the musicians gathered and the critics took notes. At first his ideas were rejected by jazz conservatives: when he shattered the status quo that had persisted since Coleman Hawkins first established the tenor saxophone as a jazz voice in the late twenties, there were cries of resentment. Prez was not moved by them.

But Prez was temperamentally unsuited to the complexities of twentieth-century life. His growing eccentricity was a means by which he could disguise his uncertainties.

Many who thought they knew him well believed him to be a junkie. He wasn't, but his dull, parchment complexion and generally distracted manner matched the junkie stereotype. His heavy-lidded eyes, resting on grayish bags, gave him a vaguely Asian look. They would become illuminated unpredictably with a gentle twinkling that accompanied quiet, slow laughter. Often Prez would shuffle onto the bandstand with ridiculous, mincing little movements, or move across the stand with crablike sidesteps until he reached his destination. Once there, he'd stop and shiver slightly, as drummer Dave Bailey put it, "like a chicken spreading its feathers."

His idiosyncrasies were part of the masquerade, the massive characterization. Prez used an almost entirely personal language most of the time, some of which became standard jazz argot. "Bells!" and "Ding-dong!" signified approval. "No eyes" indicated reluctance. He sprinkled his speech with double-talk words, punctuating with "oodastaddis!" or "vout" or the suffix "-oreeny." "I feel a draft" was his signal of racial discomfort. White musicians weren't "ofays" to Prez, but "gray boys." He greeted strangers with "How are your feelings?" The more Prez lost his battle with the forces of life, the more he depended on such hip talk to keep out intrusions: memories of his Army experience; countless rebuffs from his nonjazz acquaintances; days in Bellevue and nights on booze.

Prez was earning more than $50,000 a year during his better days with the Norman Granz troupe in the early 1950s, but the money evaporated as Prez withered. The beginning of the end was signaled when he entered Bellevue in the winter of 1955. Liquor and marijuana, combined with the masochism they fed, had humbled the tenor saxophonist no other jazzman could defeat in blues combat. After a short time at Bellevue, Prez resumed his destructive life. A complete mental breakdown put him in King's County Hospital late in 1957. He had been totally inactive before his collapse, and had left his third wife and two children. He was living in a dingy room in a cheap hotel, having been fired after a few nights on a job in Harlem because, too weak to stand, he had attempted to lead his combo from a chair. The hotel room was desolate except for Prez's horn, his phonograph, and a few snapshots of his parents.

His career had ended. His life would soon follow.

Lester Young was born on August 27, 1909, in Woodville, Mississippi, but his family soon moved to New Orleans. At the age of five he began studying music with his father.

In conversations with Dr. Luther Cloud, a psychologist-physician who tried to save Prez during his last days of degradation, Lester recalled his early experiences, particularly with the family band headed by Young *père*.

"My father was a fine musician," Prez told Cloud. "He studied at Tuskegee Institute. He knew a lot about music and he tried to teach me everything. He taught all the instruments and could play them all, especially trumpet and violin. . . . He traveled with carnival minstrel shows, a week in each town. . . ."

Lester started playing drums when he was ten because the family band needed a drummer. "They were too much trouble to carry around, so when I was thirteen I switched to alto," he told Cloud. "And all the time I was learning, with my brother Lee and my sister Irma. My father would try to teach me scales and I'd goof off and learn everything but the scales. One day my father discovered that I wasn't really learning to read—I was doing it all by ear. He got so mad he put me out of the family band." After that, Lester learned to read music out of spite.

Young Lester attended church with his family, but did so more as a chore than as a conviction. "There was some shyness about him when it came to church-going," his mother recalled. "I think it was shyness, too, that made him drink later on—it gave him courage with which to face the public."

The official break with the church came during his teens and was linked closely to his extreme sensitivity to Jim Crowism. Lester and his sister visited a small country church and were among the few Negroes present. When he heard the minister shout "black sin" and "black as hell" he felt slighted both personally and racially. In later years he owned religious figurines and spoke of God but rarely attended church.

The initial flight from paternal discipline and Jim Crow came when Young was eighteen. When his father told him that the family band had been booked on a string of dates in the South, Lester left to join a band known as the Bostonians, in which he played baritone, alto, and tenor. The arbitrarily named band actually was based in Salina, Kansas.

"It's too bad more people couldn't have heard Lester play alto sax," says Benny Carter. "When I was on the road with McKinney's Cotton Pickers in 1932 we hit Minneapolis and somebody told us about a wonderful alto player in a local club. I went to hear Prez and was enraptured. It was the greatest thing I'd ever heard. He had a definition and a mastery that I don't think he ever felt necessary to display on the tenor."

During the early thirties Young wandered through Kansas, Missouri, Oklahoma, and Minnesota with King Oliver's band,

Walter Page's Blue Devils, and several others. "Those were the tough times," he once said. "The Blue Devils band was getting bruised, I mean *really* bruised, playing to audiences of three people. One time all our instruments were impounded and they took us right to the railroad tracks and told us to get out of town. There we were, sitting with those hobos, and they showed us how to grab the train. We made it—with bruises. We got to Cincinnati, no loot, no horns, all raggedy and dirty, and we were trying to make it to Kansas City."

He moved on alone. In Kansas City he acquired a tenor sax and borrowed clothes from Herschel Evans. It was at this time that he played his first job with Basie.

"I was working at the Cotton Club in Minneapolis, and I used to hear Basie on the air," Prez remembered. "Everything sounded great except his tenor man [one of Evans' predecessors], so I sent him a wire. He'd heard me before, so I joined the band. It was very nice. Just like I thought it would be."

"When Prez first came to me at the Reno Club in Kansas City," Basie recalls, "it was like nothing we'd ever heard. And it was consistent. In all the years he was with our band he never had a bad night. No matter what happened to him personally, he never showed it in his playing. I can only remember him as being beautiful."

Prez took his first wife, Mary, along with him when he left Minneapolis to join Basie in Kansas City, but all that is known about the marriage is that it soon failed. Prez never talked about it. The accumulating traumas of racial pressures, parental discipline, woman trouble, and musical rebellion were aggravated when he left Basie to accept an offer of more money from Fletcher Henderson in 1934. He replaced Coleman Hawkins in the Henderson band, but he could not erase Hawkins' image.

"I came to New York with the band and I got bruised because I didn't play like Hawkins," he said. "They rang the bell on me. So I really did a lot of teardrops there, you know?

Some people just didn't have eyes for certain things. I was rooming at Fletcher's house and Mrs. Henderson would come in every morning and that bitch would start playing me them records with Hawkins and everything, to show me what to do, and I would listen, because I didn't want to hurt nobody's feelings."

But Prez had feelings, too. Proudly bearing a letter from Henderson stating that he had *not* been fired, he returned to Kansas City. After six months with Andy Kirk's band, he rejoined Basie; within a year John Hammond had arranged for the band to head east. A combo record date, with Prez and Basie, was held along the way, in Chicago, and the first Basie big-band date was cut in New York early in 1937.

Later, bop-era tenor man Dexter Gordon said, "Hawk had done everything possible and was the master of the horn, but when Prez appeared we all started listening to him alone. Prez had an entirely new sound, one that we had been waiting for, the first one to really tell a story on the horn."

It was during these decisive years with Basie that Prez reached his peak. His porkpie hat became famous, and his unique sounds and conceptions on tenor attracted musicians, fans, and critics. He leaped and they followed. But with fame his eccentricities became pronounced. He claimed to have psychic and prophetic powers, and when he left the Basie band in 1940 it was ostensibly because a recording session had been called, in defiance of one of his superstitions, for Friday the thirteenth. But according to drummer Jo Jones, a Basie compatriot and one of Prez's closest friends, the reason for the walkout was the culmination of a sorrow Prez had been bearing for almost two years: the death of Herschel Evans.

"They were supposed to be battling on the bandstand, but actually Lester had the greatest respect and admiration for Herschel. It was just like a twin dying. Soon afterward, Lester would be so restless that he would keep his coat and hat underneath the music stand and other guys would have to pull him back down to his seat to keep playing." According to Jones, Prez didn't drink heavily until Evans died. Jones feels that "after Herschel died, Lester felt it was his duty to play Herschel *and* Lester. He had a dual thing going—he'd play four bars of himself and four for Herschel. He was lost."

After leaving Basie, Prez tried heading his own combo. When this proved unrewarding, he sat in on jam sessions at Minton's and the Village Vanguard, then went on the road with Al Sears's band, touring for USO camp shows. He engaged in musical battles with tenor man Budd Johnson and spent his nights warming dice. "He had the damnedest bad luck," recalls Johnson. "I never saw him win once, though he'd stay up all night long. He wouldn't quit; he just loved to see 'em roll."

Three years later Prez rejoined Basie as abruptly as he had departed. Jo Jones ran into him at a Fifty-second Street bar and, on behalf of Basie, invited Prez to return. "I bought him a short beer," Jones says, "and told him, 'Now don't forget we're at the Lincoln Hotel. Be at work tonight at seven.' And at seven o'clock there he was."

This was to be his last regular tour of duty with a big band. When he was asked if he might organize his own orchestra, he said, "Would I care to form a big band? Oooh, I would love to, but I wouldn't go for the okey-doke—them headaches, them evil spirits. I can barely make it with five. Like the old lady told me, there's always a bastard in the bunch, and you never know who it is. . . ."

He discovered several in the bunch when the Army called him in 1944. He survived for fifteen months, beginning as a mess orderly in the infantry, but the experience sent him plummeting downhill.

"First he had his horn and they took that away from him," says Charlie Carpenter, Prez's manager from 1946 to 1957. "They wouldn't let him play in the band. And he had his hair long and they made him cut it off. Maybe that's why later on he let it grow so long it started to curl up and he told me he wanted to braid it real long down his neck like an Indian.

Anyhow, the Army was a terrifying experience for him."

Prez entered an Army hospital for minor surgery and, in completing a routine form, admitted to having smoked marijuana. Despite a move by a sympathetic officer-jazz fan to discharge him, several Army men were waiting for him when he emerged from the hospital and returned to the barracks. Jo Jones, who was stationed with Prez at Fort McClellan, Alabama, remembers the details.

"I got back before noon and all hell had broken loose. Lester's locker had been searched. The major who made the search found some photographs. 'Who is this?' he asked Lester, and Prez said, 'That's my wife.' Well, the major was from Louisiana and this was Lester's second wife, also named Mary, who was white." Ironically, Prez later claimed to have had little affection for the girl, a jazz follower much younger than he. He was conscious of her whiteness and was often made uncomfortable because of it during the brief period the couple lived in California before Prez's induction. The marriage ended during that Army term. "The major just slammed down the pictures and said, 'Place this man under arrest.' His excuse was that he had found some pills. Actually there was nothing that Prez hadn't obtained from the dispensary—they were just pills to deaden the pain from the surgery. In addition, the major resented the fact that people had tried to arrange a discharge for Prez.

"So he found an article of war that gave him a chance to bring charges against Lester. They might as well have turned him in for having aspirin on him, but somehow it was maneuvered so he got a five-year sentence. Later on, when the truth came out, to save face for the major, they didn't reverse the decision entirely, but reduced it to one year and sent Prez to the detention barracks at Camp Gordon, Georgia. It was the most agonizing period in his life.

"A soldier at Camp Gordon, who was a bass player and knew Prez, managed to send him out on a detail to build a bridge. By this time he was so terrified that he actually tried to run away. I don't think he ever told a soul about this except me. 'But then I got into the bushes and I saw those people with the guns,' he said, 'and I came back.' "

In a desperate search for escape Prez managed to swap candy bars for liquid cocaine. With a friend (a dental corpsman) he rigged up a still behind his bunk, mixed the cocaine with 180-proof alcohol from surgical supplies, and fermented whatever fruit the amateur distillers could find. Inevitably the MPs found the still and Prez's sentence was extended by several months. Finally he was granted a dishonorable discharge. Too distraught to appeal, he returned to New York. "I'm out," he would repeat. "I'm out. That's all that matters."

But it wasn't all that mattered. Prez returned to a jazz world in upheaval. "It was pitiful," says Billy Taylor, "to see him walking along Fifty-second Street, hearing all those young kids playing the ideas he had discarded. He came back looking for some roots, and he failed to find them. You could see him wondering where to turn."

Away from fans and reporters Prez found little time for his imitators. He preferred to listen to records by Frank Sinatra or Dick Haymes. Lured by the economic promise of Norman Granz's Jazz at the Philharmonic tour in 1946, he found himself pitted for a string of hopeless years against honking, crowd-begging tenor men. He played his best after hours. When not on tour, he had trouble maintaining his own group; his sidemen invariably were less intense about the music than he was. "It takes pretty people to make the music pretty," he said after a dismal rehearsal, "and ain't a single pretty bastard in my band."

"Lester had already reached the point of no return by 1946," says Charlie Carpenter. "He was tired of the responsibilities of the world and was looking for an escape. It just seemed that everything had to go wrong for him."

Prez continued to ramble. And decay persisted, physically and artistically. On a concert package tour with the Basie band and several name combos, he worked a set in front of the band. His performance, a frightening, distorted image of his past, inspired laughter among the musicians. As he played absurd, audience-taunting figures, some laughed with Prez, some laughed at him.

Yet the obsession with beauty continued to compel him. On one occasion he found a wounded bird and took it to work with him. He nursed it between sets, admiring its loveliness and pitying its helplessness. Later, when the bird disappeared, he explained that he had given it the strength to fly—with a small nip of bourbon.

When his second marriage failed, Prez found hope in yet a third. It produced two children, and it provided him with a potentially satisfying home life in St. Albans, Long Island.

But after his second trip to the hospital—for malnutrition and a nervous breakdown owing to alcohol—Prez left his family. His wife was a fragile, proud, introspective woman, the only one who had ever wanted to create a home for him. But she never fully understood him, nor was she able to lead him. "It wasn't that the marriage ever really broke up," she points out. "He just wanted to be in New York where things were happening."

The final year of Lester Young's life was spent with Elaine Swain, whom he had known for a few years. Miss Swain had been a companion of several well-known jazzmen, including at least two Prezian tenor men, and had maintained a close friendship with Billie Holiday. She confined her activities to Prez during his last days, spending hours recording his rambling reminiscences in notebooks, to date unpublished. But she was unable to save him. Despite her care his physical condition deteriorated rapidly. He could not get out of bed without help. Elaine and his doctor persuaded him to eat, and tried to dilute his gin with water. Prez spent most of his time listening to popular records and staring out of his window at Birdland. Tranquilizers and vitamin pills by the dozen helped. Gin and bourbon were replaced by wine. He began to gain weight.

Birdland staged a tribute to him. Dozens of jazzmen attended and a jam session ensued. Set after set Prez played valiantly. Stepping forward to cut the special cake prepared for the occasion, he held the knife with one hand and with the other fingered his horn to play *I Didn't Know What Time It Was* to express his surprise on being so honored.

Late in 1958, further improved, Prez prepared eagerly for a booking in Paris, anxious to return to the sympathetic environment he had relished on earlier visits to Europe with JATP units. At this time his brother Lee, now a solid success as Nat Cole's drummer, visited Prez and upbraided him for his way of life. It was their last meeting. Prez resumed his heavy drinking. When Dr. Cloud told him, "We all have our worries," Prez replied bitterly, "You have no problems. You're a white man."

He departed for Paris early in 1959. Because he was refused permission by two hotels to cook meals in his room, he forgot about food. He found little time for sleep. Too feeble to travel, he required a week to muster sufficient strength for the trip home. He cabled Elaine that he would leave Paris for New York. The cable was dated Friday, March 13.

He shuffled weakly from the plane at the New York airport. Back in his hotel room he returned to the stare-at-Birdland, records-on-the-phonograph, bottle-in-hand routine. That first afternoon he began to fade. By midnight he had consumed a fifth of vodka and most of a pint of bourbon but had not eaten. At one o'clock the following morning, March 15, while lying in his bed half-asleep, he began to move his mouth as if playing his horn. Elaine, alarmed, phoned for aid. Twenty minutes after Prez had stopped breathing, a doctor arrived and pronounced him dead.

The police were concerned with tangibles. They impounded $500 in traveler's checks, Prez's horn, a ring, and a wallet—pending settlement of the $76 hotel bill from Prez's earlier stay there.

Four days later, at a funeral home on East Fifty-second Street, those who had heard Prez and had not forgotten him listened to Al Hibbler sing *In the Garden* and trombonist Tyree Glenn play a muted solo of *Just A-Wearyin' for You.*

"Prez would have liked that part," said one musician later. "But the photographers snapping flashlight pictures while it was going on—he wouldn't have wanted that to happen. Wasn't no beauty in that and Prez wouldn't have wanted anything that wasn't pretty."

Prestige

Bop and Bird

LESTER YOUNG was probably the first musician to make the public aware of the rhythmic qualities later to become part of bebop, but no one man was responsible for the phenomenon. Dizzy Gillespie did not create bebop in Philadelphia any more than Charlie Parker distilled it in Kansas City or Charlie Christian in Oklahoma or Prez on the road with Basie.

Bebop actually was a synthesis of many musical ideas, created by a disparate group of musicians who were often unaware of the startling impact their innovations would have. They had, after all, been doing what came naturally for a long time before it was branded as "new" music and named "bebop." Many of these artists, in fact, found the term "new music" ironic; only a few years earlier, the same performers playing the same way had been stigmatized as rebels or fools.

In that he symbolized the move from hot to cool jazz, Lester Young was indeed a radical. Although Charlie Christian's instrument was the guitar, his playing incorporated qualities that were remarkably similar to Young's. When Christian was heard for the first time in 1938 by a young guitarist named Mary Osborne, the sound that greeted her, she remembers, "was so hornlike that I thought it might be a tenor sax, played through a microphone that distorted a little."

What impressed Christian's listeners most of all, Miss Osborne recalls, was "his extraordinary sense of time. He had a very relaxed, even beat that would sound modern even today. The group he worked with was doing everything that the Benny Goodman Sextet played later, and doing it even better . . . Charlie didn't play bop exactly, but he did things with augmented and diminished chords that were completely new to me, and rhythmically some of his ideas sounded very much like bop."

John Hammond heard Christian in Oklahoma City in 1939 and arranged for him to join Benny Goodman in New York. There he came to the attention of some other jazzmen who had been experimenting with new harmonies and rhythms. Every evening after his job with Goodman at the Pennsylvania Hotel, Christian would take his guitar and amplifier to a dining room in the Hotel Cecil on West 118th Street in Harlem. Henry Minton, a former saxophonist who had been the first Negro delegate to Musicians' Union Local 802, converted the dilapidated room into a club, named it Minton's, installed ex-bandleader Teddy Hill as manager, and created an open house for musicians where jam sessions were held almost nightly.

Kenny Clarke, the drummer at Minton's, declared that "Charlie contributed an infinite amount to the new jazz. He was always very firm about a beat, and we made it our business to swing all the time. He wrote some wonderful tunes; one of them, 'Pagin' Dr. Christian,' had exactly the same four-bar opening as the number Woody Herman recorded seven years later under the title 'Keen and Peachy.' Another was 'Chunk Charlie Chunk'—Jimmy Mundy arranged it and Charlie recorded it with the whole Goodman band as 'Solo Flight.'

"One night I was fooling around with a ukulele and Charlie took it out of my hand. 'Look, Kenny,' he said, 'you can make all the chords you want on this, if you just stretch your fingers right.' I started experimenting. I got an idea that sounded good and wrote it down. Later on Joe Guy, the trumpeter, showed it to Cootie Williams, and Cootie had Bob McRae make an arrangement. I called it 'Fly Right,' and Cootie used to broadcast it from the Savoy Ballroom; it became his theme. This was right after he'd left Benny Goodman and formed his own band."

It was typical of the prevailing resistance to change that a recording of "Fly Right" by Williams' band was not released until almost thirty years later after a researcher discovered it. Meanwhile Clarke had recorded it with a small group of his own in 1946 under its other title, "Epistrophy."

Clarke, who had worked with Dizzy Gillespie in the Teddy Hill band and was a key figure among the Hill personnel, played at Minton's in 1940. He felt certain that it was Charlie Christian who first used the word "bebop." "Charlie and Diz used to hum that way, to illustrate some of their ideas," he recalled.

It was in the Hill band, Clarke said, that he first began to move away from the steady 4/4 drumming style. "On an arrangement of 'Swanee River,' I began kicking, playing off-rhythms. Diz was fascinated; it gave him just the right impetus he wanted, and he began to build things around it."

Later, as he began using the bass-drum pedal for special accents rather than regular rhythm, and the top cymbal to maintain the steady four beats, Teddy Hill would imitate the sounds he produced. "What is that klook-mop stuff you're playing?" he would ask. And that, says Hill, is what the music itself was called before it became known as bebop. In fact, Clarke was nicknamed "Klook."

The sessions at Minton's brought together men who had been producing new ideas independently and who crystallized their concepts into a new music. One of the youngsters who impressed Clarke most at the time was the late pianist-composer Tadd Dameron. Many years later he remembered that Dameron had flatted fifths in certain chords as early as 1940: "It sounded very odd to me at first. Tadd also was one of the first musicians I heard playing eight-note sequences in the new legato manner."

Dameron, who later became one of the leading bop arrangers with Dizzy Gillespie's band, always liked to depart harmonically from the rigid traditions of swing. Working in the Midwest in 1938 with small bands or accompanying singers, he used harmonic variations that few liked or understood. The following year, in Kansas City with Charlie Parker, he overheard people saying, "They're crazy." But when Gillespie heard him at a jam session two years later, he said: "I've been looking all over for a guy like you."

Gillespie, Clarke, Dameron, and kindred spirits soon became a clique, from which it was easy to bar outsiders. As Kenny Clarke pointed out, "We'd play 'Epistrophy' or 'I've Got My Love to Keep Me Warm' just to keep the other guys off the stand, because we knew they couldn't make those chord changes."

Gillespie changed a Hit Parade song of 1940 called "How High the Moon" from a slow ballad to an up-tempo instrumental. The song, or its chord pattern equipped with new melodies and new titles ("Ornithology," "Bean at the Met," "Indiana Winter," "Slightly Dizzy"), became the national anthem of the bebop movement and certainly the most recorded jazz tune of the 1940s.

The bop pioneers often turned to the Cole Porters and the Gershwins as well as to some of the less distinguished popular composers of the day for their chord sequences because of the limitations of the blues and other standard formulas. But their basic ideas did not come from Tin Pan Alley. On the contrary, some of the most successful bop themes were born at Minton's.

The bopsters played simple jump tunes based on repeated riffs; others had eccentric harmonic departures like "Epistrophy"; a few were slow-tempo, "pretty" tunes with unusual chord changes. This last was exemplified by " 'Round Midnight," written by a pianist-composer who frequented Minton's, Thelonious Monk. Monk's technical shortcomings made him a controversial figure whose contribution was both over- and underestimated. Teddy Hill remembers Monk wandering in and out of Minton's and sometimes falling asleep at the piano. "He'd stay there for hours after the place closed, or get there hours before we opened. Sometimes the musicians would appeal to me to see if I could wake him up. Suddenly he might wake up and go into some intricate, tricky little passage, with Kenny playing those funny offbeat effects on the bass drum."

Monk, like all the other bebop musicians, was a strikingly inventive writer: such themes as his "Straight No Chaser," "Well You Needn't," "Hackensack," and "I Mean You" were among his most durable products. However, Kenny Clarke felt that Bud Powell, the pianist with Cootie Williams' orchestra in the first days of " 'Round Midnight," "used to do all the things that Monk wanted to do but couldn't. Bud had more technique. Monk was a teacher, a creator rather than a soloist." (In retrospect, technical considerations seem less relevant; during the 1940s Monk, in his own heterodox way, was a unique and valuable pianist.)

There is very little disagreement among the musicians who witnessed the birth of bop as to who were the major innovators. Almost all credit Christian, Young, Gillespie, Dameron, Monk, and Clarke; but without exception those who were part of the expanding art of improvisation during the catalytic years of the 1940's and 50's still pay tribute to the man they characterize as an undisputed genius, the proven legend of their time—Charlie "Yardbird" Parker.

The same Kansas City that so influenced the newly organized Count Basie band and its most prestigious hornman, Lester Young, inspired Charles Parker, Jr. But with this significant difference: Parker did not immediately appear destined for competence, let alone greatness.

According to Ross Russell, author of *Jazz Style in Kansas City and the Southwest,* "Charlie considered himself a man of the world and a jazz musician of unlimited if unrecognized talent" during the days when, at the age of fifteen, he would sneak into the Reno Club or stand at a back entrance, holding an alto sax his mother had bought for him in a pawnshop. He would finger the keys silently, mentally playing along with Lester Young's solos.

To those around him, and particularly to those who played with him, Bird for years seemed to be a born loser.

His father, a former dancer and singer in black theaters, had left home when Charles was small. Because Mrs. Parker worked at night, young Charlie was free to wander around the city—the Kansas City of the Pendergast era. Bird liked to say that he "spent three years in high school and wound up a freshman." He played baritone horn in the school band, then switched to alto, and joined an undergraduate dance band led by a senior, Lawrence "88" Keyes. Bassist Gene Ramey, who knew him well, said that "Bird wasn't doing anything, musically speaking, at that period. In fact, he was the saddest thing in the band, and the other members gave him something of a hard time." He recalled that Parker's tone was as weak as his conception, and that he was seldom allowed to sit in at the frequent jam sessions.

As Bob Reisner described it in *Bird: The Legend of Charlie Parker*, when he did sit in, the results could be unfortunate. One night a session with some of Basie's men was getting under way. "Jo Jones waited until Bird started to play, and suddenly, in order to show how he felt about Bird, he threw a cymbal across the dance floor. It fell with a deafening sound and Bird, in humiliation, packed up his instrument and left."

With some parting remark such as: "All right, I'll fix you cats—you're laughing at me now, but just you wait and see!" Bird proceeded to disappear for several months. He spent the summer working in the Ozark lake region with George E. Lee. Aided by the few Lester Young records then available, and helped informally by Lee's guitarist, Efferge Ware, and pianist Carrie Powell, Bird studied harmony and practiced the saxophone incessantly.

By the time he returned to Kansas City in the fall of 1937, Bird had justified his exit line. "The difference was unbelievable," Ramey said. "And after this sudden development in his style, he began to get lots of work."

During the next few years Parker sat alongside Buster Smith (who was such an important influence that Bird called him "my dad") in the reed section of a band led by Smith and the drummer Jesse Price. In 1938 he began an intermittent association with the Jay McShann band and worked briefly with another of the important Kansas City groups of the period, Harlan Leonard's Rockets.

For all the jobs and the improved musicianship, Bird remained a loser. At sixteen he had contracted a short-lived marriage with Rebecca Ruffin; around this time, perhaps even earlier, he was introduced to heroin by a local hipster. The details of this period are vague and frequently contradictory, but it has been established that after the breakup of his marriage Charlie bummed his way to Chicago.

Budd Johnson remembers seeing him wander into a Chicago dance hall one night in 1938, looking beat, and without a horn. He wanted to sit in with King Kolax's band. The alto saxophonist lent him his horn; upon hearing the astonishing results, he told Charlie that he happened to have an extra horn and it would be all right for him to keep the borrowed alto.

Bird was hornless once more when he came to New York in 1939. He worked very little as a musician, but while holding down a job as dishwasher at Jimmy's Chicken Shack he could listen to the star of the show, Art Tatum. It was not until he returned to New York a couple of years later, as a member of the Jay McShann orchestra, that he met some of the young rebels of the Manhattan jazz world. Parker remembered meeting Dizzy Gillespie first when Diz sat in one night with McShann at the Savoy Ballroom in Harlem. Gillespie's version is that they had met once before, at Monroe's Uptown House in Harlem. The Savoy, once a jazz mecca and nicknamed "The Home of Happy Feet," was the New York *pied-à-terre* of the Teddy Hill, Benny Carter, and Chick Webb bands in the late

1930s. Savoy audiences comprised local jitterbugs who wanted dance music that jumped, and a scattering of white jazz fans who wanted to listen.

Although McShann's music had "the Midwestern beat," it conformed closely to the requirements of the Savoy's customers. Primarily a blues band, it featured one of the better blues shouters of the day, Walter Brown. The arrangements and the solos were generally based on the traditional blues pattern and other simple forms. Bird wrote a few tunes in this style and played solos on some of the band's first recordings, made in 1941 and 1942. His work at that time, typified by "Hootie Blues" and "Sepian Stomp," had certain qualities that lifted it above the level of its surroundings. The phrasing was more involved, the tone a little more strident, and the pulse of each performance had a way of swinging that seemed to owe nothing to any source. His grace notes and dynamic inflections differed from anything previously heard.

"Charlie Parker offers inspired alto solos," wrote Bob Locke in the July 1, 1942 *Down Beat,* "using a minimum of notes in a fluid style with a somewhat thin tone but a wealth of pleasing ideas." Barry Ulanov, in the March 1942 *Metronome,* said: "The jazz set forth by the Parker alto is superb. Parker's tone tends to rubberiness, and he has a tendency to play too many notes, but his continual search for wild ideas, and the consistency with which he finds them, compensate for weaknesses that should be easily overcome." Because of Bird's unpredictability, it is entirely possible that Locke ("a minimum of notes") and Ulanov ("too many notes") were both right, but heard different sets.

The foundations of Parker's ultimate style were probably defined before he left Kansas City, but he began experimenting with new harmonic ideas in New York. "I used to hang around with a guitarist named Biddy Fleet," Bird once said. "We would sit in the back room at Dan Wall's chili joint and other spots uptown, and Biddy would run new chords . . . After I left McShann in Detroit and came back to New York,

I used to sit in at Minton's with men like Scotty [Kermit Scott, tenor sax], John Simmons on bass, Kenny Clarke or Kansas Fields on drums, and Monk. Those were the guys who'd play everything on the *right* chords—the new chords that we believed were right . . ."

Parker found little room for expansion within McShann's spirited but tradition-rooted band. It was not until he began playing with a small group at the Uptown House that the young inquisitive New York musicians began to talk about him. At that time, Kenny Clarke said, he was playing alto with a sound and manner of phrasing evocative of Lester Young's tenor.

His style was becoming more and more personalized, but Bird did not begin to acquire a reputation among his fellow musicians until a few years later. He worked at various jobs, even spending nine months with the Noble Sissle band, which had always been further removed from jazz (and closer to the Broadway commercial concept of dance music) than any other black orchestra. "Sissle hated me," said Parker, "and I only had one featured number in the books. I doubled on clarinet for that job."

Clarinet was not his only double; in Earl Hines's orchestra, the first big band to incorporate bebop, he played tenor sax. Hines had originally tried to hire Bird for an alto chair as a result of pressure from progressive members of his band; but he was reluctant to take Bird away from Jay McShann. He called McShann to give him fair warning about his designs on Parker, and to his astonishment, was told cheerfully: "The sooner you take him the better. He just passed out in front of the microphone right in the middle of 'Cherokee'!"

A year later, early in 1943, Bird was out of work, and so he finally joined Hines. Because there was no alto job available then, Earl bought him a tenor and Charlie replaced Budd Johnson.

Hines's band was slowly becoming a nursery of new ideas. The leader, although personally of the old school, encouraged experimentation and gave the men a free hand. Even Billy Eckstine, between vocals, took up the trumpet and became interested in the new music.

One of the great regrets of bebop students is the lack of recordings during that crucial period (1942–44), one of the consequences of a Musicians' Union strike. Thus the first joint engagement of Dizzy and Bird, a decisive phase in the history of bop, was not preserved.

After almost a year with Hines, Parker worked briefly with Cootie Williams and Andy Kirk, then went on the road with the original Billy Eckstine band in 1944. This was to be his last regular job with a big band; the post-Eckstine period was spent in and out of Fifty-second Street, with Ben Webster, with Dizzy's small band, then with his own group at the Three Deuces featuring an eighteen-year-old trumpeter named Miles Davis. He rejoined Dizzy, went to California, and remained there after Gillespie returned East.

Shortly afterward Bird's physical and mental decline began.

Parker returned to New York in April of 1947 to find that some of his friends barely recognized him. His weight was up from 127 to 192. He looked healthy and happy. When I saw him he was candid about his bad years and his "regeneration." He was, moreover, eloquent and honest, with none of the pseudo-hipness so characteristic of less articulate musicians. "It all came from being introduced too soon to night life," he said. "When you're not mature enough to know what's happening—well, you goof."

Bird's dissipation had begun as early as 1932, taking a more serious turn in 1935 when an actor friend told him about a new kick. One morning, very soon afterwards, he woke up feeling sick and not knowing why: the panic, the eleven-year panic, was on.

"I didn't know what hit me . . . it was so sudden. I was a victim of circumstances," he told me. "High school kids don't know any better. That way, you can miss the most important years of your life, the years of possible creation.

"I don't know how I made it through those years. I became bitter, hard, cold. I was always in a panic—couldn't buy clothes or a good place to live. Finally out on the Coast last year I didn't have *any* place to stay, until somebody put me up in a converted garage. The mental strain was getting worse all the time. What made it worst of all was that nobody understood our kind of music out on the Coast. They *hated* it, Leonard. I can't begin to tell you how I yearned for New York."

The climax came one night after a recording session at which Bird had showed alarming signs of imbalance. He finally lost control completely. He was never to remember anything about the next few days. Ross Russell, of Dial Records, spoke up for him, and the authorities had Bird sent to Camarillo State Hospital, where he gradually regained his health. He could hardly wait to return to the east. "When I left the Coast they had a band at Billy Berg's with somebody playing a bass sax and a drummer playing on the temple blocks and ching-ching-ching-ching cymbals—one of those real New Orleans style bands, that *ancient* jazz—and the people liked it! That was the kind of thing that had helped to crack my wig."

Bird then was charged with an enthusiasm and ambition such as he had never known in the bad old days. He declared (and every great musician admits it sooner or later) that he played best when he was under the influence of no stimulants at all. He felt sorry for the kids who think: "So-and-so plays great, and he's on such-and-such, so I should do like he does and then I'll blow great too."

The night we talked, Bird was preparing for several weeks out at a farm in Pennsylvania; he was hoping to persuade two other members of the frantic Fifty-second Street clique to come along with him—drummer Max Roach and pianist Bud

Powell, both fine musicians who had had experiences similar to Bird's. When he came back, he said, he'd have a small band playing concerts. "Big bands are limited—you can do so much more with a combo."

He cited a nonjazz parallel: "Have you heard that album of music by Schönberg with just five instruments playing while an actress recites some poetry in German? It's a wonderful thing—I think it's called *Protee.*"

And speaking of classical music, "Have you heard *The Children's Corner* by Debussy? Oh, that's so much music! . . . Debussy and Stravinsky are my favorites; but I like Shostakovitch . . . Beethoven, too . . . you know, life used to be so cruel to musicians, just the way it is today—they say that when Beethoven was on his deathbed he shook his fist at the world; they just didn't understand. Nobody in his own time really dug anything he wrote. But that's music."

In the jazz field Charlie paid his respects to Thelonious Monk as the man responsible for many of the harmonic changes that came to be a part of bebop. But, he added, "Let's not call it bebop, let's call it music. Everyone got so used to hearing jazz for so many years, finally somebody said, 'Let's have something different,' and some new ideas began to evolve. Then people brand it 'bebop' and try to crush it. If it should ever become completely accepted, we should all remember it's in just the same position jazz was. It's just another style. I don't think any individual invented it. I was playing the same way years before I came to New York. I never consciously changed."

Of those playing in the style at the time, he selected as outstanding exponents Sonny Stitt, Fats Navarro, and Miles Davis. And he pointed out that Curly Russell, Chocolate Williams (the bass player), Bud Powell, and Thelonious Monk were among the "originals."

His favorite arranger? "Jimmy Mundy . . . Calvin Jackson, who writes for MGM . . . and he can play, too! . . . Ralph Burns; anybody who's writing for Dizzy's big band; and of course Dizzy himself."

Of his own records Charlie said, "I still haven't produced any that completely satisfied me. I hope to some day." He made two Dial dates before returning to New York; one was with a group of musicians unfamiliar to him, and he wasn't too happy about it, but the other was a trio date with Erroll Garner which he believed was highly successful.

It appeared then that Charlie Parker, at twenty-six, had his best years—as a man and as an artist—before him. But this was not to be the case. After a series of recuperations and re- lapses he died on March 12, 1955, at the age of thirty-four.

The death-cult manifestations were quick to surface. "Bird Lives" graffiti appeared on Greenwich Village walls; an over- flow crowd jammed Carnegie Hall three weeks after his death to hear what *Down Beat* called "the largest jazz concert in the history of New York City." For many years Joe Segal held an annual series of Charlie Parker Memorial jam sessions in Chicago.

Only now is it possible to gain a clear perspective of Bird's contribution, and even now it is unfortunately true that to a great degree he is as misunderstood in death as he was in life. When he and Dizzy Gillespie were creating a new spirit and form in jazz, their bebop movement was mercilessly denounced by almost every critic, whose support could have meant so much to them. Nor did Bird's mistreatment at the hands of the lay press stop with his death. That he died in the home of Lord Rothschild's sister was much more important to the headline writers than the premature loss of an artist whom most jazz musicians had proclaimed the greatest musical influence of our generation.

Bird continues to be the subject of a morbid, James Dean- like reverence on the part of cultists; yet denigration of him for his personal weaknesses has continued.

To me he was, quite simply, a genius who was my friend.

In all the years I knew him, I never heard Charlie refer to himself as "Bird." To me he was Charlie, or, occasionally in jest on the telephone, "Leonard? This is Yardbird." There are many conflicting theories, none of them important, concerning the origin of his nickname.

Charlie and I originally got to know one another slightly through his combo work with Gillespie, and through just one record date he made for me—a Sarah Vaughan session, for which he showed up so late that we cut only three somewhat ragged sides, with Dizzy, Flip Phillips, and a rhythm section. He kept in the background for the ballads but took a superb solo on "Mean to Me." This was May 25, 1945.

At that time many of us in jazz knew little or nothing about hard narcotics. Marijuana was in common use, but heroin, cocaine, and opium were just commodities we had read about in paperback novels or seen in B movies. We had never heard terms like "busted," "fuzz," or all the other jargon that came into common use in bop circles once a vast clique of junkies had fanned out from Bird. (Even the word "junkie" was unfamiliar.) Perhaps for this reason it was not unusual for some of his admirers to observe Bird with a mixture of reverence for his music and morbid revulsion at what they had heard about his addiction.

By the time Parker had gone to California on the disastrous trip that ended with the "Lover Man" record date, his breakdown, and seven months in Camarillo, we knew a great deal more about the curse that had struck deep into the world of jazz. During the eight years of life that remained for Bird we were to witness a series of rehabilitations and relapses not unlike those of Billie Holiday. In both instances the road to hell was paved with good but easily shaken intentions. The temptations were too close and too constant; yet there were some stretches of relative calm and adjustment, periods when Charlie and his wife Doris found an almost bourgeois happiness in conventional living. But for Bird the normal was abnormal. The kindly Doris was too straight for him.

His deepest instincts, as I observed them, were grounded in the need to give and receive affection, including sexual gratification, and to maintain a fruitful relationship with his art and with society. His kindness was often evident. When I was immobilized by a serious automobile accident at a time when Charlie must have had trouble digging up the cab fare, he took the long trip from his Lower East Side apartment to my Upper West Side hospital bedside not once but several times. During those visits he found common ground for amiable conversations with my father, an Englishman in his sixties whose world could not have been more completely removed from Charlie's.

My starkest recollection goes back to the time when it was Charlie who was in the hospital. When I uttered some platitude about taking better care of himself, he sat up in the bed and said, "I can't afford not to. The doctor told me if I don't quit drinking, I'll die. I've had my last drink."

Three or four years and several thousand drinks later, he made one final effort to rally. At a Town Hall concert in the fall of 1954 he looked well, talked well, and played magnificently. "I have a new life," he told me. "I come in every day from Pennsylvania to take psychiatric treatment at Bellevue." His private life had seen a series of changes: he had an attractive common-law wife, Chan Richardson, and was passionately proud of their two children, Laird and Pree. Then Pree died of pneumonia. To most observers the loss of his infant daughter was the major factor in Charlie Parker's final breakdown.

One night at Basin Street, soon after Pree's death, I was watching the show when I felt a tugging at my pants leg. I turned to find Charlie squatting at the side of the table. He refused to get up, take a seat, or move from this awkward spot. He mumbled for a while about the need to talk to someone, about the tragedy of Pree, the cruelty of life. After a while he edged away.

It was after Pree's death, though, that Charlie made the last attempt to straighten himself out. Had he moved away entirely from the environment of jazz and the nightclub world and the pushers, perhaps he would be alive today. But he might have found such a life too constricted to be worth living.

Early in 1955, a few months after the Town Hall concert, I received a letter from Chan.

"We've moved to New Hope, Pa.," it read in part. "It's in Bucks County, and the nicest. We're on nine acres—two horses and sheep. I adore it, and Bird is playing the commuter—4:30 to Trenton and I pick him up at the station. Let's hear from you."

In March, 1955, I saw Charlie again. He was standing, raggedly dressed, in a bar located above Birdland.

"New Hope?" he asked. "No, I haven't been back there lately." The name of the town now seemed to take on an ironic significance. Charlie's eyes looked very sad, and the bloated excess fat had returned.

There was the final weekend of work, when Birdland (whose management for a while had banned him from the club named after him) changed its mind and put him in for two nights with Bud Powell, Kenny Dorham, Art Blakey, and Charlie Mingus. It was a dismal sight. Bird quarreled with Powell, walked off the stand after playing a few bars, and within minutes was around the corner at Basin Street (then on Fifty-first near Broadway). Tears were streaming down his face. He begged a couple of old friends to come over to Birdland and see him.

"You'll kill yourself if you go on like this," said Mingus, who loved Charlie and was mortified by the spectacle of his self-destruction.

A few days later, before leaving for a booking in Boston, he stopped off at the home of his friend Baroness Nica De-Koenigswarter.

Bird, appearing quite ill, refused a drink. Shortly afterward he began to vomit blood. A doctor summoned by the Baroness insisted that he be hospitalized, but Parker would not hear of it; he had had more than his share of hospitals.

Bird's sense of humor remained with him until the end.

When the doctor asked him whether he drank, he replied with supreme irony, "I take an occasional sherry before dinner."

The doctor warned the Baroness that Parker was suffering from ulcers and advanced cirrhosis of the liver, might die at any minute, and would have to leave in an ambulance if he left at all.

During subsequent visits the doctor revealed that he had been a musician. Bird played him some of his own recordings and was pleased at the favorable reaction.

After two or three days Bird's condition was improved and it was agreed that he could sit up and watch the Dorsey Brothers' television program. Propped up in an easy chair, he enjoyed the show. During a comedy juggling act he began laughing loudly, but the laugh turned into a choke; he tried to stand up, choked again, and fell back. The Baroness checked his pulse, felt it moving, then felt it stop.

"At the moment of his going," she said, "there was a tremendous clap of thunder. I didn't think about it at the time, but I've often thought about it since, how strange it was."

All the details of Bird's passing, of the disagreement between Doris and Chan concerning the disposition of the body, are too familiar to call for any repetition here.

One detail will never be known, however. Reflecting on those last moments, on the final torture of those thirty-four years, I sometimes wonder whether, in his mind at least, Charlie Parker shook his fist at the world.

Grover Sales, Jr.

Diz

Although Dizzy Gillespie was by no means the only musician who originated, developed, or popularized bebop, his history, at least from 1940, is largely the history of bebop. Gillespie was so prominent in every development from that year through the entire bebop cycle that the stories of Bird, Monk, Klook, and the others all dovetail into Dizzy's biography. It is possible to follow the winding course of bop as we trace his own peregrinations.

John Birks Gillespie was born to Mrs. Lottie Gillespie on October 21, 1917, in Cheraw, South Carolina. The ninth and last child, he was the only one to make his living as a musician, although his father, a bricklayer, was an amateur musician who led a local band as a sideline and kept its members' instruments at his home. Dizzy's introduction to music thus equipped him with a working knowledge of several other horns in addition to the trumpet.

"My father treated my mother good," Dizzy told Richard Boyer, who wrote a profile of him for the *New Yorker* in 1948. "He got my mother real expensive stuff. I was scared of him, though. When he talked, he roared. He was a real man. He didn't have a voice like this." Dizzy ended the sentence in a falsetto. "I got a beating every Sunday morning." He exploded into mirth. "At school I was smart, but I didn't study much. I'd fight every day. Ev-er-y day I'd fight. I was *all*-ways bad, you know."

The elder Gillespie died when John was ten. Within the next few years John's musical talent earned him a scholarship to a Negro industrial school in North Carolina, the Laurinburg Institute. He started on trombone at fourteen, taking music seriously for the first time. Nine months later a neighbor loaned him a trumpet, and not long after that he was given one of his own at Laurinburg, where an instructor whose name he recalls as Shorty Hall taught him theory and harmony. Although he did not become an expert reader until many years later, he soon mastered the horn well enough to play with a ten-piece band of youngsters that featured such early swing arrangements as the Casa Loma Orchestra's "Wild Goose Chase."

When Dizzy's mother left Cheraw in 1935 to live in Philadelphia, he had to quit school several months before his class graduated. Not until he visited Laurinburg in 1947 for a special ceremony did he receive his diploma and football letter.

Arriving in Philadelphia with his trumpet in a brown paper bag, John Gillespie was still a rough and rowdy country boy, his hat cocked to one side and a smart-alecky manner to match. It was around this time that he acquired the nickname Dizzy.

Charlie Shavers and Carl "Bama" Warwick were the other trumpeters in the local band led by Frank Fairfax, who gave Dizzy his first important job. While listening to Teddy Hill's band broadcasting from the Savoy Ballroom over NBC, Dizzy had found a musical idol in Hill's star trumpet man, Roy Eldridge; after that, he played in a style approximately Roy's.

Dizzy's next job ended before it started; Lucky Millinder heard him and hired him, but after he came to New York to join Millinder, something went wrong and he wound up jobless. At this point luck, in the person of Teddy Hill, stepped in. He had lost Roy Eldridge to the Fletcher Henderson band in Chicago. Frankie Newton was holding down the chair, but Teddy was looking for someone who could play like Roy, and he invited Dizzy to a rehearsal.

Bill Dillard, later to make a name for himself as an actor,

was playing first trumpet, and Shad Collins was on second. Teddy switched Collins to third and gave Dizzy the second book. Dizzy, dressed as if for a polar expedition, climbed on the bandstand. He did not remove his topcoat and gloves throughout the rehearsal, according to Hill, and during their subsequent years together Dizzy studiously avoided any attempt to belie his nickname. He was likely to start a new arrangement with an interlude, or the last chorus, instead of taking it from the top. While somebody else took a solo, Dizzy might stand up in the corner, imitating the soloist, holding up his horn and pretending to blow. Often he'd play an extra bar or two at the end of a number, a habit that persists today.

Dizzy would always respond to Teddy Hill's attempts at discipline. If reprimanded for putting his foot upon a chair, he would remove it promptly—and rest it on a music stand. No less disturbing were such early antics as dancing in the middle of someone else's act, putting the trumpet derby on his head, and playing with his chair turned away from the audience. But his musical value was nevertheless established by the time Dizzy made his first record session with Hill in March 1937. His solos on "King Porter Stomp" and "Blue Rhythm Fantasy" attested to his careful study of Roy Eldridge. Howard Johnson, the lanky, smiling first-alto man who was to play in Diz's own band a decade later, encouraged the similarity by writing out some of Eldridge's solos for Diz to copy.

Although some of the men in the band resented Dizzy, Teddy decided to take him along on a European tour. A few of his colleagues threatened to leave if Dizzy were not fired, but Teddy called their bluff and kept Dizzy, and the others stayed. The band spent a happy summer in London and Paris, serving as background for a Cotton Club show.

For British jazz fans the Teddy Hill tour marked the first visit of an American band in several years. The British Ministry of Labor had clamped down on all imported music, lifting the ban only with the strict provision that Hill's orchestra be used as mere accompaniment for the acts.

I can remember straining my ears at the London Palladium to catch a few bars of trumpet obbligato by Bill Dillard or Shad Collins while the Berry Brothers danced. The other trumpeter, John Gillespie, was of no concern to me or to any of the audience, whose interest lay in the names they recognized from records, such as Russ Procope, who was playing alto in the band, and Dickie Wells, the trombonist. Wells subsequently made some splendid records in Paris featuring a brass contingent from the band—but omitting the unfortunate nineteen-year-old trumpeter.

Dizzy was having a happy time, however. Off the job he would sit in with a small, experimental interracial band at London's only after-hours jazz spot, the Nest. On the job he would help supply ideas for head arrangements and work on new material with the brass section after rehearsals. When he returned to the United States he devised choruses for the band's production numbers at the Apollo and other theaters. For Diz the European trip was a chance to see the sights, take pictures, and indulge in such eccentricities as wearing a British regimental busby with a strap under the chin—a forerunner of the beret fashion he was to set later.

Back in the States Diz decided to transfer to New York's Musicians' Union Local 802. While he waited for his union card he took odd jobs. He recalls that he worked with "one cat in the Bronx who doubled on bass and musical saw."

When he rejoined Hill he worked steadily: out of the $45 a week earned at the Savoy by Hill's sidemen, plus a few extras for one-nighters, Dizzy somehow managed to save a little, send money to his family, and even make frequent loans to other men in the band, just to avoid throwing his money away.

Dizzy was soon playing lead trumpet with Hill, as well as taking most of the solos. The other two men in the section in 1939–40, Al Killian and Joe Guy, were learning from Dizzy rather than teaching him.

He impressed people outside the band, too. One day Lorraine Willis, a young chorus girl at the Howard Theatre in Washington, heard him, and that, declares Dizzy, was how he won his wife. They were married in Boston on May 9, 1940. (Lorraine might have married him for his cooking. Earlier, when she was working at the Apollo and he was idle, awaiting his union card, he would prepare elaborate meals and take them to the theater for her.)

Dizzy did no more recording until Lionel Hampton invited him to an all-star small-band date for Victor in September, 1939. He took one solo: the muted opening chorus on "Hot Mallets." He showed a divergence from his old Eldridge style and hinted at the typical Gillespian cascades of eighth notes that eventually marked his work.

Around the same time Dizzy worked at the New York World's Fair, where Teddy Hill was installed in a supposed replica of the Savoy Ballroom. He also spent a couple of months with Edgar Hayes, a pianist whose schmaltzy record of "Stardust" had made him a Harlem jukebox favorite. While he was rehearsing with Hayes, Dizzy heard some weirdly different effects in an arrangement by the clarinet man Rudy Powell (later known as Musheed Karweem). "I played it over and over," he recalled, "and realized how much more there could be in music than what everybody was playing." This may well have been the beginning of Dizzy's real musical awakening. He stopped copying Eldridge and began to create his own personal style.

Dizzy returned to the Teddy Hill band briefly until managerial difficulties broke it up. Then, late in 1939, he joined the orchestra of Cab Calloway.

Record collectors need hardly be told of the important developments that took place in his two years with Calloway. He cut some fifty sides with the band for the Vocalion label (later known as Okeh) and, although Cab dominates many of them with his vocals, there are numerous examples of the emergent new Gillespie. On "Pickin' the Cabbage," a simple minor-key riff tune Dizzy wrote for the band, he played a full chorus whose continuity and smooth flow of notes was quite unlike anything normally expected in the swing era.

The job with Cab ended abruptly in September 1941 after Cab accused Dizzy of throwing spitballs at him in the middle of a stage show. A scuffle backstage followed, and Dizzy readily admitted afterward that he had been far from blameless. The story made him a talked-about name in music circles for the first time, but for the wrong reason. "Cab Calloway still has a sore rear end," said *Down Beat* delicately in a long news story on the fracas. "Cab took ten stitches from a doctor."

For a few weeks Diz worked with the Ella Fitzgerald band, which Ella had inherited from her boss, the late Chick Webb. Gillespie's old friend Kenny Clarke, who had been helping Teddy Hill to establish Minton's, was also with Ella. Dizzy liked the job, especially when he heard Dick Vance, the lead trumpet man, play a clean altissimo B flat on the end of an arrangement Diz had just written called "Down Under." But Dizzy never recorded this or any other number with Ella. A few months later he sold "Down Under" to Woody Herman, who cut it for Decca. His talent as a composer-arranger was becoming more and more evident. One of his new tunes, slower and more exotic than "Pickin' the Cabbage," was used later to feature trombonist Benny Green in the Earl Hines band. Hines titled it "Night in Tunisia." Dizzy also placed several originals with Jimmy Dorsey and Ina Ray Hutton. But selling arrangements was an arduous and undependable business; much less gratifying, for instance, than settling down on an easy Fifty-second Street location in a six-piece band, especially when you were now working for a leader as talented and amiable as Benny Carter.

It was with Carter that Dizzy played his first jazz concert, at the Museum of Modern Art in November 1941, co-starring with Maxine Sullivan. ("Dizzy Gillespie's trumpeting is top-notch . . . he fits in excellently with the Carter ensemble," wrote Barry Ulanov, covering the event for *Metronome*.)

Diz interrupted his stay with Carter to go on the road for a few weeks with Charlie Barnet during the Christmas season. Barnet says he now realizes that his impatience with Dizzy's nonconformity at that time was due to unfamiliarity with his musical motives. "Dizzy's the greatest," Joe Guy reported some time afterward. "I was in the Barnet trumpet section when he was. He has an extraordinary style. He never gets tired of playing, he'll do sixteen sets and then go across the street and jam with someone else. The other evening Oscar Pettiford and I went to his house about 6:30 A.M., woke him up, and started a jam session. And I've spent whole evenings listening to his collection of records—classical and jazz."

After playing the Famous Door and Kelly's Stable for several months, the Carter group broke up in February 1942. Before long Dizzy had another big-band job, working for Les Hite. Walter "Gil" Fuller (later a frequent associate in Gillespie's own big bands) was contributing some arrangements that lent the ensemble a modern flavor. Hite and most of his sidemen regarded Diz with a mixture of amusement, irritation, and respect. That the respect was justified was clearly evident in Dizzy's half-chorus on "Jersey Bounce" (a long-forgotten 78 on the short-lived Hit label), probably the first example of pure bebop on records. By now his style was clearly formed and his tone distinctive; his innovative ideas came faster than ever.

Nothing much, however, was happening for Diz around New York; a little work with Lucky Millinder, a job with Calvin Jackson at the Sky Club. He decided to go home to Philadelphia, where he formed a quartet at the Down Beat with Johnny Ace, piano; Oscar Smith, bass; and a succession of drummers, one of whom was a local white boy named Stan Levey. New ideas still kept coursing through Gillespie's mind; sometimes he would spend as much time at the piano as he did blowing trumpet. His use of flatted fifths had now become commonplace, although many fellow musicians still heard them as wrong notes.

"Little Benny" Harris, a young trumpeter and perennial Gillespie acolyte, was in the Earl Hines band now, and straining to work with colleagues who could provide him with a challenge. Before long Gillespie joined Hines.

Although Charlie Parker was in this band, Dizzy paid little attention to him at first: his awareness of Parker's talent came about indirectly. Little Benny had copied out Bird's alto solo from the McShann record of "Sepian Bounce." One night with Hines he played it on trumpet, much to Dizzy's delight. "You like that?" said Benny. "Well, it's Bird's." Dizzy soon realized that many other impressive new concepts were Bird's work.

Dizzy's insatiable love of music was constantly rewarded in the Hines band. One night in Chicago he persuaded Oscar Pettiford to trudge through ten long city blocks in a snowstorm, carrying his bass, to join him in a hotel room for an all-night jam session. Often in New York, up at the Dewey Square, or at Dizzy's apartment nearby, there would be Bud Powell and Benny Harris and Freddy Webster, to all of whom playing and talking and thinking meant more than eating and drinking.

On April 23, 1943, Hines opened at the Apollo in Harlem. The curtains parted to reveal two pianos. At one sat "Fatha" Hines; at the other was a shy young girl from Newark whom Billy Eckstine had recommended for a vocal spot. Later she left the piano and came front-and-center to sing "Body and Soul." This was Sarah Vaughan's debut in the big time, and her first alliance with a group of progressives who were to play vital parts in her career—Eckstine, Parker, and Gillespie. Her own influence as a musician must not be discounted. She would sit at the piano after the dance, working out new ideas, and it was for Sarah that Dizzy began to write arrangements for the Hines band. But his "East of the Sun" was too unusual; it "didn't catch on," said Hines, and they couldn't use the arrangement. (A year later Sarah sang this number, with Dizzy in the background, on her first record date.)

In the summer of 1943 Billy Eckstine's defection shook up the band. Hines decided to try a new pseudosymphonic sound, with a female string section, and he replaced Gillespie with a young white trumpeter, Paul Cohen. After playing briefly with Coleman Hawkins, Dizzy subbed in the Duke Ellington band for three weeks at the Capitol Theatre on Broadway.

Musicians who were in the band at that time recall that the Ellington-Gillespie alliance was not a particularly happy one. Dizzy was not attuned to Ellington's music and the band didn't dig Dizzy. Everyone was glad when the three weeks were over, with the possible exception of Duke himself, who later became one of Dizzy's most distinguished admirers.

By this time the war had brought Fifty-second Street to its zenith. As many as five or six spots featured small jazz groups: the Onyx, the Three Deuces, Kelly's Stable, the Yacht Club (or Famous Door), and the Spotlite. The music on the street was heterogeneous; there were a couple of neat little arranged groups such as Red Norvo's, an occasional semi-Dixieland unit like Red Allen's, and by early 1944 a few reflections of the Minton and Hines sounds. With the wartime manpower shortage affecting the availability of musicians, competition was keen, and bands were often formed expressly to fill the jobs. Thus Dizzy and Oscar Pettiford had a chance to open with a small group. Pettiford wanted Dizzy to be the leader; after an Alphonse-Gaston exchange of "No, you" and "Why not you?" it was decided to put both names on the banner outside. With Don Byas on tenor, George Wallington on piano, and Max Roach on drums, Diz and Oscar opened, for $75 a week apiece, while Byas got $60 and the other men union scale, which was around $50.

Their music was a synthesis of ideas that had never before found a regular outlet. Although Byas was never exactly a bop musician, all five men thought very much alike. New tunes grew out of improvisations so fast that they had to remind one another to write them down. Oscar had one featuring Roach which he called "'Max Is Making Wax"; he spotlighted his own work on "Bass Face," which was later revised as "One Bass Hit" and played by Ray Brown. Dizzy conducted a simple octave-jump riff tune on which, instead of playing the octave jump, he sang "Salt peanuts, salt peanuts!" And he had a minor-key number which, because its main phrase could best be verbalized by repeating the sound "bebop!" later came to be given that title. In fact, so many of the rhythmic ideas developing at that time ended with a staccato two-note phrase, suggesting the onomatopoeic word "bebop" that the term soon began to be applied to all the music initiated by Dizzy and his fellow radicals. Thus it was late in 1944 before most of us who were around Dizzy and his contemporaries began to be conscious that there was a musical genre emerging, sufficiently distinct to have earned a special name. "He plays all that bebop stuff," people would say, or perhaps "rebop," since either sound suggested the musical phrase.

While Dizzy and Oscar were bringing bop to Fifty-second Street, Coleman Hawkins, working a block away at Kelly's, used them for an historic record session. Hawkins, an enthusiast of the new music ever since he had first heard Dizzy, assembled a ten-piece band for a date that set three precedents: it was the first session cut for the new Apollo label, the first date Dizzy had made since the lifting of the recording ban, and the first strictly bebop unit ever put together for recording.

Three of the compositions were clearly bop. One was Dizzy's own "Woody'n You," named for Woody Herman (but never recorded by him) and later retitled "Algo Bueno" when the Gillespie band cut it for Victor. The others were Budd Johnson's "Bu-Dee-Daht" and a blues riff called "Disorder at the Border."

Because of the problems of finding trombonists who could face the fast-moving technical passages involved in the new music, Hawkins' band comprised simply trumpets, saxes, and rhythm.

Budd Johnson, who played baritone sax on this session, was one of the few older swing-era stylists (he was born in 1910) who were readily converted to bebop. During the tenure of the Gillespie-Pettiford combo at the Onyx he replaced Byas on tenor saxophone. The music at the club was providing the most catalytic sounds in town, and business was good enough to keep the quintet in residence for three months. It was Johnson who helped to develop the ensemble styles that became definitive in small-band bebop; he and Oscar suggested that Diz write down some of the things he was doing, so that the two horns could play them in unison.

After the Onyx job, when Dizzy and Oscar split up, Diz took Budd and Max with him into a spot right across the street known temporarily as the Yacht Club. On the same bill was Billy Eckstine, working as a single. (Thanks to some brainstorm on the part of his manager, Billy Shaw, he was billed as Billy X-Tine.) He had fared poorly at the Zanzibar, the Yacht, and other clubs. Shaw, uncertain about what to do with him, finally decided to have him booked as a bandleader, heading a large unit.

By the time Eckstine started lining up his personnel, Dizzy had closed at the Yacht Club and was filling in time with John Kirby's sextet at the Aquarium on Broadway. (Kirby evidently did not trust Dizzy because he brought in Charlie Shavers to play the combo's broadcasts.) Eckstine, who wanted Dizzy to help him form the band and act as its musical director, fought Billy Shaw about the kind of music to be featured. Disarming Shaw with such statements as, "Billy, this is the music of tomorrow and we've got to fight it through!" he hired Sarah Vaughan as his girl vocalist, then went to Chicago to get Gail Brockman, another Hines trumpet section alumnus; Jerry Valentine, the trombonist and arranger; and Charlie Parker, who was working with Carroll Dickerson at the Rhumboogie. Bird played first alto for Eckstine; Dizzy led the trumpet section.

The news that Dizzy was to be so prominent did not meet with unanimous rejoicings. The road manager whom Shaw had hired to travel with the band refused the job when he was told the news. "I've heard too much about Dizzy," he declared. Shaw called Diz into his office for a lecture. "If you do well, this'll be your big chance to straighten out. After Eckstine is established, I'll go to work on you and build you up with your own band." Dizzy nodded wisely and gravely. On the band's first date, a theater booking in Baltimore, he overslept on the train, woke up in Washington, and arrived in Baltimore in time to see the end of the first show.

Eckstine's confidence in the new music was justified. The band, instead of hampering him, helped to sell his singing. Moreover, Billy was experimenting on a valve trombone as a medium for the same style. Within the first six months his band became one of the biggest money-making black orchestras in the business; it broke the house record at the Earl Theatre in Philadelphia. Billy was a casual leader, loyal and unselfish, although the task of handling a group of eccentrics was too much for him at times.

Eckstine's and Vaughan's images as singers admittedly sold the band; bebop registered on many audiences as a strange and meaningless noise, epecially in the Southwest, where, Charlie Parker recalled, nobody liked it: "In the Middle West the colored audiences liked it but the whites didn't. In New York *everybody* liked it." And in the South, of course, black audiences still preferred to hear the blues.

After a while on the road Dizzy began to assume the responsibilities of his position as musical director. He worked hard, sometimes sitting in for a missing pianist or drummer, and trying to make the band sound clean and full. Men like Leo Parker, baritone; Lucky Thompson, tenor; Fats Navarro, trumpet, passed through the lineup. Much of the band's style was due to the writing of Jerry Valentine and Tadd Dameron.

After several months with Eckstine, Dizzy returned to New York, where he organized Charlie Parker, Al Haig, Curly Russell and Stan Levey to go into the Three Deuces on Fifty-second Street. He had been signed to a new recording company, Guild, and his first two sides were greeted enthusiastically. They were "Blue 'n' Boogie," featuring Dexter Gordon and an all-white rhythm section, and "Groovin' High," Dizzy's bop version of "Whispering," with Bird, Clyde Hart, Remo Palmieri, Slam Stewart, and Cozy Cole. The last four trumpet measures of "Groovin' High" later provided Tadd Dameron with part of the theme for a beautiful ballad recorded by Sarah Vaughan, "If You Could See Me Now." But Dizzy's numerous other dates were making his name familiar to musicians and jazz fans; I had finally found a company willing to record Sarah Vaughan (for $20 a side), and I had Dizzy on the New Year's Eve date that marked her debut as a solo singer. With Clyde Hart, Diz also made four sides for Manor which later came out under his own name: "Good Bait," "I Can't Get Started," "Bebop," and "Salt Peanuts." He even sat in on blues sessions with Rubberlegs Williams and Albinia Jones.

The Three Deuces engagement was a turning point in jazz. The group cut four sides for Guild, with Sid Catlett sitting in on drums and Sarah Vaughan taking the vocal on "Lover Man." Dameron's "Hot House" (a bop treatment of "What Is This Thing Called Love"), plus a new "Salt Peanuts" and the fast and dazzling "Shaw Nuff," were perfect examples of the new Fifty-second Street small-band style, with cleanly played trumpet and alto unison, tricky rhythmic intros and codas, and fantastic solos by Diz, Bird, and Haig. It was the New Jazz in excelsis.

The name value of Diz and Bird was given further impetus when the New Jazz Foundation, consisting of disc jockey Symphony Sid, promoter Monte Kay, and publicist Mal Braveman, presented two Town Hall concerts in May and June of 1945, starring Gillespie and Parker in performances similar to those on the Guild records.

While the small group was at the Spotlite, a few doors up the street from the Deuces, Billy Shaw tried to help Dizzy become a leader of a full-sized orchestra. When bookings were not forthcoming, Shaw put together a unit comprising the orchestra, the Nicholas Brothers, comedians Paterson and

Jackson, and June (Mrs. Billy) Eckstine as vocalist. This "package deal" made the Gillespie band acceptable to some of the less cautious bookers. Gil Fuller wrote all the arrangements and rehearsed the band. The "Hep-Sations of 1945" took to the road—and headed South.

This meant trouble right from the start. As soon as it was known that the unit would penetrate the Deep South and would have to travel under the most humiliating conditions, the men started dropping out like flies. It was hard enough to find trumpet and trombone men who could play fast enough for Dizzy's requirements, let alone those willing to make the Southern trip. By the time Diz got below the Mason-Dixon line, his original band had been almost totally replaced. Worse, promoters told him that the customers couldn't dance to his kind of music, so Diz forgot all the elaborate arrangements in the books and just played the blues. Nor was he sufficiently experienced to front a big band. Previously lighthearted and at ease, he now tightened up with his new responsibility. He would take stiff, awkward bows and generally showed no signs of the comic, personable Dizzy of the past.

Later, in the course of some ninety one-nighters through the Southwest that co-featured Ella Fitzgerald, Dizzy loosened up, started mugging, spinning around, and dancing, and became the complete showman. He even made a big impression at the Apollo, where he had flopped on an earlier appearance. But the problems of personnel and bookings were still too much for Shaw and Gillespie. As 1945 came to a close he found himself booked with a small band again, on his first trip to California.

Nobody who witnessed Gillespie's engagement at Billy Berg's in Hollywood is likely ever to forget it. The booking was an unhappy one from the start. Charlie Parker was in the unit, but was so sick that he often showed up either late or not at all; as a safeguard Dizzy had to add a tenor saxophonist, Lucky Thompson. There were also adverse comments about the presence of two white musicians, Al Haig and Stan Levey.

Ray Brown's bass and Milton Jackson's vibes completed a superb musical combination and a commercial disaster. On top of all this, tension developed between Slim Gaillard, who led the alternating group, and Dizzy. Not long after he and Bird had sat in on a recording date with Slim, a tension developed, which was brought to a climax backstage at Berg's when Dizzy characterized Slim as a musical Uncle Tom. There was a brief altercation and an even briefer exchange of blows. It seemed safe to predict that Dizzy would never again make records with Slim Gaillard. (He never has.)

Dizzy's bad luck continued. A new company, Paramount Records, set up an unusual date for him with a string section to play some Jerome Kern music for a memorial album dedicated to the late composer. After the records were made, Kern's publishers refused to grant a license for their release on the grounds that Dizzy had departed from the orthodox Kern melodies. Although they would sound very conservative years later, they have never been issued.

Dizzy did make one successful session on the Coast, however, when Ross Russell cut several sides with the combo (but without Bird) for his new Dial label. Made on February 7, 1946, they consisted of "Dynamo," which was a new version of the "Dizzy Atmosphere" cut previously for Guild; "Diggin' for Diz" (a bop "Lover"), " 'Round Midnight," "Confirmation," and "When I Grow Too Old to Dream" (from which title the final word was omitted on the label).

Business was miserable at Berg's. Except for a small ingroup of young musicians, hardly anybody in California understood or cared about bebop, and the clique in question had so little money that it couldn't help much. Dizzy was further hampered by the reactionary local critics and disc jockeys, who were not merely passively disinterested in his work but actively hoping to see him fail. All told, the band was happy to get back East to the Apple.

By now Gillespie's contract with Guild was invalid, the company having gone out of business, and he was due to sign soon with Musicraft. Just in time I corralled him for an album I was recording at Victor, to be called *New Fifty-Second Street Jazz.* (At that time it would have been useless to try to persuade any major record company to title an album *Bebop.*) Victor wanted an all-star group featuring some of the *Esquire* Award winners, so we used J. C. Heard on drums and Don Byas on tenor, along with three of Dizzy's own men—Milt Jackson, Ray Brown, and Al Haig—and the new guitarist from Cleveland, Bill de Arango. Thanks largely to Dizzy's name we outsold every jazz album of the past few years. By now he was the object of enough curiosity to ensure a fairly substantial value for him as a recording artist. He reorganized a big band and made his first records with it in the summer of 1946. A stronger personnel and better arrangements gave this group a chance to make the grade commercially, especially since Dizzy was fast developing into a showman. Gil Fuller's "Things to Come" typified the beauty of modern jazz. Although imperfectly executed at a breakneck tempo, this dynamic and exciting arrangement impressed musicians who had previously scorned bop. "Emanon," on the other side, was a medium-tempo blues, a simpler example of big-band bop, but swinging all the way. Both tunes showed off individual talents other than Dizzy's, notably Milt Jackson.

Musicraft was impressed enough with Gillespie's importance to release an album by him, featuring big- and small-band reissues. Although it was a dismal failure in Detroit in July, the band returned the following February to produce such a turnout that police had to be called to keep the crowds from getting out of hand.

With a light-hearted disregard for contracts, Dizzy made records for several small labels in his spare time and under various names. On the California Dial date he had been "Gabriel"; on Savoy, in a session with Ray Brown, he became Izzy Goldberg; with Tony Scott, for Gotham, he became B. Bopstein. For other labels he simply stuck to John Birks, omitting his surname. But by now his fans were in close enough touch with his activities and familiar enough with his style to spot pseudonymous appearances and buy the records promptly.

In January 1947 Dizzy outdistanced Roy Eldridge to win the *Metronome* poll on trumpet—an auspicious opening for an auspicious year. John Lewis, a brilliant young pianist and arranger, joined the band and wrote a "Toccata for Trumpet and Orchestra." George Russell, a visionary young composer from Cincinnati, penned an Afro-Cuban drum suite, "Cubana Be" and "Cubana Bop," combining a couple of Dizzy's ideas with conga drums and chanting by Chano Pozo. These works were given premieres when I presented the Gillespie orchestra in its first concert appearance at Carnegie Hall on September 29, 1947. A capacity house paid tribute to Dizzy, Ella Fitzgerald, and Charlie Parker. The entire evening demonstrated how far Gillespie had outstripped his contemporaries in distilling a new kind of big-band jazz. The orchestra included Howard Johnson and John Brown, altos; James Moody and Joe Gayles, tenors; Cecil Payne, baritone; Dave Burns, Elman Wright, Raymond Orr, and Matthew McKay, trumpets; Taswell Baird and William Shepherd, trombones; John Lewis, piano; Al McKibbon, bass; and Joe Harris, drums, plus Milt Jackson on vibes and Kenny "Pancho" Hagood on vocals.

There were still faults, to be sure. The band was rough at times—the bop singing was overdone, a few of the arrangements were pretentious, and the leader's showmanship was occasionally tasteless—but these faults were compensated for by some of the most challenging and attention-riveting performances ever created by a big jazz ensemble.

Now that Dizzy and bebop were national names, a widespread movement to get on the bopwagon arose. Bop even crossed the border into the respectable, conservative world of commercial radio and recordings. Jo Stafford's arrangement of "The Gentleman Is a Dope" began with four bars of unmistakably boppish riffing; other popular songs would find little phrases borrowed from Diz and Bird edging into the backgrounds of their Hit Parade tunes. The Cuban-plus-bop rhythmic alliance, too, was expanding rapidly. Stan Kenton had pioneered in this genre on the West Coast around the same time, using Jack Costanzo on Latin percussion while Chano Pozo was with Gillespie.

Recording company executives who had previously scorned bop as uncommercial searched frantically for bop talent. Disc jockeys who had held out against the new movement suddenly found that bop paid off, and became avid Gillespie supporters. One jazz concert promoter who for years had presented nothing but Dixieland bashes and had gone to some pains to insult Dizzy and his supporters now begged for his services at a concert.

So fast did the new word catch on with the public, and so frequently was it abused by opportunists, that utter confusion resulted: Eddie Condon, whose traditionalist concerts had established him as a symbol of Dixieland, was introduced on a television show as the King of Bebop.

National magazines, having heard that Dizzy's followers were aping his whiskers, beret, and glasses as well as his trumpet playing, ran feature stories in which the musical importance of bebop was virtually ignored while the eccentricities of some of its disciples were exaggerated tenfold. "How Deaf Can You Get?" sneered *Time* in its headline, belatedly acknowledging Dizzy's existence in a piece on bop (May 17, 1948). A nadir was reached (with Dizzy's own acquiescence) with a six-page spread in *Life* magazine in the fall of 1948. Packed with errors of fact and judgment, it culminated in a picture of Dizzy, supposedly a Mohammedan, bowing to Mecca.

Unpleasant though all this cheap publicity might seem, it was no worse than the confusing articles that had flooded the press when the word "swing" had become popular a decade or so earlier. At least the word bebop and the name of Gillespie got into print often enough to stir up some curiosity about the music.

Bop acquired a permanent New York home in the spring

of 1948 when, through the efforts of Symphony Sid and Monte Kay, a small bop group was installed at the Royal Roost, a fried-chicken emporium on Broadway that had been experimenting unsuccessfully with standard jazz talent. The Tadd Dameron group, featuring Fats Navarro, Allen Eager, Kenny Clarke, Curly Russell, and sometimes Charlie Parker, paved the way for a big-name policy at the Roost. Before long the Gillespie, Charlie Ventura, and Woody Herman bands played the Roost, which became so popular that it was soon known as "The House That Bop Built" and the "Metropolitan Bopera House." In April 1949 the Roost moved across Broadway to the larger Bop City. Bop had taken jazz out of the small Fifty-second Street clubs and into bigger, better gathering places where a thousand jazz fans could be entertained nightly.

The new music had spread across the world, too. In England, France, Sweden, and a dozen other countries, jazz pundits argued learnedly over the relative merits of the old and the new jazz. Bop was a factor in the violent split between Charles Delaunay, pro-bop head of the French magazine *Hot Jazz*, and Hugues ("Bop-Is-Not-Jazz") Panassié, the didactic critic and impresario. As rival factions sprang up supporting Delaunay or Panassié, the feud developed to such a ridiculous point that when Louis Armstrong (an outspoken opponent of bop) visited Paris early in 1948 he was given extensive police protection, occasioned by a rumor that the new-jazz crowd were out to injure Pops and prevent him from playing.

In England bebop produced the customary reaction: most of the musicians were for it and most of the critics against it, with the noteworthy exception of Edgar Jackson, the *Melody Maker* record reviewer.

Scandinavia was bop-conscious enough for Chubby Jackson to tour successfully in the winter of 1947–48 with a sextet featuring Frankie Socolow, tenor; Conte Candoli, trumpet; Lou Levy, piano; Terry Gibbs, vibes; and Denzil Best, drums. Just before Jackson left for home, the Gillespie band arrived in Sweden on the first leg of what turned out to be a financially disastrous tour. One fact emerged quite clearly: the tour was seriously mismanaged. Reactions to Dizzy's music ranged from outraged indignation to unqualified enthusiasm. When the tour wound up in the south of France, Dizzy had to cable his booking office for fare home. Soon afterward he signed with a new manager, Willard Alexander, who had helped build the Benny Goodman and Count Basie bands during the swing era.

By the end of 1948 bebop had achieved a success for which its most fervent supporters had not dared hope. Benny Goodman, quoted a year earlier as strongly anti-bop, formed a new band featuring bop soloists and arrangements. (This romance was short-lived; Goodman soon went back to Fletcher Henderson.)

Everywhere—in the United States and Latin America, in Europe and even Asia, Africa, and Australia—young musicians waited for the latest bop orchestrations to arrive, striving eagerly to copy the original Diz and Bird solos, while youthful jazz fans traded rare Savoy and Dial 78 rpm single discs for as much as $10 apiece.

Now that bebop had been absorbed into the mainstream of jazz, it remained to be seen whether it would expand, escape its limitations and clichés, lead the way into something still richer in musical texture and subtler in artistic concept. Most musicians of the immediate post-bop years agreed that if jazz was to remain a separate entity at all, the element of swing, the implied steady beat and tempo, would still be a vital part of every jazz performance, as would the art of improvisation on a given set of chord patterns. It was still possible to develop fertile new soil within this territory. The history of bop, like that of swing before it, like the stories of jazz and ragtime before that, was one of constant struggle against the restrictions imposed on progressive thought in an art that had been commercialized to the point of prostitution; of struggle against reactionaries who resented anything new that they could neither understand nor perform themselves.

Thanks to the uncompromising attitude of Gillespie and

others in the face of these obstacles, the history of jazz moved inexorably ahead. Bop, once stigmatized as a weird, eccentric dialect, survived to become a central part of the living language of contemporary music.

The extent to which a creative artist's musical direction can be governed by economic conditions has seldom been more graphically illustrated than by Gillespie. After his first tremendous impact he had a roller-coaster career during which he seldom had the opportunity to express himself fully as trumpeter, composer, or bandleader.

Dizzy has always relished his auxiliary role as comedy singer and entertainer, and so has always been able to work. But too often, frustrated in his real ambition, he has taken the line of least resistance, going through familiar motions as leader of small combos in nightclubs.

When his second big band broke up in 1950, Dizzy told friends: "It really breaks my heart that we can't stay together, but the whole band business is disintegrating. Besides, everybody wants you to play that ricky-ticky dance music.

"What I'd like to do now is tour with Charlie Parker and his string ensemble. I'd like to lead a woodwind group, too, with arrangements by Johnny Richards. We can pick up musicians on the road, cats who just have to read the music while Bird and I do the swinging."

The tour with Parker never materialized, but some months later Dizzy made some records with a twenty-three-piece strings-and-woodwinds orchestra directed by Richards.

Starting in 1953, Norman Granz produced all of Gillespie's recordings for seven years, allying him with various Jazz at the Philharmonic groups as well as with special studio units that offered him somewhat more stimulation than the small group he led for in-person work. Granz teamed him with Stuff Smith, Sonny Rollins, Sonny Stitt, and Stan Getz. Later there was an orchestral album of Ellington compositions brilliantly arranged by Clare Fischer.

Gillespie's longing to lead a large touring orchestra again was satisfied in 1956; at the same time he set an historic precedent. The U.S. State Department delegated Dizzy to organize a sixteen-piece band for its initial attempt to aid jazz and to improve foreign relations under its official auspices. Quincy Jones selected the musicians, hiring such eminent sidemen as the late Joe Gordon on trumpet, Melba Liston on trombone, and Phil Woods and Ernie Wilkins on saxophones. Dizzy was in his element. A tour of the Middle East was so successful that soon afterward he was sent to Latin America.

Anti-American feeling was intense there, but Gillespie was an ideal ambassador. He made no speeches but mingled with crowds, pointed to his interracial personnel when the subject of American racism was raised, bought gifts for fans, and made countless new friends in every city. In some areas where radios and jukeboxes were unknown, Gillespie's music was puzzling, but the team spirit and dynamism of the orchestra proved irresistible.

"Those were some of the happiest days of my life," Gillespie said years later. "We were accomplishing something musically, and we did what we set out to do in terms of goodwill."

Back home, he tried to keep the band together, and succeeded for a year or so, but by 1958 was once again reduced to the quintet format. Outwardly he was not discouraged. Even when Miles Davis became the fashionable (and indisputably important) new influence, supplanting Gillespie in popularity polls, Gillespie refused to become embroiled in controversies about their relative contributions. Sometimes, however, he was caught offguard and revealed his suppressed hurt.

"I know my own contribution to jazz," he said in 1960. "I know just what I did that other people didn't do, and what Charlie Parker did, and Monk. I hear people playing things today, on tunes like ' 'Round Midnight' and 'All the Things You Are,' and even in Frank Sinatra arrangements, that are taken directly from things I did with Bird and them, and the people playing these things don't even realize where they got them from! But *I* know. It will all come out in the wash, baby —whether or not I get the recognition now, the records I made will tell posterity the whole story."

Soon after that statement two works by Lalo Schifrin, the composer-pianist Dizzy had met during his 1956 State Department visit to Argentina, were introduced. Schifrin spent three years on the road playing with Gillespie's quintet, during which time he wrote the *Gillespiana Suite* and *New Continent*. With Dizzy's horn at the head of a large orchestra, the former was introduced in 1961 at Carnegie Hall and the latter the following year at the Monterey Jazz Festival. Both works were recorded; both inspired Gillespie to creative heights he had long been prevented from reaching. During the same period he recorded *Perceptions*, with an orchestra conducted by Gunther Schuller. This was an album-long suite composed by J. J. Johnson, fusing jazz with classical music.

But even when working with a small combo over the last ten years, Dizzy has had occasional innovative spurts. Because of the presence of Schifrin and Dizzy's long-standing ties with Latin-American rhythms, he was among the first U.S. jazzmen to incorporate bossa nova into his repertoire, before Stan Getz initiated the fashion. He also demonstrated a piquant West Indian amalgamation in *Jambo Caribe*, an album for the now-defunct Limelight label.

By 1970 Gillespie had no record contract and was limited to occasional albums for different companies, with mixed results. An attempt to align himself with the rock generation in an album called *Souled Out* sounded too much like its title; it failed to work either musically or commercially. Results were happier when he teamed with his old friend Bobby Hackett and with Mary Lou Williams for a recital recorded in 1971 at the Overseas Press Club in New York. The provocative interplay brought out the best in both men.

Moments like these compensate for the nights when Dizzy goes through the ritualistic comedy lines ("Thank you, ladies and gentlemen, for your magnificent indifference") and the cliché trumpet phrases that, despite their extraordinary technical difficulty, roll off the bell of his horn as if he could play them in his sleep. He should remember that no matter how many Miles Davises and Freddie Hubbards come to prominence, John Birks Gillespie has no peers in the genre he helped create. Today, in his mid-fifties, he still has the spirit of men half his age as well as a continuing flow of ideas. Although he ignores setbacks, he is far from complacent.

"What I want to do," he said once, "is extend everything I've done. You know, when an architect builds a building and decides he wants to put on some new wings, it's still the same building. He keeps on until it's finished, and when he dies, somebody else can take over."

Gillespie still has the tools, the bricks, the mortar, to put on all the new wings he might care to add. But he must first be assured professional and financial security. Peace of mind undoubtedly would lead to a new burst of the artistic energy that established him, almost thirty years ago, as one of the two greatest living exponents of contemporary jazz.

The Granzwagon

A GLANCE AT the names of the artists discussed in the preceding chapters would probably reveal no striking common element beyond the fact that all were major contributors to the evolution of jazz. Yet one man is a link, important to them all: at one time or another, each recorded for one of Norman Granz's labels, and four of them (Ella Fitzgerald, Lester Young, Charlie Parker, Dizzy Gillespie) were frequently members of Granz's Jazz at the Philharmonic (JATP) concert unit.

The contemporary observer of the jazz scene may know little or nothing about Granz's contribution to the advancement of jazz, and his ultimate success in getting the public America, where JATP originated and flourished between 1944 and 1957. Younger jazz fans are doubtless unaware of the to accept it as a valid art form. Granz is no longer active in degree to which his efforts secured the recognition, welfare, and human dignity of the musicians with whom he was associated.

Granz is that rare paradox, a businessman with a strong social conscience; an aggressive proponent of civil rights, and a non-musician with a deep understanding for, and love of, jazz and jazzmen. Nobody who remembers the Granz years can doubt that he upgraded the course of American jazz from a virtually underground art, rarely presented for serious listening and often confined to segregated dance halls and nightclubs.

The Granz phenomenon reached its peak in the middle 1950s, at which time the jazz world revolved around him and the near monopoly he had built by shrewdly interweaving a Midaslike commercial instinct with an uncompromising love for the music.

Norman Granz's jazz career began in the early 1940s in Los Angeles, where he ran jam sessions without payment at a small nightclub; he presented his first full-scale jazz concert in July, 1944, at the Philharmonic Auditorium—until then the exclusive preserve of symphony orchestras. (Also in 1944 his short film, *Jammin' the Blues*, directed by Gjon Mili, won an Academy Award nomination.) Before long he was releasing records made at his concerts—at a time when every previous phonograph record had been made, not surprisingly, in a recording studio. Within a few years the success of the live Jazz at the Philharmonic, as well as that of the records, led to the establishment of a jazz empire. In due course he became the owner of four record companies, shepherded his Philharmonic flock through European, Japanese, and Australian tours, promoted concerts for innumerable units other than his own, managed Oscar Peterson and Ella Fitzgerald, and extended his interests far outside jazz to record Spike Jones, Bing Crosby, and Fred Astaire.

To the musicians for whom his patronage guaranteed upward of $50,000 worth of work annually, Granz was a paterfamilias, a benevolent giant who strode through the world in seven-league boots, knocking down the Jim Crow pygmies as he went. To competing promoters, nightclub operators trying to buy talent, booking agents, and other businessmen who needed him more than he needed them, Granz was a petulant grudge-bearer and a hard man with a buck. To Henri Soulé at New York's famed Le Pavillon restaurant, he was a gourmet sufficiently acquainted with the culinary craft to earn an apprenticeship in Soulé's kitchen. To disinterested observers he was and is a tough, ruthless businessman as well as a tireless worker who expects everyone else to have the same endless reservoir of energy and determination; a sensitive man of highly developed tastes who appreciates the beauty of perfect workmanship, who can be warm, thoughtful, and lovable to close friends, and whose acquired fund of knowledge reflects limitless curiosity.

The man who has given rise to this disparity of characterizations is just the chameleonlike individual one might expect. Depending upon the company in which he finds himself, Granz may act and talk at times like a four-beat Oscar Levant, while at other moments he may take on the warm grizzly-bear characteristics of a Paul Muni, the martyred air of a homeless evictee, or the pristine enthusiasm of a movie producer showing his Picassos to the new house guests. (Granz has an art collection with a estimated value of $2 million.) The failure of the volatile Granz to come into clear focus is more a credit to his adaptability than a reflection on his integration as a personality. He is the product of a middle-class family whose members, living at the time of his birth in what is now the Central Avenue epicenter of Los Angeles, moved first to Long Beach, where Granz's father owned a department store, and later to the Los Angeles area known as Boyle Heights, when Granz, Sr., lost his store and entered an era of diminished affluence during the Depression years.

"Long Beach was predominantly a Midwestern community in its thinking," Granz says. "We were one of about half a dozen Jewish families in the whole city. I remember there used to be a gag about all the retired businessmen from Iowa settling in Long Beach. And I think I remember the Ku Klux Klan used to parade there in nightshirts, but I don't recall that it had any impact on me at all at the time. I suppose that the reason I can mix so easily with minority members arose from my playing with the kids on Central Avenue, when it was a heterogeneous district with all minorities represented."

Boyle Heights, although it constituted a nadir in the Granz family fortunes, failed to upset him. (Granz once recalled this era when, in a mood that seemed characteristically out of character, he began a diatribe against Billie Holiday, whose escapades in jails and recording studios caused him frequent trouble and expense. "Why the hell should I sympathize because of her childhood?" he complained. "Mickey Cohen and I came from the same area in Boyle Heights. Mickey Cohen became a gangster; I didn't. Nobody forced him to become what he became.")

After attending Roosevelt High in Boyle Heights and graduating in 1935, Granz took a job in a brokerage house in order to work his way through UCLA. "There was never enough money for a car, so I spent the better part of my life in buses and streetcars. I'd have to be at work at 6 A.M., and during that time I played basketball at UCLA, and stayed up studying at night."

The years of marking time, of late nights and early mornings, lasted until Granz entered the Army in 1941. Originally in the Air Corps, he was later transferred to Special Services. After a medical discharge in 1943 he went to work on a labor gang at the Warner Brothers studio, cleaning up the premises for a dollar an hour. "I was fired from the labor gang," he recalls with an air of quiet satisfaction, "and the next time Warners saw me was when I went back there later to make my own picture."

By now a casual interest in jazz, fed in the late 1930s by a hobby of collecting phonograph records, had developed to the point where he had begun to stage jam sessions. His reasons, he states now, were mainly sociological rather than musical. The Hollywood nightclubs had a fixed rule against admitting Negroes as patrons. "I remember once when Billie Holiday was complaining that some of her friends had come to see her and they weren't allowed in. She was crying and everything: it was a real drag." (Granz's conversation was always a jagged mirror of his various backgrounds: intellectual rhetoric rubbed syllables with normal jazz jargon: musicians were "cats" and money was "bread" or "loot.") Granz proposed to Billy Berg, a leading nightclub operator, that he run a series of jam sessions, one night a week, to fill the gap caused by a new union ruling that guaranteed the regularly employed musicians one night off weekly.

As has always been the case when Granz offers a deal, he stated his terms in an abrupt, take-it-or-leave-it manner. There were three main conditions: first instead of relying on musicians to drop in and play for nothing, the men would be paid, and this would enable Granz to announce their presence in advance. Second, tables were to be put on the dance floor so that there could be no dancing; in defiance of all established nightclub standards, listening would thus be almost mandatory. Third and most important, Negro patrons were to be admitted.

"I think the cats got $6 each," Granz recalls, "and those were good days for getting musicians in Los Angeles. Duke Ellington's band was around town; Jimmie Lunceford's men were available; Nat Cole, who had the trio at the 331 Club, was my house pianist; Lester Young and his brother Lee were regulars."

Lee Young, the drummer who was the first musician to become friendly with Granz, remembers him as "a real Joe College type, with the brown-and-white shoes, the open collar, the sweater, and the general Sloppy Joe style; he was just a guy that was always around, and at first we wondered what he did for a living. He was a lone wolf. We'd drink malteds together—neither of us ever drank liquor—and before long I'd be going over to his side of town and he'd be visiting mine, and we'd be playing tennis."

Nat Cole, who at that time led a local trio for $35 a week and had not started singing, knew Granz around 1941. "He'd bring a whole bunch of records over and we'd listen to them together and have dinner. He had that sloppy Harvard look, and even in those days he wouldn't knuckle down to anybody. A lot of people disliked him, but I understood his attitude; he just knew what he wanted and exactly how he was going to get it. I remember when the booking agents used to call him a capitalistic radical, which of course wasn't right."

Before long Granz had a little circuit going: because several clubs had a different night off for their regular musicians, he was able to rotate his jazzmen in several clubs on these odd nights and offer them four or five nights' work a week. The time was ripe for his next logical step, into the concert field.

In the summer of 1944 a defense fund was organized for the liberation of a group of Mexican youths who had been sent to San Quentin after a killing during Los Angeles' so-called zoot-suit riots.

Granz says: "There were so many kids accused that it smacked of a prejudice case. Orson Welles and Rita Hayworth and a lot of other Hollywood people were involved in the thing, which was called the Sleepy Lagoon Defense Committee. I don't even remember where Sleepy Lagoon was, and I didn't know what the hell was going on with the case, but it did seem to be a prejudice case, and this was a chance to try out one of my ideas, which was to put on a jazz concert at the Philharmonic."

Granz's cast for the benefit show, held on a Sunday afternoon in July, included Les Paul, a guitarist who was later to sell several million records through the development of electronic techniques that enabled him to twist his music into many lucrative distortions: Meade Lux Lewis, a pioneer boogie-woogie pianist; Nat Cole, and a saxophonist named Illinois Jacquet who, according to *Down Beat,* "had the kids wild with the screaming high notes of his tenor sax."

Granz's millions were preordained by this last item. The erotic appeal of freak high notes played on the saxophone proved to have a commercial lure far beyond that of any jazz hitherto performed. Critics belittled it, but during the rest of 1944 Granz was able to present his concerts at the Philharmonic as monthly events.

Year by year the Granz concerts assumed a firmer pattern. Some musicians acquired a loyal following and would remain with the unit for each tour. They included Roy Eldridge,

Dizzy Gillespie, Illinois Jacquet, Lester Young, Gene Krupa, Ella Fitzgerald, Billie Holiday, and Oscar Peterson. Of all the performers who worked with him, only three had serious differences with Granz. One was Billie Holiday. Another was Lester Young, who was fired summarily in the middle of a show but was taken back into the fold two years later. The last was Buddy Rich, an explosive drummer whose temperament clashed with Granz's on many occasions. Once, after a break with Granz, he denounced the entire concert unit in a *Down Beat* interview as "a lot of junk" with no musical value. Granz thereupon condemned Rich publicly as a liar and an adolescent. Less than a year later Rich was back in the show, playing the same "junk" he had so vehemently attacked.

During the concerts, both backstage and onstage, Granz's temper could be a raw nerve on which electricians, sound engineers, musicians, and audiences acted like so many dentists' drills. Often accused of attracting unruly audiences, he was known to stride angrily onstage and threaten to stop the show immediately if the noise could not be stopped.

Some of his critics complained that Granz's audiences were the creatures of his music, with its intensely exciting appeal. Granz doesn't see it that way at all. "I don't like to talk about exciting an audience," he has said, "because it always implies *inciting* them. Jazz has always been, to me, fundamentally the blues, and all the happy and sad emotions it arouses. I dig the blues as a basic human emotion, and my concerts are primarily emotional music. I've never yet put on a concert that didn't have to please *me*, musically, first of all. I could put on as cerebral a concert as you like, but I'd rather go the emotional route. And you know, the public's taste reflects mine—the biggest flop I've ever had in my life was the tour I put on with some of the cerebral musicians like Dave Brubeck and Gerry Mulligan. A critic can tell me Bud Powell's a better pianist than Oscar Peterson, but I could put Powell on the stage and he'd die like a dog."

Granz's loyalty to the brand of jazz and the particular musicians that made up the core of his entourage for several years was reciprocated by the musicians, who knew that accommodations in the best hotels, travel by plane instead of bus or train, four-figure salaries and an antisegregation clause written into Southern contracts bore out his credo of treating them with dignity as human beings. On at least one occasion he chartered a plane simply to avoid having to spend a single night in a Southern town.

The phrase "spare no expense" has been as much a part of the Granz story as if it were a slogan framed on the wall of his office. "I have a feeling of tremendous pride in whatever I do," he once explained, "so I may do things that are unsound economically, but they pay off in another form. For example, I hired Lionel Hampton for my Carnegie Hall show last year. We weren't allowed to advertise him, and I paid him a huge salary, but I just dug the idea of his coming over for a few minutes to play with my cats."

Similarly, "I don't know another promoter in the country that can promote like me. The reason is simple: I spend more loot. You don't have to be a genius to be a good promoter, you just take bigger ads than anyone else."

Granz was no less lavish with his recording sessions. "Anyone else could take my company and make a lot of money if they ran it economically," he said in 1956. "Who needs that album I just made of Dizzy Gillespie with his big band? It cost me $5,000; it can't possibly make money. But Dizzy wanted to do it. He's happy."

When the contentment and dignity of his artists might be at stake, Granz was even more reluctant to tighten his purse strings. When two musicians were found shooting dice in Ella Fitzgerald's dressing room in a Houston auditorium in 1955, Granz and others in the room were arrested. After posting $10 bail apiece, the group forfeited the bail and left Houston. For weeks after the incident Granz was on the phone to lawyers in New York and Houston, attempting to have the charges quashed. Ultimately the cases were dismissed and Granz was told he could collect the bonds any time. To get the few dollars back and have the incident expunged from the record, it had cost him slightly over $2,000 in phone bills and legal fees.

I remember an afternoon in 1956 when Granz and I were watching Ella Fitzgerald record with a large orchestra. "You know," he said, "I'd been thinking for years about taking over Ella's personal management. Finally, one day on the plane between Tokyo and Osaka, we talked about it. Ella was afraid —she thought I was too much of a blowtop. So I told her it was a matter of pride with me, that she still hadn't been recognized—economically, at least—as the greatest singer of our time. I asked her to give me a year's free trial, no commission. But she wound up insisting on paying the commission. We have no contract—mutual love and respect is all the contract we need. I went to work right away on getting her into the class of clubs where she'd never been booked. I can get her into the right clubs with just a few phone calls. And now that she's on my own label she'll make more records during the first year than she made in the whole nineteen years she was with Decca. What's more, she'll have complete freedom to record anything she likes. Eventually I want Ella to make enough bread so she can afford to take a couple of months off every year—if she can make 200 grand a year, and without dieting, why should she knock her brains out? That's what I'm looking out for. That, and her dignity, which hasn't been respected enough."

As the evening drew to a close Granz's thoughts took a speculative turn. "I don't want to be king of the mountain in America," he said. "I don't dig ostentation. What does one live for? I want to be casual, I don't want any big rush; and I'd like to be in a place where your competitors think and operate the same way. That's why I dig Italy. I'm going to spend six months a year there from now on. I'm not as eager as some of our friends along Broadway; I want a peaceful existence."

Somehow it was difficult to imagine Norman Granz subsiding from around-the-clock productivity to quasi-immobility.

It seemed unlikely that he would ever carry out this threat completely, thereby throwing many office employees and musicians off the payroll. For one thing, he had enlarged his record domain in the past year and was bound to be needed on the scene to nurse these new children past the infant stage. For another, beneath his new interests lay an undimmed love for jazz and the friends it brought him. Aside from that, there was one factor he was bound to take into altruistic consideration: the cats needed the bread.

Sometimes many years pass before you realize that your crystal ball was clouded. In 1956 the American jazz world seemed to be Norman Granz's blues-point oyster. Although by that time other jazz packages were competing with him in the concert tour marketplace, and the Newport Jazz Festival had begun, the JATP phenomenon still seemed definitive and unsurpassable. Nevertheless during 1957 Granz abruptly gave up the U.S. concert scene; two years later he moved to Switzerland; in 1960 he sold Verve Records to MGM for $2,750,000. Since then the American concert halls, once his basic territory, have barely seen a trace of him. He is seldom in the United States for more than a few days, and then usually on business involving Ella Fitzgerald and Oscar Peterson, both of whom he still manages.

Working from his home base in Geneva or from London and Paris, he continued to tour with JATP in Europe but during the 1960s expanded far beyond jam sessions; he presented Duke Ellington, Ray Charles, and Count Basie all over Europe and financed such nonjazz attractions as Leonard Cohen, Richie Havens, and the Mothers of Invention.

Granz returned to America for a valedictory whirl in 1967. With him were Benny Carter, the late Coleman Hawkins, and several of his old standbys, including Ella and Oscar. As the tour ended, he said: "Never again. I made a profit, but it's too much of a production, too much work, and above all, too much aggravation. It's no fun any more, at least not in the States."

Thus far, he has lived up to his "never again"—except for an appearance at a nostalgic "Salute to JATP" evening in 1971 at the Monterey Jazz Festival.

However, he has kept in close touch, mostly via records, with the new post-JATP developments in jazz. In the early 1960s he brought the late John Coltrane and Eric Dolphy to Europe. He recalls meeting Ornette Coleman in Paris and discussing the possibility of sending him out on a continental tour. "My reaction to his music is zero—whether it's some lack on my part or not, I really don't know. On the other hand, I don't care for what the Mothers of Invention are doing either, but I feel strongly that certain artists at least deserve a hearing." He maintains no office anywhere; as always his main base of communication is the long-distance telephone. During a visit late in 1971 he summed up his attitude toward the current state of jazz. Although many American musicians who have toured Europe depict it as a jazz haven, Granz disagrees. "The scene is shrinking," he said. "Scandinavia is hopeless for jazz concerts now, they all want rock. Germany used to be an eight- to ten-city tour—now it's four or five. In England and France there are no cities worth playing except London and Paris.

"Actually America doesn't stack up too badly, in proportion to the population. But why should I promote jazz here? If I want to take the Los Angeles Music Center or Santa Monica Civic Auditorium, my rent is going to be the same as if I'd booked Creedence Clearwater; my ads will be just as expensive; so why gamble? You just can't come in and do a nice, quiet inexpensive jazz concert. . . .

"There's more stability in Europe. You find the same successful people still enjoying the same reaction. Oscar, Miles, Erroll Garner will always do business. I've been bringing Ray Charles over every year for five years, Ella and Oscar annually for much longer, and Basie every year since I stopped bringing Duke."

Granz and Ellington were closely involved during the mid-

1960s. Perhaps inevitably, a relationship between two such strong individualists led to clashes, and to a breakup in 1966. Granz says elliptically, "Duke's story is that I discharged him. I was his unpaid manager for five or six years. Voluntarily I never took a penny in commission from him—I did it all as what I thought was my contribution to jazz. I heard the band recently, and for a lot of reasons I don't care for it, but I still believe Duke's the greatest thing that ever happened to jazz."

At fifty-four, Granz is busier than ever. "Whenever there's any writing about jazz nowadays," he says testily, "people write me off as though I were retired. Shit, I do more jazz concerts than any man in the world, including George Wein. I've had everybody in Europe for me from the Modern Jazz Quartet to the Basie band, from Stan Kenton's band to the Glenn Miller Orchestra led by Buddy De Franco.

"If I had the time or the inclination, I'd get back into recording. In 1971 I tried to buy back Verve Records, but the deal fell through. Assuming all the conditions today, I could run Verve profitably. But this country has changed, the recording companies have changed. Executives nowadays are only concerned with the fact that they can gross $9 million with the Rolling Stones. They forget that a profit is still a profit, that you are still making money if you only net $9,000. I keep telling people that, and they think I'm crazy. Oscar Peterson, for example, is available. When I ask someone to record him, they want to know how much he sells and I'll tell them 25,000 or so, which would be profitable—but they don't want to hear about it.

"It's a disgrace what the jazz artists today are being forced to do, recording material that is all wrong for them. I let them try it with Ella and they wanted to create a new image for her by having her work the Fillmore, to promote this album of pop songs she'd recorded. I said, 'What for? She's making half a million a year as she is, why should I change that?' If I had my way Ella would never make another record —at least not by those standards. Who gives a damn?

"It's criminal, too, that someone like Sarah Vaughan was allowed to go without making a single record for five years. It's an outrage that of the twenty-seven albums I produced with Art Tatum for Verve, not a single one is available—they've all been deleted from the catalog. The son of a bitch who did that ought to be hung from the nearest lamppost. I even tried to buy the Tatum masters back, just so I could get them on the market again, but they wouldn't let me have them. They'll never sell the rights to anything, and yet they won't make it available to the public. And you wonder why I don't want to come back?"

Perhaps it is just as well that Norman Granz left the U.S. jazz world when he did. He had an idea whose time had come, and he knew just how long to sustain it. Had he decided to continue JATP domestically into the 1960s, let alone the 1970s, it is unlikely that there could have been any other consequence than an anticlimactic winding down.

He quit at the right time, leaving on our scene an ineradicable mark. Although his courage and initiative are sorely missed, American jazz to this day is the stronger for having experienced Granz's presence.

Salle Productions, Inc.

Oscar

OF ALL THE musicians who were closely associated with Norman Granz when Jazz at the Philharmonic flourished in the United States, Oscar Peterson has remained most consistently faithful to Granz's values. At once a skilled, self-searching performer and a jazzman unalterably dedicated to the proposition that his music had to swing, Peterson emerged during the 1950s to become perhaps the most widely known, and certainly the most extensively recorded of virtuoso jazz pianists.

If there had been a Norman Granz in the 1930s, it is conceivable that Art Tatum, who was Peterson's direct stylistic antecedent and (according to many classical and jazz musicians) probably the most thoroughly accomplished musician ever to play improvised jazz, would have enjoyed a career like Peterson's. His art properly belonged in concert halls, yet during his most creative years Tatum was limited to appearances in small nightclubs. Toward the end of his life Tatum recorded a memorable series of albums for Granz, but only after his health had begun to deteriorate. By this time Oscar Peterson's star was rising. After Tatum's death in 1956 Peterson became identified with Tatum's kind of music, by many critics as well as a segment of the jazz public.

The opinion of the experts is of little consequence to Peterson, according to his often reiterated and strongly worded views.

"I've sat and listened to records with critics," he once said, "and I've seen things that are important jazzwise go right over their heads, whereas the musicians in the room were aware of this. That's why I don't think criticism is an honest thing." Peterson's point was graciously admitted by one critic, Nat Hentoff, in *Down Beat*: "Peterson, of course, is quite right. . . . Very few of us have the musical equipment to pick up on everything that's happening in a given performance, or even everything *important* going on."

Certainly Peterson's own music—subtle and technically superb—has often been bypassed in favor of lesser jazzmen with more glamour. And although this Canadian giant of the piano is basically a happy man, he resents the worship of mediocrity and the incompetence that he feels has affected jazz adversely. "We put up with standards in jazz that are intolerable in classical music," he says. "The public is being fooled; people are trying to create, and appreciate, all kinds of miracles overnight. If we can manufacture geniuses so fast in jazz, why did Ellington have to spend all those years earning his way into the list of giants? Why did Armstrong? Why did Tatum? Why is it impossible to rave over an early Ellington as we do about the blue period of Picasso? Or the cubist period? Why did a beautiful saxophonist like Ben Webster have to give up and move to Europe? A Picasso created many decades ago may today bring a six- or even seven-figure price, but because of this sick attitude on both sides of the fence in jazz—the musicians and the critics—everything has to be strictly today.

"If I happen to make a record today, and impress this critic who is popular at the moment, then I've got a valuable record. But five years from now, if this particular school of criticism has gone out of favor, we look up and suddenly this 'great' record is outmoded. Why?"

These complaints are not fashioned from sour grapes. Peterson's trio has all the work it can handle, is neither old-fashioned nor avant-garde, and bears out his contention that good musicianship is imperative in the effective performance of jazz. Moreover, as a critic, let me be the first to cry *mea culpa*. Too often I have neglected artists who have been around for years, in order to concentrate on some new sensation whose significance and durability may be far from proven. All of us at one time or another have been affected subliminally by the aura of excitement surrounding some colorful new discovery.

The requirements for glamour in jazz too often include eccentricity, limited technical scope (supposedly compensated by "soul"), a personal background of social problems, and a tendency to show up for the Wednesday matinee at midnight on Thursday. By these standards Oscar Peterson was a cinch to be voted Least Likely to Succeed.

There are musicians who find it incomprehensible that Peterson has never made the cover of *Time* although this honor was accorded many years ago to a musician greatly favored by the critics, Thelonious Monk.

"Monk is a good composer," says guitarist Herb Ellis, who spent almost six years as a member of the Oscar Peterson Trio. "But he's *not* a piano player. Even within his own technical limitations he can't play any logical swinging jazz. Ray Charles has no technique, but at least what he plays swings and makes jazz sense. Monk's piano is ugly, contrived, and dumb. He just doesn't know any better. To quote Ray Brown, who once played with him, Monk has got the people buffaloed— the critics and even some musicians. On the other hand, Oscar has thrilled Ray and me to unbelievable heights."

By the standards of anyone who tends to favor artists with maverick personalities, Peterson's mistakes have been numerous. He is not self-taught, not weird in any sense of the word, and dresses in neatly-pressed suits. A well-educated, sophisticated man, he was born neither in poverty nor the South, and shows up for the 8:30 show at 8:15. He is as normal as heterosexuality, as gentlemanly as David Niven. He worked hard and systematically in developing himself professionally; he is a contented husband with five of the best-raised children in Toronto. Jazzwise, an unglamorous cat in a most unglamorously northern town.

Peterson is tall and heavy, with an athletic appearance that belies his background: at the age of seven he had to give up the trumpet because he had contracted tuberculosis. After Oscar had spent a year in a hospital, his father, a Canadian Pacific porter, shifted him to the role of pianist in the family band. There were three boys and two girls. One sister, an excellent classical pianist who helped to launch his career, later became a teacher. A brother, Chuck, took up the trumpet professionally.

"I used to practice from nine A.M. till noon," Oscar recalls, "then after lunch I'd go from one to six. After dinner I'd practice again from seven-thirty until my mother would drag me away so the family could get some sleep."

After playing hymns and classics Oscar turned to jazz. He won an amateur contest at fourteen, used the $250 prize to buy a new piano, soon landed his own fifteen-minute radio show, and later worked for Johnny Holmes's dance band. Although his studies enabled him to play classical and popular music and jazz, as a teen-ager his scope was limited. "I was overdoing boogie-woogie and was completely lost for slow music," he once said. "Holmes was responsible for changing this; he built up my technique and was responsible for the style I put on records." But Peterson's first recordings for the Canadian RCA label sound limited and mechanical compared with the exultantly swinging persona that had evolved by the time he invaded the States.

Throughout the 1940s his career had gone about as far as any jazz pianist's could in Canada. Visiting American jazzmen heard him, first with Holmes and later leading his own trio, but he turned down the many offers to join U.S. name bands; he felt he wasn't ready.

Peterson's discovery by Norman Granz was the result of chance, impulse, and the impresario's ear for talent. "Musicians like Coleman Hawkins had told me about this cat as far back as 1945," says Granz, "but I never bothered to listen to him. Then one night in 1949 I had been visiting Montreal to prepare a concert, and was on my way back to the airport, when I heard some music on the taxi radio. I asked the cab driver what record that was and he said, 'It isn't. It's live—a trio playing at the Alberta Lounge.' I said, 'Turn around and go back into town.'

"Oscar later told me that he saw a pair of suede shoes entering the lounge; he'd heard that I always wore suede shoes and guessed it must be me; then he got panicky. We talked, and I persuaded him to come down and make one appearance at Carnegie Hall in September."

Down Beat reported that Peterson "stopped the concert dead in its tracks." In 1950 he became a regular member of Granz's peripatetic Jazz at the Philharmonic unit. At first he worked in a duo with Ray Brown, then in 1952 added guitarist Irving Ashby, who was succeeded by Barney Kessel, then Herb Ellis; after Ellis' five-year tenure ended in 1958, he used drums instead of guitar. Peterson's trio became the highlight of dozens of Jazz at the Philharmonic tours, at home and abroad. "Oscar leads the fullest and most varied life of any musician I know," Granz once said. "He's so well informed and well organized that I'm sure, if he wanted to, he could run for office in Toronto."

Granz may have been referring to the intensity that Peterson brings to all his interests, be they photography, painting, or teaching. Certainly he applies to his pastimes the same perfectionism that brought his musicianship to its present level. For example, having started taking photographs with a small box camera, he soon acquired a Leica, a Hasselblad, a Bolex, a 3-D, a Lenhof, a Gami, four or five other cameras, and a color enlarger. Several photographs have been published and he could make an excellent living at it. He couldn't just take pictures; he had to become a superb photographer.

Peterson disengages himself when perfection seems inaccessible. He once refused to play with the Toronto Symphony, on the grounds that a classical concert would require six months' preparation. ("I don't want to go up there and just play the notes.") A first-rate singer, he made two fine vocal LPs, but insisted that he sounded too much like Nat Cole and so gave it up.

He has the gift of total recall, and can return to the trio after a month's holiday, jump on the bandstand, and remember every note of every arrangement. On the personal front he is a family man, an inveterate practical joker, and a tireless conversationalist.

"Oscar enjoys discussing things," says a friend, "whether it's with a bank president, a brain surgeon, or the car-hop at the Century Plaza." He is high-strung, hypersensitive, easily touched by kindness, and easily wounded by malice. Once, in a rare display of anger, he flattened a cab driver who refused him a ride and called him a name. And when a fan once asked why he didn't hire a Negro guitarist instead of Ellis, Oscar offered an impassioned lecture on race prejudice in reverse.

In the early 1960s Oscar Peterson, Ray Brown and Ed Thigpen taught jazz at their Advanced School of Contemporary Music in Toronto. John Norris, editor of the Canadian jazz magazine *Coda*, said: "These teachers don't just separate the men from the boys—they make men *out* of the boys. I heard one bass player before and after he studied there. I could hardly believe it was the same guy." The school attracted students from all over the U.S., but after a few years Peterson's traveling commitments forced him to shut it down.

Peterson's own expertise has continued to grow. Although he was very much influenced by the bebop movement during the 1950s, and particularly by Bud Powell and George Shearing, his true idol, musically rather than just technically, was Tatum, to whom he grew very close during Art's last years. As Gene Lees wrote in *Down Beat*, "If there are pianists who rival Oscar's speed, they lack his virility and blues-rooted power. If there are those who rival his power, they lack his absolute mastery of the instrument." That assessment could as well have applied to Tatum.

It seemed symbolic that when Tatum lay dying, Peterson rushed to his bedside. In the opinion of this writer and many musicians, the passing of the foremost pianist in jazz annals left Peterson in the position of heir to the crown.

Why? Peterson himself may have supplied the answer in a statement he made some years ago: "Let's face it, jazz piano is an instrument most pianists have forgotten. A piano can be as subtle as a French horn in the distance or as driving as the Basie band. Because a man is working within one esthetic framework, that's not to say he shouldn't therefore use the rest of the scope of the instrument."

Yet he has always been musically conservative. For example, he feels that it's "crazy" to say that jazzmen can learn anything from rock. "People call this the Big Beat," he has said, "but as often as not it's harder to discern the beat in rock than in jazz, because they have so many confusing things going on. Talking about a big beat in that kind of music is just a shuck, an excuse. . . .

"I'm not trying to be a stoic by pretending you can't acquiesce to any particular trend. For instance, I dig the feeling of bossa nova as it has entered our music. I even dig rhythm-and-blues—I did tunes with this feeling years ago, but without completely selling out and losing my identity . . .

"You have to try and grow. You can't take your own creative talent and put it into some new mode, washing away your own image to become a part of whatever movement is prevalent at the moment. Too many artists have visions of dollar signs and contracts to work in the big rooms. Sure, you can play some of the pop things that are adaptable to your style, but you don't have to go all out and prostitute yourself."

Peterson also does not believe in defiling the piano's natural sound by hitting its belly with hammers and tongs, or by clawing at the strings. The so-called "prepared piano," he says, is a gimmick; the artists, not the instrument, should be prepared, to play it according to the designer's original intentions.

"I despair about the lack of proper respect shown for the piano. If you want it to sound like a traffic jam, go out in the street and create a traffic jam and forget the piano. That's not a piano sound.

"I still like Hank Jones, Bill Evans, Phineas Newborn, Jr. —people who play the piano as a piano. Nobody has done anything concrete enough in any other manner to convince me that this is not where it's at anymore.

"I've been criticized for overuse of technique, but I've heard many of the important new soloists doing things that no so-called 'soul pianist' or rhythm-and-blues novice could play.

"Technique is something that can be acquired in any field. If I wanted to build houses, I could learn the technique of architecture. I have told many students that I could teach anyone off the street to play the 'Revolutionary Étude.' But after that, it's the interpretation that becomes the vitally important thing."

Analyzing his own contribution and that of the trio, he says: "My group has always retained that fire, that feeling of pressure, of playing with honesty.

"I could never think of giving up what I'm doing. I could never, for instance, settle down and become a studio musician. That kind of job was offered to me years ago, but it doesn't represent the way I want to live."

Oscar and his second wife, Sandy, live in a penthouse apartment on Toronto's lakeshore. Unlike most jazz musicians Peterson can be happy when totally removed from his usual surroundings; he and Sandy have a cottage in the beautiful Halliburton area of Ontario, where they go during his vacations for water skiing, underwater swimming, snowmobiling.

In recent years he has devoted more time to composing. His best-known work is the exquisitely fashioned *Canadiana*

Suite, each movement of which signifies some area that has captured his imagination: "Wheatland" for the Canadian wheat fields, "Land of the Misty Giants" for the Rocky Mountains, "Place St. Henri" for Montreal, "Hogtown Blues" for Toronto, and "March Past" for the parade that initiates the Calgary Stampede rodeo. Peterson has also written and published several jazz études for piano. Some compositions dedicated to close friends bear their nicknames: "Blues for Smedley" (Norman Granz), "Blues for Big Scotia" (Lil Peterson, his first wife), "Goodbye, J.D." (for Jim Davis, producer of many of his Verve records) and "Nightingale" (for Sandy).

He has always believed music to be self-sufficient, and beyond the realm of politics or propaganda. Nevertheless a touch of social relevance informed what has generally been acclaimed his most stirring composition, the gospel-oriented "Hymn to Freedom."

Despite personnel changes from time to time, his trio has maintained the high standards it established in the 1950s. Its incumbents early in 1972 were drummer Louis Hayes (who rejoined him after a three-year absence) and Niels-Henning Orsted Pederson, the phenomenal young Danish bassist.

Peterson's musical attitude has remained unchanged throughout the turbulence that has racked jazz during the past decade. His conservatism has not affected his popularity; he is still one of the three leading pianists, according to such yardsticks as the *Down Beat* readers' poll; he still plays in jazz spots suitable to his music and continues to have a healthy following in Europe, where he tours annually. For several years in the late 1960s Peterson recorded only for a German company which has a studio in the Black Forest and controls the world rights to his sessions. It is probable that if Oscar were to record rock tunes, add a fender bass, switch to electric piano, and turn his drummer onto the boogaloo beat, he might be a howling domestic success. But he has done none of these things. While other jazzmen lie awake figuring out ways to beat the system with such stratagems, Oscar Peterson continues to sleep well at night.

"When I stop playing the way I'm playing," he says, "I'll just close the piano lid one night and stop for good."

One can only hope that day is still far off. Peterson has remained through the years a paragon of the virtuoso musician. Erroll Garner has his impishly rhythmic, predominantly chordal style; Horace Silver, his mercurial single-note lines; Thelonious Monk, his jagged melodic formulations and unconventional intervals. Each leading jazz pianist, as Peterson has said, tends to follow one particular avenue of the instrument's potential. But Peterson's eclecticism has entitled him to the Tatum legacy; unlimited technique can facilitate unlimited style. Along with this capacity Peterson and his sidemen demonstrate as viably as any group on the scene today a faculty critical to the survival of jazz: the time-honored art of swinging.

Ray Charles

IT CAN BE said that both Oscar Peterson and Ray Charles are products of the black experience—that blanket term commonly used to characterize the environments, experiences, and life styles of some twenty million Americans. But what in fact is the black experience? If it is waking up black every morning, if it is an acute awareness of what is in the typical white man's mind when he observes your blackness, they indeed have that in common. Beyond that an almost endless diversity of life-styles unfolds.

For Ray Charles, poor and black and blind in Georgia, blackness had demonstrably more significance than it could have for Peterson in Canada, who never knew real poverty and whose brushes with racism have been relatively slight and transient. If social background is the esthetic determinant, one would expect to find almost no relationship between the music of the two. Although contrasts exist, there is a hidden link, one that can be attributed perhaps more to the music they heard on records and radio than to the live sounds in their respective geographic vicinities. Both men were strongly influenced by Nat King Cole.

The instrumental trio format popularized by Cole in the early 1940s—piano, electric guitar, and bass—became a dominant influence throughout the decade. Cole's piano style, an outgrowth of the percussive and rhythmically volatile Earl Hines sound, also made a pervasive impact.

As leader of a Cole-oriented combo deliberately patterned along the lines of Nat's "Straighten Up and Fly Right" days, Charles established a modest reputation around 1949. During most of the 1950s Peterson too led a trio composed of piano, guitar, and bass. Although Peterson was influenced basically by Art Tatum, his debt to Cole is not always recognized. In an album called *With Respect to Nat,* recorded shortly after Cole's death, their instrumental resemblance and vocal similarities are strikingly evident.

Despite their early mutual indebtedness to Nat Cole, Charles and Peterson soon developed individual styles. By the end of the 1950s a "return-to-roots" movement took place within jazz; it was exemplified by some of the works of Horace Silver (*Opus De Funk, The Preacher*) and later by Cannonball Adderley and Art Blakey. It was characterized by a shift away from the sophistication of Shearing, Brubeck, and the Modern Jazz Quintet, for instance, which had been the hallmark of the early 1950s. But the trend had already reached gut level with the first Atlantic recordings of Ray Charles. Charles's audience, at first almost exclusively black, had expanded by 1960 to include not only white jazz fans but a large part of the general American audience.

Until his first album came out, his single-record releases had been moderately successful. Charles's polymorphous talent was known only to a few musicians, most notably Quincy Jones, who like Charles was living in Seattle in the early 1950s and who credits Ray with having taught him most of what he learned in those years. Without losing the Southern jukebox market for whom his gospel-flavored early hits were geared, Charles the pianist soon became famous as a singer. In this respect his career closely followed that of Nat Cole and, as in Cole's case, many who followed his development as a singer were unaware of his musical background.

Charles has played piano, organ, saxophone, and clarinet professionally. Using a Braille notation system, he was active for many years as a composer and arranger. His piano style is curiously adaptable; sometimes the bop influence is apparent (he has named Powell, Peterson, Tatum, and Cole as his favorites). But because he was swept up in the soul movement, his funky, blues-drenched solos became more commonly identified with him.

Like many noted performers from Armstrong and Teagarden to Fats Waller and Nat Cole, Charles essentially is a jazz instrumentalist who drifted into a singing career. Yet many who have heard his jazz piano have wondered how a bop-influenced instrumentalist emerged as a folk- and church-influenced singer.

The answer is not hard to determine. In the first place, no jazz soloist whose style has matured logically is likely to have developed without first acquiring roots in the basics of the art. Many modern jazz artists can play convincingly in traditional styles, but the contrary is almost never the case.

Second, the vocal art in jazz is more directly linked to certain qualities of timbre and emotion that play a less conspicuous part in the performance of many modern instrumentalists. Unless he deliberately imitates a horn solo (in the style of Eddie Jefferson, King Pleasure, or such groups as Lambert, Hendricks & Ross), the jazz artist is likely to be more earthy in his singing style than in his complex eight-note-infused piano or horn solos. To cite a famous example, one need only point to Dizzy Gillespie's occasional blues vocals. They are about as basic as one can get—as down home, in fact, as Ray Charles.

Ray Charles's "Georgia on My Mind" was a smash hit record of a popular standard song rather than a blues-funk-soul composition, and with it his process of diversification got under way in the 1960s. His album entitled *Modern Sounds in Country and Western Music* was the first of several highly successful attempts to reconcile his timbre and phrasing with material that seemed antithetical to everything he had symbolized during the previous ten years.

Charles has always been a pragmatist. While critics attacked the alleged "whimpering lachrymose sameness" of the pop hit songs and Western vehicles, his enlarged band stormed France, Belgium, Sweden, Germany, and Switzerland, and he had his first acting role in a motion picture filmed in Ireland.

This is not, however, an instance of artistic integrity sacrificed in the interests of commercial success. Opponents of the direction Charles has taken in the past ten or twelve years overlook the fact that he still sings *What'd I Say* and *Hallelujah, I Love Her So* with the gritty honesty that was apparent in the original recordings. He has rejected none of his past, preferring to incorporate an ever wider range of elements into the present.

As an instrumentalist, too, he has kept the faith, if somewhat sporadically. An LP, scarcely noted in the press, was issued in 1970 on his own Tangerine label bearing the title *My Kind of Jazz*. It featured his own regular orchestra in arrangements by Charles, Quincy Jones, Teddy Edwards, and others, and included reminders—in Ray's solos on such instrumental numbers as Lee Morgan's "The Sidewinder," Toots Thielemans' "Bluesette," and Horace Silver's "Senor Blues"— of his undiminished affection for the eternal and happy verities of jazz. Except for a little soulful humming on one tune, there are no vocals in the album.

In sum, Ray Charles is aligned with no special group. He has successfully demolished the borderlines that separated bop from funk, soul from country and Western, popular music from jazz, artistry from show business. No matter how carefully his show is planned to attract maximal box-office returns, no matter how heavily choreographed the gyrations of his Raelets, he is a performer whose contribution to the music scene is as valid as it is long-standing.

During the fall and winter of 1965–66 Charles voluntarily withdrew from the public scene. When he returned six months later, after having been hospitalized, he was willing—even eager—for the first time in his life to talk freely about the narcotics problem that on several occasions had nearly cost him his career. Although Charles's troubles with the law made the front pages, the news of his projected cure went unnoticed. Neither the statements from hospital officials nor the dutiful "Mr. Charles is taking a vacation" reports from employees in the Charles office were picked up. A curtain of silence covered the activities of Ray Charles from August 22, 1965, when he entered St. Francis Hospital in Lynwood, south of Los Angeles, until shortly before his release some months later when the following news item appeared:

Ray Charles, the blind Los Angeles jazz pianist and singer, won a continuance for a year after pleading guilty to a Federal charge of possession of narcotics. The judge continued the case after Charles' lawyer said the singer was trying to cure himself of drug addiction. He said Charles was under treatment at a California clinic.

Even after his release, Charles remained in seclusion until he gradually resumed work at RPM Enterprises in Los Angeles. I met with him one afternoon in the two-story office building on Washington Boulevard which he had bought some years earlier.

Charles had always been an enigma to interviewers. Blindness, which for George Shearing means self-deprecating jokes, was not a subject he would discuss. In fact, I had to talk and act as if his handicap did not exist, which was exactly what Ray seemed able to do himself. Another strict taboo had been the subject of his addiction. Now, however, he was willing to talk. After all the years of anguish he seemed to have come to terms with himself and with society, and spoke like a man who had sought and found his own answers.

Ray Charles is, in equal parts, a deeply committed artist and a shrewd businessman. He understands the fine print of every contract he has signed. When he speaks for the record, he knows exactly what he wants to say and how it will be interpreted.

I mentioned the one-sided publicity about him and said that I wanted to hear about the changes he had evidently gone through during his retirement. He first told me that he was more relaxed—"You have to understand that I've been able to get quite a bit of rest.

"*Nobody* forced me into this. I just decided it was something I wanted to do. After all, my kids are much older now, and there comes a time when you realize that, even if you don't give a damn about yourself, you must try to consider your kids and the other people involved. I've always heard that children can be very cruel to other children, and I certainly didn't want my kids to have somebody make some remark to them, and then they'd get themselves in trouble, just because of me."

(*I've known Ray Charles since we were both in our midteens in Seattle, when he had that King Cole-style trio, and even then noticed that when he made up his mind about something, he couldn't be stopped. I'm sure he meant what he said about being concerned for his children.*—Quincy Jones)

"Some people may say, 'You're a little late,' and I may be; but like the old cliché says, it's better to be a little late than never.

"I'm 100 percent against the idea of taking a person that may have some problem and just locking him up. It doesn't solve anything. In my opinion, for what it's worth, the whole system is wrong because it's been proven time and time again. You take some guy and give him five or ten years. They come out, and the very next day they hit the street, if they can find anybody who they ran with, they're right back where they started. So putting somebody away is not the answer."

(*I began using stuff when I was sixteen and first started in show business . . . I really need help. I'd like to go to Lexington. I guess I've always wanted to go, but it was easier the other way . . . the daily grind gets to be too much. A fellow who lives in the dark has to do something.*—Ray Charles, after arrest in 1962, to a policeman in Indianapolis)

I asked him how long it had taken for him to kick his habit, and he replied that "the chemistry part" had only taken a couple of days; the remaining time was spent in resting, reading, and writing "two or three songs." As for advising anyone else with the same temptations, he said, "It's kind of like saying to a kid, 'Don't smoke.' And you know darn well that entices him *to* smoke. . . . The only thing I would suggest is not so much to talk to the kids, but to say something to the parents. That's where the problem lies."

(*What could Ray's parents do? His father, Bailey Robinson, was a handyman in a little town called Greenville in Florida. And Ray went blind at six, and his father died when Ray was ten. When he was fifteen and studying at St. Augustine School for the Blind, his mother died. After she died he couldn't eat, couldn't even break down and cry; they had to put him in the hospital for a week*—Quincy Jones)

Had he listened to radio during his recent hospitalization?

"It's very difficult for me to turn on a radio and listen to the same damn music every day, all day. It's pretty hard to take. Some of these things you hear, for instance, the way they fix these *git*-tars, the way they sound like you're playing through a paper comb . . . Believe me, I don't like to knock anybody's means of making a living, because each man has to eat and take care of himself, but, personally, it is not my cup of tea.

"I'm not against rhythm-and-blues or rock 'n' roll, it can be played well, but what bothers me is the way it's being messed up. There's a good way to do everything and a bad way—you can make a bad thing out of a church if that's what you want to do."

Charles thought it remarkable that *The In Crowd*, a recent Ramsey Lewis record, had become a top seller. "I don't know how that happened," he said, "but it just goes to show how the public can't be predicted. Well, look, I love rhythm-and-blues and I play it and sing it because I like it, but I try to perform it in a way that has some meaning, wherein you can understand it, for heaven's sakes.

"I heard a record when I was in the hospital, and it was called something about 'I Can't Get No Satisfaction' by some group or other—which may be fine if the kids love it, but as an entertainer I can't wake up to that. Because this was a smash hit for the Rolling Stones or whoever it was, I'm not going to go out and try to make a record just like it. It's not my bag. I'm still back, as far as rhythm-and-blues is concerned, back in the 'What'd I Say?' bag or the 'Hallelujah, I Love Her So' bag. And with regular instruments that come out with a clean sound! And a clean beat!

"I don't think you could say music is on the downgrade because of the present situation. This is like what you might call a side order of music, not the main dish. You take some of the great songs that have lived through the years. Most of them never were No. 1 on the Hit Parade. Take a song like 'I Didn't Know What Time It Was' or an 'Over the Rainbow,' it isn't important what happened to them when they first came out; they're still around. The music that comes out on these records today that you're talking about, the top 40 things, people like 'em for a few minutes and then they're gone and forgotten. After all the gimmicks and new sound groups have come and gone, you'll still have your Ella Fitzgeralds, your Sinatras, people like Sarah Vaughan and Nat Cole, bless his soul—people like this will still be around, we'll still be buying their records."

Soon the conversation turned to Charles' overseas travels and his experiences in the Irish-made film.

"It's the first movie I've been in where I actually did some acting," he said. "I can't tell you whether I was good or bad in it. I've decided that when they show it here, I'm going to get a seat in the back row so if it turns out real bad I can just sneak out of the place."

I asked him how he had taken to acting; whether or not he needed much direction.

"I would say that acting was fairly natural to me. Because, strange as it may seem, singing honestly is a part of acting, and I'll tell you why. In order to project to the people, to transmit so they can feel what you feel—not necessarily hear what you hear, but sense the same emotions—this is precisely the same thing as when you are acting."

As for audience reaction to his singing in Europe: "What always amazes me is that when you sing where very little English is understood, they seem to enjoy the songs just as if they understood every word! It's fascinating. When we went to Japan, for instance, they gave me a standing ovation. I was very surprised at this, because I thought the language barrier would make it impossible . . . They wanted things not only from the Atlantic period, they even wanted to hear some things I recorded when I was on the Swingtime label, way back, around 1948–49. They'd come up and say, 'Do you do "Baby Let Me Hold Your Hand?"' or 'How about "Confession Blues"?' They remembered things I'd completely forgotten I had ever recorded. It makes you feel very good."

As a black artist Charles has strong views on every aspect of the racial scene but prefers not to express them through message material or protest songs. Pressed for a statement, he will come out firmly against the war in Vietnam; but as a black singer whose following might enable him to take an evangelical stand, he is among the least likely ever to sing an anti-Vietnam blues. (In 1972, unexpectedly, a Charles album entitled *A Message from the People* included a number of socially meaningful compositions.)

Answering a question in a 1970 *Playboy* interview concerning performers' increasing use of militant material in their shows, he replied: "Personally, I think everyone can see that I'm black, so I guess I don't have to tell anybody about it. Furthermore, I'd like to think that when I sing a song, I can let you know all about the heartbreak, struggle, lies and kicks in the ass I've gotten over the years for being black and everything else, without actually saying a word about it." No sensitive listener could possibly take issue with Charles on this

point. Even when nominally singing the praises of his home
state in strict accordance with the intent of Stuart Gorrell's
original "Georgia on My Mind" lyrics, it is impossible to miss
the black sob of misery ingrained decades ago.

Professionally the last five years have been notable more
for economic achievements and official honors than for new or
surprising musical developments. Like Nat Cole during the last
decade of his life, Charles in recent years has more or less
coasted on the strength of his early successes. As with Armstrong, Gillespie, and other innovators, there was one significant phase during which Charles profoundly influenced his
contemporaries—something that almost never happens twice
in the life of a contributor to any of the arts.

Ray Charles's era of maximum impact began in the mid-
1950s, when his Atlantic records attracted widespread attention, and ended in the early 1960s when he won Grammy
awards from NARAS (the recording academy) for "Georgia,"
"Let the Good Times Roll," "Hit the Road Jack," "I Can't Stop
Loving You," and "Busted." Although the NARAS victories
often tend to serve as a gauge of popularity rather than the
measure of artistic merit they are supposed to imply, it may
be noteworthy that except for "Crying Time" in 1966, none of
his records since 1963 has captured a Grammy.

Perhaps more significantly, during the past few years
Charles's entertainment business operations have grown to
multimillion-dollar proportions, involving personal management, publishing companies, and the recording company. While
the number of gold albums has continued to increase, it is entirely possible that the recordings with which he has reached
the widest audience, at least domestically, are the commercials
for Coca-Cola for which he was teamed with Aretha Franklin.

Now in his early forties, with poverty many years behind
him and narcotics five years in the past, Charles has a measure
of economic and psychological security he would never have
dared hope for during the formative days in the South, or even
in Seattle and on the road during the early 1950s.

Some critics feel that in yielding to the temptation to broaden his audiences, Charles has lost something along the way and is no longer the King of Soul. Others strongly disagree; Whitney Balliett probably was closest to the target when he commented not long ago that Charles "has solved the Midas-touch-versus-artistic-integrity problem with extraordinary grace."

"I don't profess to be a modern jazz artist, or a rhythm-and-blues artist," Charles once said. "I like to stay away from titles hanging onto me, you know. I would just like to be a good entertainer, period."

The fact is that how often he plays or sings jazz, or what proportion of rhythm-and-blues songs he now incorporates in his repertoire, is not relevant today to the phenomenon of Charles's success. What is important, whether he sings the raw materials of his black roots, the country corn of Buck Owens, or the contemporary creations of Jimmy Webb or Paul McCartney, is that Ray Charles in the 1970s can reach out and touch, with unerring accuracy, the hearts and souls of uncounted millions who at one time were far beyond his grasp. Alongside this irrefutable fact, the quibbles concerning his relationship to jazz, to soul music, to blackness, become secondary issues. Ray Charles is one of those rare folk heroes of the arts who has reached his goal without any deliberate concession or compromise. Surely this is achievement enough for one lifetime.

Don Ellis

Just as Ray Charles has succeeded in wiping out artificial barriers between jazz, rhythm-and-blues, and related idioms, so has the general trend of recent years indicated an increased anxiety on the part of innumerable musicians not to think or operate in terms of categories.

More and more often we have heard such statements as, "I don't want to be labeled a jazz musician," "Jazz and rock must draw from one another," "Jazz is a white man's word," and various dogmatic remarks telling us that jazz in some way inhibits the performer's freedom, and must yield the right of way to a new music, free of the stigma allegedly implicit in that word.

It remains unquestionably a matter of fact rather than opinion that jazz today is alive, that even those artists who abhor the word continue to play the music, that it is taught more extensively than ever at the school and college levels, that concerts and festivals are staged in its name.

Since the late 1960s the changes in jazz have been more fundamental and have evolved at a more accelerated pace than at any previous period. On the one hand, musicians are demolishing the fences, opening the way toward the new, nameless idiom that represents their concept of a musical utopia; on the other hand, factionalism, particularly in the form of racial separatism, has tended to draw the performers away from each other, polarizing a music in which unification has long been an objective.

These contradictory cross-currents are nowhere better illustrated than in the cases of Miles Davis and Don Ellis. Both are generally accepted as innovative jazz musicians; both are composers who play trumpet and flügelhorn; both have become deeply involved in the use of amplified instruments, wah-wah pedals, ring modulators, and other devices that control and distort what we have always thought of as "natural" sounds.

Despite these superficial similarities, however, the worlds of Ellis and Davis overlap only minimally. The most conspicuous difference between them is that while Ellis is primarily interested in experimentation with big-band jazz, Davis has given new directions to small combo music. Don talks to his audiences at length about the subdivisions of 9/4, 7/8, 9/8, or 3/2 they are about to hear; Miles, who does not find it necessary to tell his listeners anything, allows his musicians almost limitless latitude and is far more concerned than Ellis with freedom and spontaneity.

That Miles is black and Don white may be assumed by some to connote an automatic difference in their approaches. Of course, it could be pointed out that Ellis worked for quite some time as a sideman or leader in predominantly black combos, and that Miles has never had an association more fruitful than his partnership with the white composer-arranger Gil Evans in a series of ambitious orchestral ventures. The contrast actually is one of attitude determined by background and associations rather than simply of race *per se*. Ellis clearly has sprung from the roots that gave us Stan Kenton. His orchestra usually is almost or completely all-white, as Kenton's bands have been, and the composition of his audiences is similar. Miles thinks black and talks black, but his appeal is interracial, and paradoxical though it may seem, his group in recent years has been more international and more integrated than Ellis' band; in person or on records he has employed an

English bassit, a Scottish guitarist, Austrian and English pianists, and a Brazilian percussionist.

The temperamental differences between the two men are not hard to perceive. As both trumpeter and leader, Ellis exercises a tight, hard-edged discipline. He can perform with great lyricism but more often displays harmonic and rhythmic complexities. The listener is less conscious of the technical or intellectual effort that goes into the creation of a Miles Davis solo.

It must not be concluded from these observations that the jazz of Ellis and the jazz of Davis are mutually exclusive: a member of one group might find himself at ease with the other. Still, these two dominant personalities of the 1970s are representative of two clearly different directions in contemporary jazz.

On the afternoon of September 18, 1966, the audience at the Monterey Jazz Festival accorded a tall, blond, trumpet-playing composer-bandleader named Don Ellis what may have been the most thunderous standing ovation in the festival's history.

One of the most talented young musicians in America today, Ellis is also something of a paradox. As a musician he is a radical innovator, an exponent of unlimited freedom, an uninhibited experimenter who once performed a piece consisting entirely of musicians standing around a piano and looking at it in total silence. At the same time, on the personal level he is a conservative, clean-cut, all-American—totally rigorous and disciplined.

His triumph at Monterey climaxed years of experimentation with almost every kind of musical adventure. There were tours as a band sideman; combo gigs with Charles Mingus and George Russell; the formation of several groups of his own that played Greenwich Village, Stockholm, Oslo, and Warsaw; Third Stream ventures with Leonard Bernstein and Gunther

Schuller; study on the West Coast; and a long flirtation with Indian music that resulted in his Hindustani Jazz Sextet. After a year in Buffalo he went to Los Angeles where, in 1964, he launched a rehearsal band, which varied from twenty to twenty-three men and which produced the orchestra responsible for the Monterey madness.

Intermingled with Ellis' various jobs were several stretches of studying and teaching, an initiation into liturgical jazz, numerous painstaking attempts at journalism, and a number of forays into the recording field, some of which ended in frustration when the albums were never released.

Nat Hentoff, one of Ellis' earliest and most vociferous rooters, has observed that "No contemporary jazz composer makes use of as many different devices. He draws from both the classical and jazz traditions, and invents forms of his own. His writing is as varied as his playing."

Donald Johnson Ellis was born in Los Angeles on July 25, 1934, the son of the Reverend and Mrs. Ezra Ellis. A precocious child, he began to show musical talent at a very early age. His mother, a church organist who had studied to be a concert pianist, noticed Don's rapid development; by the age of five he could transpose a tune from C to G without hesitation.

"But I rebelled against piano lessons," says Don. "I hated scales. The trumpet, on which nobody ever had to talk me into taking lessons, was what held my interest."

His formal musical education included composition studies with four teachers, trumpet lessons with at least seven, and a degree in composition from Boston University in 1956.

His attraction to jazz began at West High School in Minneapolis. "The first band I ever heard in person was Tommy Dorsey's, with Charlie Shavers on trumpet. I was so fascinated I even forgot the chick I was with and just sat there open-mouthed." A few years later he heard both the classic Hot Five 78s of Louis Armstrong and "Manteca" and "Cool Breeze" by the early Gillespie band. Although Armstrong and Gillespie were far removed from each other, they both excited Ellis.

(Don himself has been compared to such diverse jazz artists as Dizzy, Rex Stewart, Roy Eldridge, Maynard Ferguson, Fats Navarro, Clark Terry, and almost every jazz trumpet giant.)

After graduating from college, Ellis auditioned successfully for the Glenn Miller band, then directed by Ray McKinley, and joined up immediately. "I'll never forget how he started his professional life," his father recalls. "He had nothing but a toothbrush, a razor, and a trumpet."

"It was quite an indoctrination," Ellis agrees. "We had three months of one-night stands with a total of three nights off, making a minimum of 500 miles a day in the bus. But I was happy to be right out of college making $135 a week. I stayed until September of 1956, when the Army got me."

The Army was more fun than drudgery; the Seventh Army Symphony and Soldiers' Show Company included a jazz orchestra, for which he was chief arranger. During his second year the band was fronted by Leo Wright, later well known as Dizzy Gillespie's sax-and-flute specialist. The personnel also included Sam Fletcher, the singer; Cedar Walton, the pianist now best known as an Art Blakey alumnus; and saxophonist Eddie Harris.

Once out of the Army, Ellis shared a cramped apartment in Greenwich Village with Fletcher, Walton, and pianist Horace Parlan. He played some local gigs, a few brief stints with dance bands in Boston, and a short tour with Charlie Barnet. Then one night Slide Hampton and Joe Zawinul of the Maynard Ferguson band heard Don sit in with a combo at Smalls Paradise in Harlem, and promptly recommended him to Ferguson. He joined the orchestra in the spring of 1959 and remained for nine months. "Maynard was a great natural talent," says Ellis. "In those days no one else could play like that."

In the next couple of years Ellis broke away more and more from standard bebop playing and the symmetrical, formula method of writing. He demonstrated his concern for freedom and expansion of tempo and meter on his first album as a leader, a 1960 cut on the long-defunct Candid label. Promi-

nently featured on the LP was Ellis' roommate, a friend from
Boston and an ex-Ferguson colleague, Jaki Byard, who was
closely associated with Ellis from 1959 to 1962.

"Ironically," Ellis recalls, "at the time of what turned out
to be the end of our professional relationship, I was set to take
a quartet into Wells' in Harlem, and found that Jaki didn't
want to play uptown." Byard, who is black, and Ellis were
feeling the first effects of the reverse racism that disapproved
of mixing.

Some observers, aware of Ellis' rightist views, find a curious
paradox in his close musical association and personal friendship with black musicians. His father is a friend of Richard
Nixon, who has visited Rev. Ellis' church, and Don is a staunch
Republican, a Reagan enthusiast, a Goldwater fan and an opponent of the Rumford Fair Housing Act. He says: "I'm for a
complete laissez-faire capitalistic economy" and believes that
"If people who have the intelligence not to be prejudiced
would simply ignore racial differences, the whole racial problem would be solved rapidly."

In his politics as in several other respects Ellis has much
in common with Stan Kenton. Like Stan, he is a restless seeker
after new musical forms. Both men are tall (Ellis six feet,
Kenton six feet four inches) and physically prepossessing; both
have a keen sense of self-promotion; both lean toward grandeur
and magniloquence rather than simplicity and soul.

Don is a firm disciplinarian. "Those rehearsals have to start
right on the button," says Dave Wells, formerly of Ellis' trombone section. "He figures out his whole life that way."

Ellis' rigid self-discipline enabled him to concentrate his
efforts on the furthering of his professional ambition. As everyone now knows (including the imitators, who are multiplying
by the minute), the door to success was unlatched by mathematics—a kaleidoscope of metric novelties that could swing
the tempo of his big band, in the course of a single set, from
5/4 to 5/8 to 13/4 to 27/16 to 6/8, with only a now-and-then

glimpse back at that quaint old 4/4 beat that used to be the basis of all jazz.

According to Third Streamer Gunther Schuller, who annotated the first Ellis album and later used him in a series of contemporary music concerts, "Ellis has found a way of expanding the rhythmic vocabulary of jazz to include rhythmic patterns heretofore excluded because they couldn't be made to swing. . . . It is evident that he has listened to Webern, Stockhausen, and others of the avant-garde."

The shape of swing to come was clearly indicated in a 1961 interview when Ellis said, "I don't know where jazz is heading, but I'd like to see it keep improvisation and swing. And it doesn't have to be sanctified to swing . . . it doesn't always have to be 4/4. There are a lot of other time signatures to try out. I think we'll go into 5/8 and 7/8. Hall Overton was showing me some things like that. . . ."

The Village years were productive both on the musical and personal levels. One night a stunning blonde ex-model named Connie Coogan walked into the Phase 2 on Bleecker Street where Don had a gig. She became Mrs. Ellis in July of 1961. Their combined experimentation has included a natural-health-food kick, which allegedly improved Don's vision, enabling him to Throw Away That Glass Mask (early photos show him wearing heavy horn-rimmed glasses). Don even gave experimental names to his sons, Brav and Tran, born in 1963 and 1964. "This was an attempt to get away from the same old familiar names," he explains. "Brav was derived from Bravo and Tran from Transcend." The Ellises were divorced in 1971.

In October of 1962 Don went through the familiar prophet-without-honor phase. He and Connie left for a couple of months of travel and study, starting at the International Jazz Jamboree in Warsaw. He wrote "Warsaw Diary" for *Down Beat*, recording the minutest details of the festival, each entry clocked to the nearest fifteen minutes.

He and the Poles, who were deeply immersed in the Third

Stream, got along famously. Soon afterward, in Stockholm, Ellis reported, "We were treated like royalty. The musicians I recorded with for Swedish radio were very sympathetic to the 'new thing' and impressed me with their natural feel for it."

It was in Stockholm that Don earned his first headlines by mixing straight playing with "jazz happenings" at Gyllene Cirkeln, a jazz restaurant. The happenings supposedly represented an acting out of something a musician might have thought or felt during the evening in relationship to what he had been playing. The concept was reflected in such gambits as using sticks on the piano, pouring salt into it, inflating and bursting paper bags, crawling around under the piano, or drawing a paintbrush across the strings.

Looking back at these attempts to become the John Cage of jazz, Don says, "I felt jazz musicians could do more than classical musicians. The idea was, everybody was too staid and stagnant, afraid to try new things. I never felt that Ornette Coleman was that new or radical.

"There was one happening called *The Death* in which we just stood around the piano looking at it. It was fascinating, because of the varying audience reactions; it was a dramatic thing.

"This was just something I wanted to try out, but I later found it didn't have enough substance to justify doing it over and over. Other areas were more fruitful."

Lalo Schifrin, the composer and pianist who collaborated with Ellis in an Improvisational Jazz Workshop in New York in 1963, had reservations about Don's motives for staging happenings. "Don was and is one of the most creative musicians on the scene," says Schifrin. "His imagination is just what jazz needs. However, sometimes he would become too bold, just to attract attention. I felt we were becoming too much actors, and for me this was not really art. Later I was pleasantly surprised to see Don come back to music. I guess he had just gone through a Dada period, like the French poets and painters in the 1920s."

In 1964 Don returned to Los Angeles, where he conducted workshops in improvisation and ensemble playing at UCLA. At this time a latent fascination with Indian music surfaced as he studied with the sitarist Hari Har Rao, who worked with him in a group they called the Hindustani Jazz Sextet. Next he formed a big workshop orchestra, the forerunner of his current band.

From the start the big group employed unconventional meters and instrumentation; Ellis added three drummers and a three-man bass section. The latter sometimes sawed away in somber unison but also were often used for intricate harmonic effects. His percussion section included cowbells, conga, cuica, and bongos, as well as conventional American drums. A later innovation was an attachment that can feed sound from Don's trumpet or any of the other horns to an elaborate amplifying system.

If the men have problems with a 5/8 or 9/4 beat, Ellis sits down with them and claps the part until everyone claps together. (Aware that drummers had difficulty learning to keep the odd time signatures, Don taught himself to play drums—"in self-defense, so I could demonstrate to my drummers how those meters went.") "He's a real teacher-preacher type personality," said Dave Wells. "I never saw Don lose his temper with the band. He covers up his emotions very well. When our morale was low, you can imagine how much this helped."

The Ellis initiative was forcefully demonstrated one night when the band arrived at the Havana Club where they were working, and found it padlocked: the owners had had a disagreement and closed it up. Ellis, unruffled, called up Walt Flynn, a trombonist friend, who was working at a Hollywood club called Bonesville. Within an hour the entire band followed Ellis into Bonesville, together with customers from the padlocked room.

"From that time on," says Ellis, "things began to pick up."

Stan Kenton, intrigued by the concept of offbeat time signatures, took Ellis under his wing. One evening in February

1966, Don brought the Hindustani Jazz Sextet to the Los Angeles Music Center. In an original work aptly entitled *Synthesis*, he grasped Kenton's entire mighty Neophonic Orchestra, stuffed it in his very hip pocket, and ran off with the show.

"We used two basic ragas," Ellis says, "with Hari Har Rao on sitar and tabla. I explained to the audience that the Indians have the most sophisticated rhythmic system in the world." He also used a jazz saxophonist, plus mallet and rhythm instruments, all fortified, of course, by the twenty-five towering neophonicists around them. The synthesis wound an idiomatic route from New Orleans to New Delhi, with brief European and African detours along the way.

The Kenton break set the ball in motion . . . now it was up to Ellis to keep it rolling. During the next few months he urged his Bonesville audiences to keep up a letter-writing campaign, pleading that the big band be introduced at Monterey. Festival chief Jimmy Lyons read the letters, heard the band, and gave his word that the deal was on. Meanwhile the fast-growing Bonesville movement took on the aspect of a cult.

On a typical Monday evening at Bonesville, Don's wife Connie sat by the entrance, ready to collect the $1.50 admissions. On the wall at her side was a placard advising the unaware that membership in the Don Ellis Jazz Society would entitle the joiner to such privileges as a reduced ($1) admission fee, a free brochure about Don and the band, an autographed photo of Don, and a free supply of "Where Is Don Ellis?" bumper stickers of the type that had publicized him at Monterey. It was 7:30. For the past hour the band had been running over some new charts. The concert was due to start at 8, but this was one of those nights when the early entrants would get in on the end of a rehearsal.

Ellis tried out a number he had scored for a vocal album. A songwriter friend had commissioned him to write arrangements of several of her tunes. After the first rundown, Ellis said, "All right, now let's transpose it from D minor to E minor, and then we'll try it in C minor, because one chick has a real low voice, and we don't know yet what singer is going to do this song or what her range will be." The band patiently went through the chart in all three keys, with Ellis taking the vocal on trumpet.

This done, Ellis looked around and, in a very even voice, said, "Are we having trouble getting blue shirts for Monday? It looks kinda nice, you know, blue shirts. Those wearing white tonight, what happened?"

An unintelligible mumble came from the three-fourths of the band members wearing white shirts. "Well," said Ellis, "make it blue every night from now on." A moment later he was busy explaining to a drummer how to get the right feeling into a 5/8 work.

By the time the rehearsal ended, the room, a sparsely decorated high-roofed bar with a seating capacity of three hundred, was half full. By the end of the first formal set, customers were standing in line outside.

After each number Ellis spoke to the crowd as if he were addressing an assemblage of loyal constituents. When he found himself becoming too technical in explaining the next number, he used a bit of humor to lighten things. For instance, after explaining a work written in a nineteen-beat meter and correspondingly titled "3-3-2-2-2-1-2-2-2," he added, "Of course, that's just the area code."

On the program that night was a composition by a Czech writer, Pavel Blatny. A couple of years before, Ellis had received a tape recorded by Blatny in Prague of an original work featuring a trumpet playing quarter-tones. "Blatny later sent me the music, then I persuaded a New York instrument manufacturer to make me a quarter-tone trumpet. I guess they were determined not to let the East beat out the West. Maybe some day I'll get a five-valve trumpet so that I can play eighth-tones."

Another finger-twisting feature of the opening set was a

boogie-woogie number conveniently shorn of one beat, which gave it a limping quality. Ellis called it "Beat Me Daddy, Seven to the Bar."

As the evening wore on, Ellis' announcements became more informal and engaging than ever. He announced his forthcoming appearance at Shelly's Manne Hole (the band's first full week anywhere). He plugged a benefit for an ailing musician. After dwelling on three or four more extraneous topics, he said, "Oh, yes, about this next tune. What did I say we were going to do?"

Early predictions of success have been borne out by Ellis' progress in the past five years. Don is very much involved now in all aspects of the music field. He led the all-star "dream band" at the Berlin Jazz Festivals in 1967 and 1968; at the 1968 Festival his cantata, *Reach*, was premiered. He has scored two motion pictures: *Moon Zero Two*, filmed in London and not released in the United States, and *The French Connection;* he also made a joint appearance with Zubin Mehta and the Los Angeles Philharmonic, playing Ellis' *Contrasts for Two Orchestra and Trumpet.*

Still as deeply concerned with teaching as with learning, Ellis has given courses at U.C.L.A. and San Fernando Valley State College. He has emphasized his role as a drummer, playing more frequently and studying with a private teacher.

The band, gaining substantially in public acceptance, has toured extensively and with notable success at colleges, and has played everywhere from the Ed Sullivan show to the Fillmore West (both of which it has fortunately survived). There has been a series of Columbia albums of variable merit. The band was nominated for a Grammy award by the Recording Academy for four consecutive years but has not yet won.

The Kenton analogy was brought to mind when, during Kenton's illness, Ellis substituted for him as leader for a week in the summer of 1971.

Of his own orchestra Ellis now says: "We went through a

heavy rock phase, but now we're getting into new colors. By early 1971 I felt I had explored as much as possible within the standard orchestral framework, even with the electronics; so I added a string quartet, which helped mellow the sound of the band when necessary, and transformed the saxes into a woodwind quartet. We don't need three bass players any more because everyone plays electric nowadays, so I switched to just one fender player. I'm enjoying all the challenges of this revised instrumentation.

"As for my political views, I don't consider myself a right-winger. I'm a radical for personal freedom and liberty. I'm disappointed in Nixon. He came in on one set of principles, then operated on another. Why, if a left-winger had made some of those same proposals, everybody would be up in arms!"

Nat Hentoff once pointed out that Ellis had done much to prove, by his own example, that musical freedom is increased rather than constricted by the acquisition of knowledge. It is safe to assume that in the years immediately ahead he will continue not only to acquire new knowledge but also to impart it to a growing audience wherever jazz is heard. Toward the end of the last decade I ventured a prophesy that Ellis would become the Stan Kenton of the 1970s. To a substantial degree that prediction has already been borne out, and I suspect, to paraphrase Goldwater, that in his heart Kenton knows this is right.

Tamas Breuer

Miles

MILES DEWEY DAVIS III has learned as well as any musician alive how to make music, women, money, and headlines, not necessarily in that order of importance but probably in that chronological sequence.

The various sobriquets he has acquired along the way— Prince of Darkness, Public Enigma No. 1—attest to his ability to build around himself an aura of cultism and mysticism.

He inspires young musicians who are awed by his presence, instills fear in the hearts of young secretaries at Columbia Records whom he has called white bitches, leaves reporters ignored or confused, talks in absolutes and with seemingly total conviction. His words are at variance with his actions, particularly in the area of race, and some of his statements are total contradictions of others.

He has been called bitter, hostile, bigoted, capricious, undependable, often by some of the same observers who at other times have found him shy, warm, generous, sensitive, and witty. After denouncing white American society, he has emulated its most materialistic values by acquiring all the appurtenances and luxuries his millions could bring him over the years: the $15,000 Ferrari; the $100,000 town house on West Seventy-Seventh Street; the vast Italian-style wardrobe, including compensatory high-heeled shoes.

Much has been made of his background: unlike most black

and many white musicians, he was born into a middle-class family with bourgeois values, and was urged by his mother to take up some genteel instrument such as the violin. That these advantages have not protected him from racism or other forms of dehumanization Davis considers irrelevant. "You don't know how to play better just because you've suffered," he says. "The blues don't come from picking cotton."

He is a maverick in much more than his social origins. It has been axiomatic through the history of jazz that once established, the great individual styles, whether conceived by Armstrong, Eldridge, Hawkins, Hodges, Young, Gillespie, or Peterson, have remained basically unchanged through the years, evolving only within the original framework. Gillespie solos recorded in 1945 and 1971 are clearly recognizable as the work of the same artist. Davis, on the other hand, has changed so radically that most listeners not familiar with all his work would refuse to believe that a recent solo, on one of his rock-dominated records, was played by the same trumpeter heard on, say, "Out of the Blue" in 1951.

Davis, for all his changes of direction, is today more than ever a player of unquestionable originality and has an almost hypnotic influence on his contemporaries, as Gillespie had in the 1940s. Miles was the first to make a definitive switch from trumpet to flügelhorn, an instrument that has since become a double for hundreds of trumpeters. He was the first to make use of modal themes, a development later associated more closely with John Coltrane, but actually dating back to the late 1950s when Coltrane was a sideman in Davis' group. Davis' early career found him as a bebopper who had listened closely to Clark Terry and Gillespie; in a second phase, as a central figure in the breakaway from bop to cooler and more orchestrated conceptions through his collaboration with Gil Evans, John Lewis, Gerry Mulligan, and others on the *Birth of the Cool* recordings (1949–50); in a third stage, as leader of various small bands, quintets and sextets, and overlapping the latter, as partner with Evans in a series of large-scale orchestral albums that are assured a permanent place in musical history. Still later came the first intimations of "space music," and not long afterward the flirtation with rock.

With each of these directional shifts in the group style came substantial changes in Davis' entire approach to the horn. According to him each new move has represented a step ahead, a development evolving directly out of the previous period. Other musicians are sharply divided concerning the accuracy of this self-analysis.

Davis revels in the present and eagerly courts the future; in effect, although at times he may deny it, he rejects his past.

LF: When you hear the old records you made with Gil Evans, or the combo albums when Herbie Hancock and Wayne Shorter were with you, how do they sound to you today?

MD: I don't listen to them.

LF: Is that because you no longer find anything interesting in them?

MD: The records sound funny to me.

LF: Wouldn't you advise young musicians to go through those stages first before getting to what you're into now? These guys that you have now, didn't they at one time play songs with definite beginnings and endings?

MD: Yeah, you have to come up through those ranks. They can always do that; but you don't hear anybody doing that old shit with me. You know, some guys are still playing all that shit we did years ago, things I did with Bird and stuff; they're still using those clichés and calling it jazz. Black guys as well as white guys. I hear it over and over again—shit that I've even forgotten.

LF: Well, that's natural, Miles, as long as they get into something eventually.

MD: No, it's not natural.

LF: You could just as well say that Dizzy is still playing the blues and "Night in Tunisia" and all those things. Does that make him inferior?

MD: How is he going to be inferior? How is he *ever* going to be inferior?

LF: That's what I mean. So why shouldn't he continue to go on like that as long as it's valid?

MD: He can do anything he wants to.

LF: Do you believe the era of the 12-bar blues and the 32-bar song is dead?

MD: No, you can add something to it. But when I write something, I don't think of anything I've ever heard. I don't try to be different; it's just that I figure, when whatever I wanted to write is finished, I stop. I don't count the bars. What's complete to me might not be complete to your ear; 'cause I never resolve anything that way. I hate to. But I'm not rejecting anything. You're not losing anything with what we're doing now; you're gaining everything you lost, because you heard all that other shit over and over again.

LF: A lot of young people haven't heard it. The kids that heard you at the Fillmore or Shelly's Manne Hole may not even know about the Gil Evans albums, let alone the Capitol albums. I think it's wrong that they should be unfamiliar with the important innovations of the past.

MD: There's so much more to music than just that. Like what I'm doing now, you know?

LF: I'm saying that they should also recognize what you did then, because you accomplished something that was important to you and to jazz at that time.

MD: I don't know whether they recognize it or not. Anyway everything that I do is recognized until somebody else does it.

This last observation is irrefutable. Whether or not today's rock fans are conscious of it, some part of each Davis contribution has eventually filtered through into the mainstream of jazz. This means that he has manifestly changed the entire course of an art form three or four times in twenty-five years—an accomplishment that no other jazz musician can claim.

The Davis family has to its credit at least three generations of impressive achievements. Miles Dewey Davis the First was a well-to-do black man who at one time owned 1,000 acres of land in Arkansas. Miles II became a substantial landowner himself in addition to pursuing a lucrative career as a dentist and detal sunrgeon. Miles Dewey Davis III was born May 25, 1926, in Alton, Illinois. Soon afterward the family moved to East St. Louis, where Miles II increased his wealth still further by breeding hogs.

Pride of family was a conspicuous trait in the Davis household. Doc Davis once said: "The Davises historically have always been musicians. I would have been one myself, but my father forbade me to play, because Negroes at that time could only play in barrelhouses. By genetics and breeding, Miles III is always going to be ahead of his time."

LF: How many were there in the family?

MD: I have an older sister, Dorothy; she's married. My brother, Vernon, was born in 1929.

LF: How old are your own children now?

MD: Cheryl is the oldest, then there's Gregory, and Miles. They're all in their twenties. I was married when I was sixteen. I have a grandson—he's five; he and Cheryl live in St. Louis.

LF: You were pretty close to your mother, weren't you?

MD: No, I've never been close to none of my family. Me and my mother fell out when I was thirteen. We were close at one time; we could talk to each other, but you know, I wasn't going to take none of that shit from her just because she was my mother.

LF: What kind of shit?

MD: Just real bullshit. It was a matter of either talk straight to me or not at all. When she did, we became real tight.

LF: How was your relationship with your father?

MD: Not bad. He just told my mother to leave me alone. He bought me a trumpet for my thirteenth birthday, and I'd only been playing two or three years when I had a chance to leave school and go on the road with Tiny Bradshaw's band. I went home and asked my mother . . . she said no, I had to finish my last year of high school. I didn't talk to her for two weeks.

LF: What advantages did growing up black and middle class give you over growing up black and poor?

MD: You're gonna run into that Jim Crow thing regardless of how wealthy you are. I can't buy no freedom. Having money has helped me once in a while, but I'm not looking for help. I'm even the one that's the helper, helping people by playing my music. There's no excuse for being poor anyway. You see, you're not supposed to wait on anybody to give you nothing. My father taught me that.

LF: How old were you when your parents separated?

MD: I don't remember, but I remember I sent my sister to school, to Fisk, when I was about sixteen—I was making $85 a week with Eddie Randall's band. That was just before I went to New York.

LF: How did you get along that far musically in just a couple of years?

MD: I just got onto the trumpet and studied and played. It would have been that or something else; a lot of black people think that to keep from being Jim Crowed and shit like that you have to be a professional man and know a little bit of something. But then if you want an engineer or an architect or something, who do you get? You don't go to a black man.

LF: Were there a lot of kids in school with you who became professionals?

MD: Yeah. One of them is going to run for Mayor of Compton, Cal. East St. Louis was so bad that it just made you get out and do somehing. . . . See, I believe if you don't go to school you can still educate yourself. I don't think you need formal schooling to get an education. There's always a library. You know, I can't *believe* the library they got in New York.

LF: Were you a good student?

MD: Well, I taught my sister mathematics. See, if I had a book, I could look at it and remember the whole page. It came to me like that. I can remember anything—telephone numbers, addresses. Even today I can just glance at them and remember. That's the reason I used to take care of band payrolls; I could remember all the tabs and shit.

Music was easy. When I was a kid, I was fascinated by the musicians, particularly guys who used to come up from New Orleans and jam all night. I'd sit there and look at them, watch the way they walked and talked, how they fixed their hair, how they'd drink, and of course how they played.

Then of course I played in the school band. Around that time I met Clark Terry. He was playing like Buck Clayton in those days, only faster. I started to play like him. I idolized him.

Clark Terry, five years Miles's senior, grew up across the river in St. Louis. "The first time I ever set eyes on Miles," says Terry, "was in Carbondale, Illinois. His music teacher, who was a drinking buddy of mine, had told me about him. 'I've got a little cat over there in East St. Louis who's a bitch,' he said. 'You really got to hear him.' I said OK, OK, I'd hear him sometime.

"Not long afterward I was working in a May Day affair when all the schools would compete against one another in athletics. He was in this school band, and he came up to me and very meekly said, 'Pardon me, Mr. Terry, but would you tell me something about the horn? I'd like to know how you do certain things.' And I was so preoccupied with all the beautiful schoolgirls around that I said, 'Why don't you get lost—stop bugging me,' which is something I never normally do. Miles was maybe fifteen then.

"A few months later, in St. Louis, I was on my way to an after-hours jam session at the Elks, a place with a long staircase. On the way up this long flight of stairs I heard this new sound, new trumpet. I thought I could recognize everybody's style, but this stumped me. So I walked up to the bandstand and there was this little fellow. I said, 'Hey, aren't you the cat I ran into at Carbondale?' And he said, 'Yeah, man, I'm the cat you fluffed off that night!' I was in the profession a long time before he was, and I guess he used to come across the bridge many times to listen to bands I was in. I know he credits me as his first influence and I'm flattered, because he's not a cat that passes out compliments too easily.

"He was a nice, quiet little kid then, and I think the changes in him are a cover-up. Deep down, basically, he's a beautiful cat. Many people have misunderstood him and don't know the true Miles.

"If he seems to go to great lengths to conceal it, he's probably been given a bad time by people who've mistreated him and he feels he doesn't have to accept these things anymore. I can understand this, because there were times in my own childhood when I was abused by Caucasians, so I could have all the reason in the world to be anti-Caucasian and make a career out of paying people back for things they've done to me. I've been attempted-to-be-lynched twice, and spat on, and had my clothes ripped off and been beaten, but I just refuse to lower myself to that level. Maybe many more things happened to Miles than to me, and some of them he just can't forget."

If Miles does not talk about childhood traumas, it is certainly not because they never existed. "One of the first things I can remember," he says, "was when I was a little boy and a white man was running down the street after me hollering, 'Nigger, nigger!' "

He is said to have been deeply hurt again when, living in a white neighborhood with his black middle-class parents, he was stopped by a white bigot who told him, "What you doin' here? This ain't no nigger street." Miles's father once told friends that his son would have won the first prize in the high school music competition, but traditionally whites had a hold on that honor.

Before leaving high school Miles had one brief fling in the big time, playing for three weeks as substitute for one of the regular trumpeters in the Billy Eckstine orchestra. This placed him in the exalted company of Dizzy Gillespie and Charlie Parker. (Eckstine recalls it differently: "When I first heard Miles, I let him sit in so as not to hurt his feelings, but he sounded terrible; he couldn't play at all.")

Mrs. Davis wanted her son to go to Fisk University, a predominantly black institution in Nashville, well known for its music department and renowned for having produced the Fisk Jubilee Singers. But Miles knew that this would be pointing him in the wrong direction for jazz. He opted for Juilliard and, with his father's blessing, headed for New York.

"I spent my first two weeks looking for Charlie Parker," he recalls. "That's who I wanted to learn from. I knew all that Juilliard shit already—I'd studied it all myself.

"Originally I went there to see what was happening but when I found out nothing was happening, I told my father to save his money. I stayed about a semester and a half. Shit, I did all the homework for summer school in one day."

"Isn't that," I suggested, "because you just naturally had a bright mind and a good feeling for it?"

"I had nothing on my mind but study. I wasn't even fuckin', man, you know?"

"I thought you said you were married when you came to New York."

"Yeah, but at that time she was pregnant."

Whatever the state of his education Davis soon drifted into the bustling Fifty-second Street scene of the mid-1940s and found a friend and sponsor in Charlie Parker. For a while they roomed together and Miles followed Bird around on gigs. "I'd make notes of the chords and stuff I was hearing, write 'em down on matchbooks, then next day at Juilliard, instead of going to class, I'd spend all my time trying out those chords."

Before long Davis was out of Juilliard for good and a regular member of Parker's quintet. As the early recordings show, his technique still had a long way to go; he had little control in the upper register and often fluffed in the middle. Over the years an elliptical sense of self-editing developed that enabled him to play less yet say more.

As a close associate of Parker he was inevitably brought into contact with the drug scene, yet to most observers around Fifty-second Street he was the abstemious, mild-mannered youth who neither smoked nor drank. A year or two elapsed before he became a part of the narcotics world. Heroin was then rampant among the young beboppers, but Miles, to all outward appearances, remained cool, taking care of business on the Bird job and subsequently with Coleman Hawkins' small band, on the road with Benny Carter's orchestra and with Billy Eckstine. By this time he was so improved, Eckstine says, that he was able to take over the parts previously played by Gillespie. He stayed with Eckstine until the band broke up in 1947, later working in the singer's small combo. It was during this period that he made headlines with his first arrest for possession.

"As strong as that man may seem to be outwardly," says Harry "Sweets" Edison, "his inward character may be a little weak just one time, and that's all it takes."

Although his private life was to remain chaotic for several years, Miles continued to progress as he became part of a workshop band, one that involved the use of two instruments never before heard in the new jazz, French horn and tuba.

"Gil Evans and I spent the better part of one winter hashing out the instrumentation for that nine-piece band," Gerry Mulligan once recalled. "But Miles dominated the band completely; the whole nature of the interpretation was his."

Miles's version of the band's evolution was predicated on his desire to play with "a light sound . . . because I could think better when I played that way. Gerry said to get Lee Konitz on alto because he had that light sound too. That whole thing started out as just an experiment; then Monte Kay booked us into the Royal Roost on Broadway for two weeks.

"As for that *Birth of the Cool* shit, I don't understand how they came to call it that. Someone just dropped that label on me. I think what they really mean is a soft sound—not penetrating too much. To play soft you have to relax . . . you don't delay the beat, but you might play a quarter triplet against four beats, and that *sounds* delayed. If you do it right, it won't bother the rhythm section."

The nine-piece band was short-lived, lasting for two public appearances and three recording dates, but it marked the beginning of the close, enduring friendship and association between Miles and Gil Evans. It was to bring out in Davis a lyricism, a soaring and ecstatic sound for which Evans provided the perfect setting.

"Gil has a way of voicing chords and using notes like nobody else," said Miles. "We work together great because he writes the way I'd like to write. In fact, years ago I used to do arrangements and give them to him to look over. He'd tell me my charts were too cluttered up, that I could get the same effect using fewer notes.

"Finally I decided the best thing to do was let Gil do the writing. I'd just get together with him—sometimes not even in person, just on the phone—and outline what I wanted. And he always has such a complete feeling for what I mean that it comes out sounding exactly like what I had in mind."

For younger jazz fans who know Davis only from his recent work, an entire new-old horizon may be opened up by the endless mixture of orchestral sounds, and the stark, mournful spareness of Davis' horn, in such masterpieces as *Miles Ahead, Porgy and Bess,* and *Sketches of Spain.* Davis and Evans were reunited in parts of the *Miles at Carnegie Hall* album and on a later LP called *Quiet Nights,* but the first three are the definitive works. (All five are still available on Columbia.)

Miles's career might have gained immediate momentum after the *succès d'estime* of the first (Capitol) collaboration with Evans, but the narcotics habit proved a formidable roadblock, wrecking his home life, limiting his musical development, and reducing him at times to a near-derelict.

"I remember one day on Broadway," says Clark Terry, "I

found him sitting in front of one of those ham-and-eggs places. He was just wasted, actually sitting by the gutter. I asked him what was wrong and he said, 'I don't feel well.' After buying him some ham and eggs I took him around to my hotel, the America on West Forty-seventh Street. I was getting ready to leave on the bus with Basie's band, and I told him, 'You just stay here, get some rest, and when you leave just close the door.'

"The bus waited longer than I'd expected, so I went back to the room. Miles had disappeared, the door was open, and all my things were missing.

"I called home, St. Louis, and told my wife to call Doc Davis to see if he could get Miles, because he was obviously in bad shape and had become the victim of those cats who were twisting him the wrong way. And you know what? Doc Davis was very indignant. He told her, 'The only thing that's wrong with Miles now is because of those damn musicians like your husband that he's hanging around with.' He was the type of guy who believed his son could do no wrong. So he didn't come to get him."

As Miles found himself facing a bleak future, it became a case of physician's son, heal thyself. "It took me four years to break the habit," he told an *Ebony* reporter. "I just made up my mind I was getting off dope. I was sick and tired of it. You can even get tired of being scared. I laid down and stared at the ceiling for twelve days and cursed everybody I didn't like . . . I lay in a cold sweat . . . I threw up everything I tried to eat . . . then it was over." He had kicked the hard way—cold turkey.

Nonetheless illness continued to plague him. He had an operation for nodes on the throat. Warned by a doctor not to use his voice for a while, he began speaking too soon; as a result he was reduced to the famous whisper that has become chronic, a source of psychological and physical discomfort, and a subject he prefers to avoid.

The post-heroin years marked the start of an invigorated,

productive phase. In addition to the large orchestral ventures with Evans, he headed a series of combos, each of which had its own catalytic effect on jazz.

In 1955, at the Newport Jazz Festival, he earned a rousing reception, scoring most strongly with a down-home swinging blues called "Walkin'." The recorded version of this number, on Prestige, became a classic. In the view of many critics it set the pace for a trend away from the cool phase, which Davis himself had done so much to initiate, into a period of funkier and more aggressive music. Even more influential was his *Kind of Blue* album, recorded after his switch to Columbia Records. Three members of the sextet heard on that LP were to develop as individual forces on disparate levels of jazz creativity: John Coltrane, who took Miles's modal pioneering many steps further and blended it with other idioms; Cannonball Adderley, and Bill Evans. (The other definitive unit flourished in the mid-1960s with Wayne Shorter, Herbie Hancock, and Tony Williams, all of whom also subsequently became leaders.)

"While I was in the band," Coltrane said, "I found Miles in the midst of a new stage of musical development. It seemed that he was moving to the use of fewer and fewer chord changes in songs. He used tunes with free-flowing lines and chordal direction. I found it easy to apply my own harmonic ideas . . . I could play three chords at once; but if I wanted to, I could play melodically. Miles's music gave me plenty of freedom."

Davis' method of assembling cohesive groups of major artists, usually finding them at the most crucial points in their evolution, is deceptively casual. Herbie Hancock, whose case is typical, recalls their first meeting, when Donald Byrd took him to the Davis house.

"I was introduced to Miles as Donald's new piano player. Donald said, 'Herbie, why don't you play something?' So I sat down and played a ballad. Miles said, 'He's got a nice touch.' And that was that until the following year, when he called me up and asked me to come over to his house.

"Tony Williams was there, and Ron Carter and George Coleman. I knew he was looking for a new group, so I figured this was an ·audition. We concentrated on one tune, "Seven Steps to Heaven." The next day we rehearsed some of Miles's older things but concentrated on a second tune. Miles didn't even play. He just came downstairs with me, said something to George, and then went back upstairs. I guess maybe he turned on the intercom and was listening to us.

"The next day, as I heard later, Miles called up Gil Evans and Philly Joe Jones and said, 'Hey, come over and listen to my new band.' On the third day Miles came downstairs and played a couple of notes, but he soon went back up. After we finished running things down, I'm still thinking that I'm auditioning, so Miles comes downstairs and says, 'You have to be at Columbia studios tomorrow afternoon at two.'

"It took me completely by surprise. I said 'Wait a minute —what? I thought you were auditioning. Are we recording tomorrow?' He said, 'Yeah.' I said, 'Does that mean that I'm in the group, or what?' He said, 'You're making the record, ain't you?'

"I left his house floating on a cloud. Just through that off-hand conversation, I had a job that turned out to last five years and then enabled me to go out on my own."

During the incumbency of Hancock, Wayne Shorter (who replaced George Coleman), Williams, and Carter, Miles veered further and further away from his 1950s concept of playing structured popular songs and jazz standards. Although he continued for some time to hold on to " 'Round Midnight" and a couple of others, most of the themes now were freer and more adventurous works written by members of the group. They became points of departure for displays of intracommunication that were tantamount to ESP—which logically became the title number of a 1965 album. Performances became longer as Davis pioneered in the concept of segueing from one theme and mood to another, so that an entire set at a club or concert would be a continuum.

Working at an ever-higher level of abstraction the quintet became more completely an expression of the leader's dominant personality as key sidemen left. The use of electric keyboards and bass, and of two or three percussion instruments, expanded the compass of the music still further. The switch from a floating, free rhythm to the incorporation of rock became a controversial element but one Davis sincerely believed in.

Herbie Hancock points out: "Miles has been going in his present direction ever since the time when I jumped on the electric piano. Back in 1968 the album *Miles in the Sky* had a hint of rock. The next year *In a Silent Way* showed the shape of things to come with its two or three electric keyboards. The essential difference was in the rhythmic complexity. *Bitches' Brew*, which shook everyone up in 1970, was totally different from *In a Silent Way*, yet you can hear the parallel; it blended all the complexities of the new modern jazz with an underlying rock beat.

"The next album, *Miles at the Fillmore,* showed how much he can be fed musically not only by his musicians but by the whole environment, the vibes of the people. This is something I totally respect. . . . But of course it didn't sound like John Mayall at the Fillmore or anyone else at the Fillmore. Miles was still playing Miles.

"The value of what Miles is doing now is that he is, in effect, setting up a criterion of excellence in the direction of rock that nobody else has achieved, in terms of instrumental efficiency, interaction, and all of those things that just hadn't happened too much in rock before.

"I realize that a lot of people were turned off by the strong rock element, especially in the sound track of the film he did, *Jack Johnson*, which was pretty much straight rock with Miles thrown on top. Obviously this has to be controversial to many of the people that were into his music during his traditional jazz days, but then periods shouldn't be compared. I don't think people should expect him to go back and play 'Stella by Starlight' again because it would only inhibit the direction he's going in.

"Sure, the best of music is timeless. But to the artist who is performing it the music has to be a reflection of where he is at any given moment, and where he is depends on the individual. Say, in the case of Oscar Peterson, there is a certain predictability about his playing, but his growth seems to be internal, whereas Miles's is external. There's room for both attitudes."

Hancock's view of Davis is of course an inside glimpse, offered by a musician who for years was an integral part of his music. Those on the outside have mixed reactions, especially musicians who were once regarded as Miles's main influences.

"I have listened to those recent albums time after time," says Dizzy Gillespie, "until I started getting cohesions. The guy is such a fantastic musician that I know he has something in mind, whatever it is. I know he knows what he's doing, so he must be doing something that I can't get to yet.

"He played some of it for me, and he said, 'How do you like that shit?' I said, 'What is it?' and he said, 'You know what it is; same shit you've been playing all the time,' and I said, 'Have I?' I said, 'Look, I'm going to come by your house and spend several hours and you're going to explain to me what that is.' But we never did get together. I'm sure he could explain it to me musically, though of course you can't explain anything emotionally.

"Miles should be commended for going off in a completely new direction, he's just as brave as shit. That's what it is, stark stone bravery, to have something that his fans all over the world liked so much, and then turn around and go on an altogether different course. Shit, I don't think I got that much guts. Sometimes I find myself playing those same old licks I used to play, till I get stale as a motherfuck. When I play something exactly the same way I did it some other time, I figure, 'Oh shit, you're getting lazy.' But I can no more change my spots. . . . Miles can, though.

"He has a knack of grabbing one of those notes in the

chord, like, suppose you have a B flat minor sixth chord with a C in the bass, Miles would stop on an A flat or something like that—and hold it! He picks the dynamic notes to lay back on. He had the same thing going on in *Bitches' Brew;* he had a blues thing going, and he grabbed one of those notes, and when the chord changed he grabbed one of those other strange ones and held it.

"Whether it'll last, what he's doing now, that's not up to me to judge. You can't judge your contemporaries; you can only say what strikes you at the moment, but you can't assess the validity of the message. Time alone judges that, so I just sit here and wait until . . . well, if he's hooked that far in front, wait for time to catch up with it. Because I had the same experience with Ornette Coleman until somebody gave me an album one day and I sat down and really listened. I used to make jokes, like I'd say, 'Ladies and gentlemen, we're going to play "Hot House" and Ornette is going to play "Night in Tunisia" at the same time.' But now I realize he had something to build on.

"Miles has even more to build on. Not only has he got me and Yardbird and Freddie Webster and whoever else inspired him, he's also got himself, to reach back and get different things. The guy's a master, so I wouldn't come out and say that I don't like what he's doing now.

"Besides, it would be out of line. Could the King of England criticize the King of France?"

Gillespie's comments may subconsciously reflect an attitude that has been lucidly explained by Herbie Hancock.

"People become accustomed to a style that's been associated with a certain individual," he says, "so when they want to hear his music, they listen with these preconceptions. This is the wrong way to go about getting involved with anything. You're better off, listening to any music, not expecting anything, because the artist you listen to may be a completely different person when you confront him at a different time. Miles is a perfect case in point. There might be a particular area of his development that you prefer, but if you walk in looking for it, you'll be disappointed. If you just go in saying, 'Let me near what's going to happen,' then you can be objective and dig what the man's output is for its own self."

Other Davis-watchers take the position that his change in direction has been at least partially pragmatic.

"I can understand exactly why he's doing these things," says Clark Terry. "Miles is the kind of man who has always wanted to stay abreast of the times. He's smart enough to realize that this is what people are buying, and if this is what they're buying, why shouldn't he sell some of it?

"Maybe he's doing it sincerely, but I do know that it's a much more lucrative direction for him. I happen to know that there was a period when in spite of all his many possessions—investments, home, car—there was a period when he needed to bolster these; he really needed to get into a higher financial bracket. And there was an opportunity for him to get into this kind of thing, so he took the opportunity to jump out and do it.

"I don't know whether or not I'm musically mature enough to understand it. I do know that there are people in that area who are incompetent, and it's an avenue where they can parallel people like Miles who have studied and worked hard. Others can reach this point through a short-cut method. Nobody could do that when Miles was playing more lyrically. I loved him much more at that time, when he was more in depth as far as chord structures and progressions. Ain't nobody around can play more melodically than Miles when he wants to. In a sense it's a waste to see him not using all his knowledge."

I asked Terry, "What do you think people hear in it that is making him so successful in widening his audience?"

"What they hear in it is less significant than what they don't hear. What they don't hear, because it's not there, is the real balls of jazz, the chord progressions, the structures, and so forth. They are not musically mature enough to cope with this and Miles is smart enough to put something where they can reach it on their own level. If they're not hip enough to know what's happening—say, the way Miles was playing with Bird years ago, with swinging groups—if they're not hip enough to grasp that type of thing, they're going to grasp whatever is simple enough for them to cop. And the simple thing for them to cop happens to be that one-chord modal bag that is so fashionable."

Other trumpeters of Terry's generation share his viewpoint. "I guess he's trying to change with the times," says Harry "Sweets" Edison, "but personally I liked the way he sounded when he had Philly Joe Jones, Cannonball, Wynton Kelly, and Paul Chambers, around 1956—that was a magnificent bunch of musicians.

"I listened to him on *Bitches' Brew* and there was just too much going on for me to really enjoy his playing. I don't think a man of his distinctive ability needs to do that kind of thing. Also, Miles is such a good writer, but what he's doing now doesn't sound like he's putting into it all that he's capable of.

"I'm not going to underestimate him; I'm sure he's true to his own convictions, but I feel he could still play the way he played years ago, with the same feeling, and people would appreciate it."

Quincy Jones, the composer and former trumpeter, who has known Davis for twenty years, has made a close analytical study of Miles's progress. "When we were kids," he says, "we all ran around with a notebook copying off all the Miles and Bird solos. Most of us didn't jump on Dizzy, though, because he was just too much to try to emulate, so we'd try to grab hold of Miles.

"Miles has always been concerned with growth, with perfecting one thing and then taking on a new challenge. That's what keeps you feeling young, man. Nobody wants to stay the same."

Asked whether he felt that to retain one's basic image was less important for an artist than the continual development of new identities as in Davis' case, Jones replied: "I think you have to trust that same mojo that led you into the first style, and go from there. It's fortunate that Miles is flexible enough to have given us the kind of contrast that separates *Miles Ahead* from *Jack Johnson*. I think he's blessed, to have that scope, that range."

Recently, as Jones points out, there has been a curious shift of focal points in the thrust of the new jazz. "A decade or two back, the velocity and animation were usually carried by the melodic instruments on top, while the rhythm section laid down the bass like a canvas, remaining essentially a time-keeping device. But in the last few years that has been reversed. Any record you hear now, the horns almost have to play time, because the complexity has moved to the basement now, and you can't take that kind of complexity on top with what the fender bass players are doing nowadays. Too many passing notes. If you play too many alterations in the top, it cancels out the freedom in the bottom.

"With this change of roles, I think Miles is trying to see what his same lyrical and innovative mind can do. We know it's the same guy, so we have to trust our group leader. He's putting himself on a different menu, and I dig it. Every step he has made, he's always been right, and always ahead of his time, so I think we'll end up in good shape.

"I think we can expect further changes. At some point he may decide, 'Hey, the rhythm section I used on *Bitches' Brew* and *Jack Johnson* was too loud,' and he'll use his wah-wah pedal and amplifier on the trumpet to match it; or he might say, 'What if we dropped the volume of everything down,' and he might bring more lyricism in. Anything can happen."

Herbie Hancock concurs. "The music of the past is not necessarily old hat, but I can understand how Miles feels, because people come up to me and ask me to play 'Watermelon Man' and that's not where I'm at now, I don't want to play it. Miles isn't up there to please everybody, or anybody. He's there to be honest, that's all; and he has to be taken for what he is."

Miles Davis remains seemingly impervious to the controversy that surrounds him. He has often been quoted as indifferent to criticism and has claimed he never reads anything that is written about him, yet there have been many cracks in the wall he has built around himself. One review (of a record made during his appearance at a rock festival on the Isle of Wight) clearly got through to him. From Milan he called the *Melody Maker* in London: "What kind of man can call me arrogant? I know where you're at. You shouldn't be a critic. You are a white man looking for white excitement, but there are more subtle forms of excitement." He went on to express contempt for the entire rock scene.

Obsessed with what seems to him to be a necessity to analyze everything in racial terms, he once told Don DeMichael, in a *Rolling Stone* interview: "Rock is social music. There's two kinds—white and black—and those bourgeois spades are trying to sing white and the whites are trying to sound colored. It's embarrassing. It's like me wearing a dress." One wonders to what extent his rebellion against the "bourgeois spade" background (that is, his own parentage) is conscious. One wonders too how he explains the fact that many of the early rock groups to which he gave serious attention (Jimi Hendrix, Sly & The Family Stone) were racially integrated.

Whatever his true feelings about the rock of whites and bourgeois blacks, he has made a palpable and self-admitted attempt to compete with the rock musicians on their own level. On listening to a record by Cream, he said: "They sure play loud. If they're gonna play loud, I'm gonna plug into an amplifier too." It was one more psychological step toward the Fillmore and the Isle of Wight.

The reception of Davis by rock fans has varied quite conspicuously from job to job. At the Hollywood Bowl in 1970 his group was the supporting attraction in a program starring

The Band. The latter was wildly received; Miles, opening the show, played continuously for forty-five minutes and walked off to tepid applause.

His own analysis of the stage at which his music had arrived around the turn of the decade is essentially that it does not call for analysis.

"See, Leonard, what you're missing, I'm not doing anything, it doesn't need an explanation. I'm reacting to what's been done and what's supposed to be happening today. Everything you've ever heard, all that shit is condensed, you know? All the clichés are so condensed that you can play 'Body and Soul' in two bars.

"If some musicians don't understand it, they just don't have that kind of an ear. Everybody I get is special. If I wanted to play songs that have a definite beginning and an ending, all that calls for is an ordinary working musician. Keith Jarrett, Jack De Johnette, all the guys I've used have changed the whole style of music today. You should know that.

"You ought to try playing some of the things we do. I could show you how. The other day I wrote down some chords and stuff for George Wein to play, and I had him playing like Keith!

"You know what I don't like? It's the playing between solos. They don't blend or nothing . . . In my group we play a lot of polyrhythms and everything, you know, a lot of different keys off of keys and scales off of scales. You ought to study it.

"I know you wrote that my group is loud. Well, that's just the times we live in. Everything is loud; everything gets higher. You take a symphony orchestra. You cannot write for two violins. You can't hear that shit. How many do they use? Dozens. They don't use one bass fiddle—they use twelve. It's the same thing. Anyhow, I still play way down sometimes, but you can hear it—every note.

"One of the things you learn in my group is, you leave drummers alone, 'cause drummers have their own inside thing.

And do like I did Herbie Hancock, take out all those fat chords and shit. And Keith—I just put him at the piano and let him go. Keith wasn't playing like that before he joined me.

"A lot of what we have in the group has been developed in clubs. I love the possibility of just freaking off on your horn in a nightclub. In Shelly's I really found out something. Actually it was a learning period in there, when I played everything and made the band play everything they could possibly play.

"That's what's good about working clubs. You play a first set, OK; second set, OK; third set, OK—and they're playing what they know, right? Then the last set they start playing what they *don't* know; which is out of sight! They start thinking, which is worth all the money in the world to me. Thrills me.

"I worked Shelly's just to help keep the place open. I lost about ten pounds in that motherfucker. I made $4,000 a week there, but I went in weighing 139 and came out weighing 129. Then I was asked to play Boston and I said to myself, if I go to Boston I'll weigh 121. I haven't worked since. That was three, four months ago.

LF: What was all the talk in the press about your retiring?

MD: What I meant was, I got a tour in Europe. I'll make about $300,000 on it. Then I won't work again until the spring and I'll make a spring tour. No more week here and three weeks off and a week there. I'm through with that shit.

LF: How about festivals?

MD: I don't care. They're all such bullshit. Just one-job things.

LF: How are you going to keep your men together?

MD: I can always get a group. The men I need, I can keep on salary while I'm laying off.

LF: Will you ever again do anything like you did with Gil Evans? Or have you put all that behind you?

MD: I can't get with that. But we have a new instrumentation for a big band that's outa sight.

LF: What does it consist of?

MD: If I tell you that, every motherfucker will be copying it. Quincy would be the first one. Quincy's always trying to pick my mind.

The slighting reference to Jones is indicative of Davis' attitude toward an overwhelming majority of musicians in every field. In judging others he cannot overcome the temptation to expect them to measure up to his own levels of originality, proficiency, and sophistication. This leaves him with very little outside the purlieus of his own music that he can enjoy and respect without reservation.

His assessment of pop and rock stars vacillates according to his moods. He has often pointed out that rock musicians are limited by their lack of harmonic knowledge and generally poor technical musicianship. He has made mildly complimentary remarks about Crosby, Stills, Nash & Young, and The Who. Concerning Blood, Sweat & Tears he has blown hot and cold. On one occasion he called the group "a pretentious imitation of me and Gil Evans," but at another point he declared that B S & T was "the only group I know that really gives people [at the Fillmore] something musically." Asked to name his preferences in the field of pop composing, he said: "Elton John and James Taylor write good songs. Valerie Simpson writes good songs."

In the fall of 1971 Miles was in Los Angeles for several weeks. As he does wherever he goes, he spent much of his time in a local gym. He has been on a serious health kick for several years, has his own personal trainer, and a white terry cloth robe with his name emblazoned on the back. Proud of his physique, he thinks nothing of working out with a heavy speed bag, sparring for several rounds, skipping rope, then doing as many as a hundred or more pushups and situps.

In his spare time he might be found watching ball games on a small black-and-white television set in his room at the Chateau Marmont, overlooking Sunset Boulevard. This fading relic of the old Hollywood is his home whenever he visits the

West Coast. One afternoon, after dispatching his lissome girl friend on a shopping tour, he was in the mood to talk about his contemporaries, his social attitudes, and his plans, such as they were, for the future.

LF: What live music have you heard lately that impressed you?

MD: I never go out to nightclubs any more. When I go, I know what to expect. It's what I can hear in my head without going.

LF: Are you going to hear Herbie Hancock's group at Donte's?

MD: I don't want to hear it. I can't even listen to that, as much as I love to hear Herbie play. I can't stand the trombone . . . and Eddie Henderson—I just don't like to hear trumpet players that keep playing like Freddie Hubbard. You know, it's the way you look at something happen that enables you to be your own self, if you're not lazy. It's easy to play a cliché. A cliché should be your musical foundation, but it shouldn't be what you do.

LF: What do you think of Tony Williams' group?

MD: Tony needs somebody to solo, other than himself. Larry, the organist, he's all right, but you know, you shouldn't bother a soloist. Like, I never bother Keith. Sooner or later Tony will get tired of not hearing what he wants to hear.

LF: What does the music of Pharoah Sanders say to you?

MD: It doesn't say anything to me, because Pharoah's not doing anything.

LF: How about Ornette Coleman?

MD: If you hear a guy, he has to be with someone that's right for him. Like, I heard a white guy with Buddy Miles, and the way Buddy plays, the white boy was playing out of sight. Now if he was playing with another white boy playing drums, he wouldn't sound like that. When Ornette was playing with Leroy Vinnegar and Billy Higgins everybody was together. But I don't know *what* he's doing now.

You know, the horn doesn't sound like it's supposed to sound. To me it's not the right background. So I check him out, and if he doesn't have the right background he's a sad mother-fucker. And he's not a trumpet player. That's something that takes years to develop. As for his violin playing, he's not going to scare Ray Nance.

LF: Have you listened to the Joe Henderson combo?

MD: Joe Henderson can play his ass off. He used to play with me. But in general there ain't much happening that I want to hear. All the groups are trying to play like somebody I know. I don't want to hear clichés: I don't want to get back into the past. What's important is what's happening now, the new music and the music of the future. I don't even want to think about what I was doing myself last year.

LF: Haven't you heard any rock groups that interested you?

MD: I haven't heard anything coming from the white kids with the long hair and shit. I like to hear the Motown sound and James Brown, them funky singers.

LF: You put it on a racial basis, yet some of your most re-warding associations have been interracial.

MD: You don't understand. What I want to hear doesn't come from a white musician.

LF: Including Gil Evans, Bill Evans, Dave Holland?

MD: No, I don't mean like that. What I want to hear, like rhythm and blues, it comes from black musicians all the time.

When you get guys that aren't prejudiced, like Joe Zawinul and John McLaughlin, I hardly ever look at their skin; they don't make me look at their skin. But when I hear a rhythm section with Tony or Jack on drums, or Buddy Miles, they do some shit that you just don't find in a white drummer.

A choreographer I know went to Africa with Harry Bela-fonte; he tried to copy some of the dances to bring them back to teach, and he said he just couldn't break it down. And he's a hell of a choreographer. It's something they have that you just can't figure out, it's a natural thing.

LF: Do you think you can tell from listening to a record whether a musician is black or white?

MD: I think you could. I still can.

LF: Would you like to do a blindfold test to prove it?

MD: If I happen to be driving along some place and I hear something—not something that you put on—if I hear something, if I say he's white, he's white; you can bet your money on it.

LF: Suppose it's a mixed group?

MD. What difference does it make anyway?

LF: You said you could tell the difference.

MD: It's because I'm black, Leonard. I'm not white. I wouldn't turn on Al Hirt, but a white guy would.

LF: I wouldn't turn on Al Hirt's show, and it's not because I'm white or black. On the other hand, if it were the Bobby Hackett show you'd turn it on.

MD: Not necessarily . . . If Herbie Hancock was on television at the same time as Al Hirt, who do you think I'd turn on?

LF: Who do you think *I'd* turn on?

MD: You'd turn on Herbie.

LF: Damn right I would, and not because of black or white, because he's a better musician.

MD: Why do you say Herbie's a better musician than Al Hirt?

LF: A musician who appeals to me more. Beg your pardon. (It had slipped my mind that a few years ago, Miles had told me: "Al Hirt is a very good trumpet player; and he's a nice guy. It's a shame they made him into a television personality —fat and jolly and bearded and funny. I guess if he was thin he wouldn't have to do it. Harry James is a good trumpet player, and he never did no shit like that." Still respectful of Hirt's musicianship, Miles was taking exception to my simplistic "better musician" explanation.)

MD: Herbie Hancock would be good for a TV program. He's the most patient guy I've ever seen. He plays all kinds of styles; and he's a nice-looking guy too, you know? Why shouldn't he have his own show?

What I'm saying is, it's not just Al Hirt, I mean because a guy is white, white people will follow him. You understand?

LF: Some white people will follow him.

MD: I'm not saying all this to be the great black father. I'm just saying that our roots are black and that's where they'll remain, and I can't help it.

When I hear a white guy, or when I look at a white girl that's supposed to be attractive, I don't feel the same thing that a white person would feel. I can understand a white girl seeing a white guy, and her screaming because she's white. But if I see a black girl screaming over a white guy . . . I'm just saying their roots won't let 'em do certain things.

There are mixed marriages that work. I'm not talking about that shit. I'm just saying that white people cater to white people and black people cater to black people. It's just a normal thing. One dog will fuck another dog.

LF: Don't you nevertheless believe that integration is the ultimate solution?

MD: I don't know whether it is or not. I think things will just come. If they work, fine. If they don't work, we just gotta accept it. You see black kids and white kids playing together, and they don't get fucked up until older people come in. Interracial couples, when they dig each other, they dig each other; it's just that outside pressure.

LF: Your ideal world basically is still an integrated world, isn't it?

MD: Right. But I think it won't work . . . Most black people would like to see everybody integrated, you know? A lot of black people want to be like white people; they think there's a level that they should be on, that white people have a level that they want to try to reach. That's sad, you know?

People can live together, but all that old shit hasn't stopped. As long as they keep on showing Army films with an all-white Army, it's not going to stop. That's a joke.

They fucked my son Gregory around, man; he went into the Army. He had to knock out a couple of white guys in St. Louis. He said, "Father, I'm going in the Army, and when I come back, if they start any shit, I'm not responsible."

LF: The Army gave him a very bad time?

MD: Shit yes, they Jim Crowed him in Germany. He's a fighter, you know, he won four titles. He brought back all those trophies. He can break your fucking neck and not even think nothing of it. He's not afraid of nothing. He would say it was supposed to be broken. He's a Muslim. He just wants to learn black things.

I can understand how he feels. If a white man bothers me, man, I don't want to touch him because I don't know what I might do. I might kill him.

Davis' need to keep his cool was never more frighteningly illustrated than in an incident that took place on a hot summer night in 1959, when his group was playing Birdland. After escorting a young white girl out of the club to a taxi, he was standing on the sidewalk when a patrolman came by and asked him to move on. When Miles said, "I'm not going nowhere— I'm just getting a breath of fresh air," the patrolman threatened to arrest him. Miles said, "Go ahead, lock me up." When the patrolman seized his arm, a scuffle ensued during which a plainclothes detective passing by began hitting Miles with a blackjack. With blood dripping all over his clothes, he was taken to the police station where, with his distraught wife, Frances, at his side, he was booked on charges of disorderly conduct and assault. At a hospital, ten stitches were taken in his scalp. After a lengthy series of legal maneuvers, a three-judge panel ruled that the Davis arrest had been illegal and the charge against him was erased. Miles decided to sue the city, but eventually dropped the whole matter in disgust. At the time of the incident he commented that it might never have happened if the girl he was escorting to the cab had been black.

LF: Have you been practicing while you've been out here?

MD: Uh-uh.

LF: Aren't you afraid your chops won't be up when you start again?

MD: Hell, I've been playing since I was thirteen. The older I get, the stronger I get. I still have the same mouthpiece I had when I was thirteen.

LF: Do you still have the urge to play, to be creating right now?

MD: I *never* have the urge to play; just sometimes when I hear something, I want to play with it.

LF: That's liable to continue as long as you live.

MD: That's what I'm saying.

LF: As long as there's something around that you can hear and want to be part of, then, you're not going to be just doing nothing.

MD: Right.

LF: The big difference between you and someone like Diz is that he will sit in with any kind of a band, Dixieland or whatever, but you still have your own thing that you want to play with.

MD: Diz may do that, but he won't stay there a long time.

LF: No, he just likes the change of pace.

MD: Right.

LF: With your children gone and no wife, don't you miss having a family around you?

MD: I don't believe in families. Like, if I die, my money ain't going to go to people just because they're close relatives. The people that are closest to me are the ones that helped me be able to do what I do, not just because somebody's my brother. If I had a lot of money, I wouldn't leave everything to my brother or sister just because they're related to me.

LF: Don't you feel close to your daughter or your grandson?

MD: No, I don't. Do you?

LF: I have no grandson, but I feel close to my daughter. I think most people feel a closeness because of family ties.

MD: Family ties are a lot of bullshit. That's what's fucking up this world. Sitting down at tea and all that shit. It doesn't go that way. In the first place, who wants to eat that much?

LF: That's not your nature, Miles, come on! If your daughter were sick and needed you, you'd go out and help her.

MD: Help her do *what?* No, man, that ain't nothing. If you said, "Miles, I need $500," and I had it, I'd send it to you, because that's the way I am. Money ain't shit, if it helps you and I don't need it for anything else, why shouldn't I send it to you?

LF: I don't see how I would deserve it.

MD: I mean I don't have anything for my family. I don't live for my family, I live for myself.

LF: But logically that should apply to your marriages too. Why did you get married if you don't believe in families?

MD: Because they asked me. Every woman I ever married asked me.

LF: Why didn't you have the strength of will to say no?

MD: Because I figured it'd make them happy.

LF: You just made an admission. You're willing to do something to make somebody happy.

MD: Of course!

LF: That's the same thing I was asking about your daughter.

MD: That's not what I'm saying, Leonard. I didn't say I wouldn't go out there. If she had any trouble I'd go out there to see what was wrong with her. I still don't have any family ties. If one of them would die or anything, I don't know how I would act; you wouldn't see me acting like they do on television. When my mother was sick I went to see her in the hospital; I knew she was dying of cancer. But when she died I didn't go to the funeral.

LF: What do you want to be doing ten years from now?

MD: Nothing. If I don't have a deal that is lined up like I want it, ten years from now, I'd give up.

LF: What does doing nothing mean to you? Sitting watching television? Going to the gym?

MD: Right now I want to find out where I want to live.

LF: You're thinking of moving out of New York?

MD: I don't know where I want to live. But the best time I ever had in my life, other than playing trumpet, was when I was out in the country riding horses.

LF: Do you still have a feeling for the country?

MD: Yeah, I like space, man.

LF: You should probably buy some more land.

MD: I don't want to have to search. I don't know where to buy.

LF: It sounds to me as though you're not that interested any more, or not deeply concerned, about continuing in music.

MD: I didn't say that.

LF: That's what you said in effect when I asked you what you wanted to be doing ten years from now.

MD: If I started thinking about music—now—then I'll have to play the trumpet. But the minute I don't think about it, I can be contented doing nothing.

Although the possibility seems remote, it is not inconceivable at this stage of his life that Miles Davis may extend his present policy of semi-retirement into almost total inactivity. For a quarter of a century he has to some extent controlled the direction of jazz, expanding the minds of his listeners along with the scope of his music. How long he can continue to grow, and take his audience along with him, is a secret as inscrutable as Miles himself seems to the young music student observing him at a distance.

For the present, though, his music remains as pervasive a force as ever, more challenging than yesterday when it seemed incomparably more complex than the day before. Now, as always, it mirrors the personality of the man, of his words and his actions. Although, as our conversation revealed, he is emotionally vulnerable, he prefers to keep his defenses up and cultivate the image that had led *Jet* to refer to him as "Terrible-tempered Miles." For all his displays of anger, cynicism, arrogance, and heavy sarcasm, he is no less capable of tenderness, generosity, and idealism. The psychological convolutions through which he moves toward these emotions are no easier to figure out than the processes involved in the creation of one of his uncompromisingly innovative solos or compositions.

In the light of Miles's life as an avocational boxer, a comment by Clark Terry seems singularly apposite: "I have a feeling that Miles is rather like Sugar Ray Robinson on the ropes, when he wants to psych out his opponent. Ray had a way of leaning on the ropes and faking, to the point where the opponent would say, 'I've got this cat now,' and then Ray would grab one hand with the rope and whale like hell with the other hand, and in most instances he'd floor the other guy. Miles uses all kinds of psychology in dealing with people, and he has found it to be lucrative."

As Quincy Jones once observed, "Miles is always trying to hide all that warmth, beauty, and romanticism; it's a tough job for him, and it shows through when he plays." And Dizzy affirms: "Basically Miles is very shy; that's the whole thing. You know, I know him probably better than he knows himself. I was talking to his daughter Cheryl in St. Louis, and I said, 'Did you know that your father is really a very bashful man?' and she said, 'Yeah, I've always known that, but nobody else can dig it; he puts up that front to cover up the shyness.'

"But what I really respect about him is he won't be a phony for anyone. He was the first one that came along in our business and figured he didn't have to smile at everyone, didn't have to tell no jokes or make no announcements, didn't have to say thank you or even bow. He figured he could just let the music speak for him, and for itself. He succeeeded in doing this, and you can't fight success. I say more power to him."

An ironic aspect of this phenomenon to which Gillespie did

not draw attention is the extent to which Miles' personality has built a mystique around him and has contributed to the hold he has on the public. The irony lies in the fact that three or four decades ago Louis Armstrong, whose attitudes were antithetical to Davis' in almost every conceivable way, also owed his commercial achievements in large measure to his personality.

Armstrong, accepted first by musicians as the supreme instrumental catalyst of his day, later reached the masses by being, onstage, exactly what they wanted him to be. Davis, after gaining similar in-group acceptance, went on to acquire his material luxuries, and massive income-tax problems, by doing precisely the opposite: defying the public to like him, insisting that he be accepted solely for the intrinsic value of his music.

That he has attained this objective is a measure of the distance traversed by pure jazz in barely half a century, from the level of entertainment and comedy, "happy music" aimed primarily at the lowest common intellectual denominator, to its present eminence as a musical idiom admired and dissected by serious students all over the world. It is an accomplishment never before registered by any of the lively arts. The jazz world may well take pride in the role played by Miles Davis—black, volatile, rebellious, and resilient as jazz itself—in bringing about this phenomenon in the twentieth-century music scene.

—Hollywood, 1972